A Whitm

Joann P. Krieg

A
Whitman
Chronology

University of Iowa Press ψ Iowa City

University of Iowa Press, Iowa City 52242

Copyright © 1998 by the University of Iowa Press

All rights reserved

Printed in the United States of America

Design by Richard Hendel

http://www.uiowa.edu/~uipress

Printed on acid-free paper

Library of Congress
Cataloging-in-Publication Data

Krieg, Joann P.

    A Whitman chronology / by Joann P. Krieg.

       p.   cm.

    Includes bibliographical references and index.

   ISBN 0-87745-647-X, ISBN 0-87745-654-2 (pbk.)

     1. Whitman, Walt, 1819–1892 — Chronology.

    2. Poets, American — 19th century —

Chronology.   I. Title.

PS3231.A2   1998

811'.3—dc21

  [B]   98-25247

98   99   00   01   02   C   5   4   3   2   1

98   99   00   01   02   P   5   4   3   2   1

For Jessica & Robert

CONTENTS

Introduction   ix

Significant Dates   xiii

Biographical Notes on Significant Persons   xviii

Abbreviations   xxi

1   1819–1854   1

2   1855–1859   26

3   1860–1863   40

4   1864–1867   61

5   1868–1875   81

6   1876–1880   107

7   1881–1887   129

8   1888–1892   158

Epilogue   178

Works Cited   181

Index   187

For the scholar or general reader interested in the life and work of a particular writer, two circumstances can be equally daunting. One is finding very little material available; the other is finding what might be considered too much. In the case of Walt Whitman, we can only rejoice at the richness of resources available, both primary and secondary, though the very richness can make difficult the task of selecting what to read. Whitman's life was both long and productive, and the accumulation of materials began with the poet himself, who oversaw six editions and numerous reprints and reissues of his major opus, *Leaves of Grass*; produced prose works that included a novel, short stories, essays, and newspaper articles; and left notebooks and a correspondence of almost three thousand extant letters. This high level of output was continued by his most immediate circle of friends, some of whom became his biographers while he was still living, and by his literary executors, one of whom — Horace Traubel — kept such detailed records of his conversations with the poet that they have yielded nine volumes.

Twentieth-century scholars have built upon Whitman's own foundation by editing the notebooks and correspondence, the early fiction and poems, and the journalism. Reexaminations and reevaluations of his life and work continue to appear, and some of the later ones cast doubt on the earlier, as, for instance, the current questions about whether some of the journalistic writings were actually written by Whitman. The public's consciousness of Whitman has been further raised in recent years as a result of the commemoration in 1992 of the centenary of his death. An outpouring of essays, books, and conference proceedings and the publication in 1993 of two monumental works by Joel Myerson, *Walt Whitman: A Descriptive Bibliography* and *The Walt Whitman Archive: A Facsimile of the Poet's Manuscripts*, have enriched Whitman studies beyond measure. The recurring question of the poet's homosexuality has also spurred new interest, yielding valuable insights often published through scholarly outlets unfamiliar to the general reader.

The intent of this book is to provide to the scholar and general reader alike a year-by-year and, to the extent verifiable, day-by-day account of selected events of Whitman's private and public life, to point out areas of major critical or scholarly disagreement, and to refer the reader to sources for further study. No claim is made for the exhaustibility of the information, for there are many details that do not appear in this chronology. Not all visits and correspondence to and by the poet are noted, but all those considered likely to be of importance to scholarship are. Not every meal taken with friends is listed, but I include as many as are meaningful in conveying a sense of the life here chronicled. Attention has been paid to items that pertain to Whitman's work, his primary relationships — with family, friends, and admirers — and the national issues and events that shaped his life. Perhaps most important, this book aims to make more accessible information that has been not just building but often sprawling at a considerable rate.

Accessibility also dictated the decision not to rely directly on the resources of the Feinberg Collection in the Library of Congress, the New York Public Library's Oscar Lion Collection, or any of the existing Whitman collections in this country or abroad. Rather, the reader is referred, in almost all cases, to the published sources which, in turn, cite collections. Unpublished manuscripts can be found in Myerson's *The Walt Whitman Archive*. Volume 1 of the *Archive* reproduces facsimiles from the Library of Congress collection amassed by Charles E. Feinberg (the largest trove of Whitman materials in the world); volume 2 reproduces the manuscripts at Duke University (especially good for manuscripts of "Song of Myself"); volume 3 reproduces the manuscripts at the University of Virginia (especially strong in poems from the 1860 edition of *Leaves of Grass*).

The task of compiling the chronology was facilitated by Whitman's almost daily (from the time he went to Washington, D.C.) correspondence; hence, there is a heavy reliance on this source, which is supplemented by his notebooks and creative writings. Individual letters are noted if they are significant or if, as in the case of some of those written during the Civil War, they are representative of many similar letters. In editing Whitman's correspondence, Edwin Haviland Miller included checklists of Whitman's lost letters; none of these are referred to here.

When deciding which events to include, I was guided by a desire to strike a balance between what seems "important" to some, especially to those mainly interested in Whitman's creative life, and the small events of daily life that flesh out the skeletal facts of the conventional outline chronology. In Whitman's life, few of the everyday events were so mundane that they had no bearing on his art. As an example, the frequent entries detailing his visits to others point up not just his sociability but also the eagerness with which he sought the company of certain individuals whose importance to him informed his creative life.

Appearances of the early prose and poetry are noted, as are first appearances of works later included in *Leaves of Grass* or in a prose volume. (For the sometimes complicated history of individual poems over the various editions of *Leaves of Grass*, Harold W. Blodgett and Sculley Bradley's *Leaves of Grass, Comprehensive Reader's Edition* is recommended; for changes to individual poems, see the three-volume *Leaves of Grass: A Textual Variorum of the Printed Poems*, edited by Sculley Bradley, Harold W. Blodgett, Arthur Golden, and William White.) Readers are also directed to the reprints of Whitman's writings. Editions of *Leaves of Grass* are described in the context of the year of their publication, with major distinctions from earlier editions and significant poems noted. The decision of the editors of the *Variorum* to consider as editions only those six settings of type overseen by Whitman (1855, 1856, 1860, 1867, 1871–1872, 1881), viewing all others as reprints or reissues, is followed here. Major reviews of the 1855 edition of *Leaves* are noted and referenced to Kenneth M. Price's *Walt Whitman: The Contemporary Reviews*, which reprints most reviews and provides checklists of others for each of Whitman's books.

In essence, I have tried to keep in mind the image of a reader confronted with the plethora of published material on Whitman's life and needing help sorting through the treasure trove. Behind that image was another, of Horace Traubel's delight at having Whitman hand him a little packet of papers tied with string, which turned out to be some very precise records of the poet's activities on specific dates. Accepting the packet gladly, Traubel, who struggled with the profusion of papers surrounding Whitman in his cluttered room, seemed to speak for many a Whitman scholar when he sighed, "I wish I had more extended records of this sort, Walt: they'd be very important data to me" (WWC, 4:513). Compiling this chronology has made me grateful beyond measure to Horace Traubel for the data he has given us and to all the Whitman scholars whose devotion to Whitman has made this work not only possible but necessary.

I much appreciate the help of the librarians at the Axinn Library, Hofstra University, and the time Hofstra granted me to complete this work. Ed Folsom and Jerome Loving have been meticulous in their reading of the manuscript and generous with their suggestions. Richard Ryan, curator of the Walt Whitman Birthplace, has provided information from the 1820 census. Robert Burchfield has saved me from many errors; those remaining are mine. My husband, John, has been as supportive in this as in all my ventures.

1819

Born 31 May in West Hills, Long Island, New York

1823

The Whitmans move to Brooklyn, New York

1823–1830

Lives at various Brooklyn locations and attends school

1830

Begins work as an office boy

1830–1834

Apprentices as a printer and at times lives separate from his family

1835

Works as a printer in New York City; loses job because of a fire in the printing district

1836–1838

Teaches in various schools on Long Island

1838–1839

Founds and publishes a weekly newspaper, the *Long Islander*, in Huntington, Long Island; writes for the *Long Island Democrat*

1840–1841

Teaches in Long Island schools; campaigns for Martin Van Buren

1841

Works in the printing office of New York City's *New World*; writes for the *United States Magazine and Democratic Review*

1842

Becomes an editor, first on New York City's *Aurora* and later on the *Evening Tattler*; publishes the novel *Franklin Evans, or the Inebriate*

1844

Publishes "My Boys and Girls"

1845

Writes for the *Long Island Star*

1846–1848

Edits the *Brooklyn Daily Eagle*; February 1848 goes to New Orleans to work on the *Crescent*; leaves Louisiana in May to return to Brooklyn

1848–1849

Edits the *Brooklyn Freeman*, a Free-Soil newspaper

1850–1854

Works as a journalist, housewright, and print and stationery store owner; takes ailing father to visit West Hills in 1853 or 1854

1855

Publishes first edition of *Leaves of Grass*; father dies

1856

Publishes second edition of *Leaves of Grass*; writes "The Eighteenth Presidency" around this time

1857–1859

Writes for and may have edited the *Brooklyn Times*; becomes one of the bohemians at Pfaff's bar and restaurant

1860

Spends part of year in Boston overseeing third edition of *Leaves of Grass*; is advised by Emerson to delete some of the *Leaves* poems but declines

1861

Civil War breaks out; George Whitman enlists in Union Army

1862

George is wounded at Fredericksburg, Virginia; Walt goes to care for him and remains in Washington as a wound dresser

1863

Takes work with the Army Paymaster's Office in Washington; begins hospital visits to the wounded

1865

Works as a clerk in the Washington office of the Department of the Interior; meets Peter Doyle; Lincoln is assassinated; publishes *Drum-Taps*; dismissed from clerkship; publishes *Drum-Taps* and *Sequel to Drum-Taps*

1866

William Douglas O'Connor defends Whitman in
The Good Gray Poet

1867

Publishes "Democracy" and the fourth edition of
Leaves of Grass

1868

William M. Rossetti publishes *Poems of Walt Whitman*
in England

1871

Publishes the fifth edition of *Leaves of Grass*,
Democratic Vistas, and *Passage to India*; reads "After
All, Not to Create Only" at opening of the National
Industrial Exhibition in New York; Anne Gilchrist
writes to Whitman professing her love

1872

Reads "As a Strong Bird on Pinions Free" at the
Dartmouth College commencement; quarrels with
William O'Connor

1873

Suffers a stroke and is partially paralyzed; mother dies;
moves to Camden, New Jersey, to live with George and
Louisa Whitman

1874

Leaves government position

1876

Republishes *Leaves of Grass* and *Two Rivulets* to
coincide with the nation's centennial; international
controversy erupts over his alleged poverty and neglect;
Anne Gilchrist arrives from England; begins friendship
with Harry Stafford

1877

Dr. Richard Maurice Bucke of Canada visits

1878

First real improvement in health since stroke

1879

Gives first Lincoln lecture in New York; Anne Gilchrist
returns to England; journeys west to Kansas and
Colorado

1880

Visits Dr. Bucke in Canada

1881

Sixth edition of *Leaves of Grass* is being published in
Boston by James R. Osgood

1882

Osgood ceases publication of *Leaves of Grass* when
Boston's district attorney threatens prosecution for
obscenity; *Leaves of Grass* and *Specimen Days* are
published by a Philadelphia press; Oscar Wilde visits

1884

Buys house at 328 Mickle Street, Camden, New Jersey

1885

Friends rally to make Whitman's life comfortable; Anne
Gilchrist dies in England

1888

Publishes *November Boughs* and *Complete Poems and
Prose*; Horace Traubel begins keeping records of his
visits with Whitman

1889

Feted at a grand celebration of his seventieth birthday

1891

Publishes *Good-Bye My Fancy* and final (1891–1892)
printing of *Leaves of Grass*

1892

Dies on 26 March and is buried in Harleigh Cemetery
in Camden, New Jersey

BIOGRAPHICAL NOTES ON SIGNIFICANT PERSONS

Parents

Walter Whitman Sr. (1789−1855) was of English descent. His forebears had large landholdings in Huntington Township on Long Island, New York. His father was Jesse Whitman, and his mother was Hannah Brush. He was a carpenter and house builder in the Huntington area and in Brooklyn and built the house in which Walt was born. He held strong opinions tending toward radical democracy and was friend and admirer of such freethinkers as Thomas Paine, Frances Wright, and the liberal Quaker Elias Hicks. In 1816 he married Louisa Van Velsor. His death in 1855 came within weeks of the publication of the first edition of *Leaves of Grass*.

Louisa Van Velsor (1795−1873) was of Dutch and Welsh descent. Her parents were Cornelius Van Velsor and Naomi (Amy) Williams of Cold Spring, Long Island, New York. The Van Velsors had a farm where they raised horses. One of her ancestors was the sailor whose death became the family legend told in Whitman's "Old Salt Kassabone." Her letters to Walt reveal a strong personality and a deep bond between them. Whitman considered her death to have been the great tragedy of his life.

Siblings

Jesse (1818−1870) was a laborer for a time but suffered from a degenerative mental condition, which caused him to be institutionalized in 1864.

Mary Elizabeth (1821−1899) married Ansel Van Nostrand on 2 January 1840. They moved to Greenport, Long Island, where Whitman visited frequently.

Hannah Louisa (1823−1899) married an artist, Charles L. Heyde, on 16 March 1852, and they moved to Vermont.

Andrew Jackson (1827–1863) was for a short time in the Union Army. He and his wife, Nancy, had two children. He died of a throat ailment while Whitman was in Washington, D.C.

George Washington (1829–1901) was in the Union Army. He was wounded at Fredericksburg, Virginia, and later was a prisoner of war. He married Louisa Orr Haslam on 14 April 1871, and they moved to Camden, New Jersey. They had one child, Walter Orr, who died in infancy.

Thomas Jefferson (Jeff) (1833–1890) was an engineer with the St. Louis, Missouri, water system. He married Martha Emma Mitchell (Mattie), and they had two daughters, Mannahatta (Hattie) (1860–1886) and Jessie Louisa (1863–1957). As a teenager he went with Walt to New Orleans, where they worked for a short time on a newspaper.

Edward (Ed or Eddie) (1835–1892), who had mental and physical disabilities, lived with his mother. After her death he lived with family members, then was boarded out. Late in life he was institutionalized.

Literary Executors

Dr. Richard Maurice Bucke (1837–1902) was a Canadian physician and alienist (psychiatrist) who supervised an asylum in London, Ontario. He was also a mystic who found in Whitman's poetry the highest form of what he termed "cosmic consciousness." The author of *Walt Whitman* (1863), he was Whitman's first biographer.

Thomas B. Harned (1851–?) was a Camden, New Jersey, attorney and the brother-in-law of Horace Traubel. A great admirer of Whitman's work, he and his wife were frequent hosts to the poet.

Horace L. Traubel (1858–1919) was a teenager when he met Whitman in Camden, New Jersey. He was later a Socialist writer. His chief claim to fame is the record he kept of conversations with Whitman from 1888 to the poet's death, *With Walt Whitman in Camden*. Traubel was a primary source for the memorial volume *In Re Walt Whitman*, published in 1892 by the three literary executors.

Friends

John Burroughs (1837–1921) was a naturalist and author who met Whitman in Washington, D.C., in 1863. He published *Notes on Walt Whitman, as Poet and Person* (1867) and *Walt Whitman, a Study* (1896).

Peter Doyle (1843–1907) was an Irish immigrant, Confederate soldier, streetcar conductor, and railroad worker who became an intimate friend of Whitman's in 1865. The two were close for at least eight years.

Anne B. Gilchrist (1828–1885) was the widow of Alexander Gilchrist, the English biographer of William Blake, and friend of many of England's outstanding literary persons. She came to the United States in 1876 to meet Whitman after having published "A Woman's Estimate of Walt Whitman" (1870).

Dr. John Johnston (?–1927) was one of the leaders of the group of Whitman admirers in Bolton, England. He visited Whitman in Camden in 1890 and later published, with J. W. Wallace, *Visits to Walt Whitman in 1890–1891 by Two Lancashire Friends* (1917).

William Sloane Kennedy (1850–1929) was a Philadelphia writer and editor who met Whitman in 1880. He published *Reminiscences of Walt Whitman* (1896) and *The Fight of a Book for the World: A Companion Volume to Leaves of Grass* (1926).

William Douglas O'Connor (1832–1889) was a political radical and author who met Whitman in Boston in 1860 and later, when both were government employees in Washington, became a devoted friend. In 1866 he published *The Good Gray Poet*, a vindication of Whitman, who had been dismissed from government service.

Harry Stafford was the eldest child of Susan and George Stafford, at whose home in southern New Jersey Whitman recuperated in 1876. Though a stormy one, his relationship with Whitman was close, lasting over a decade.

J. W. Wallace (1853–1926) was the leader of the Bolton, England, group of admirers. He came to visit Whitman in 1891. After the poet's death he maintained a voluminous correspondence with Horace Traubel.

ABBREVIATIONS

CORR

Walt Whitman: The Correspondence. Ed. Edwin Haviland Miller. 6 vols. New York: New York University Press, 1961–1977.

CW

The Complete Writings of Walt Whitman. Issued under the editorial supervision of the literary executors, Richard Maurice Bucke, Thomas B. Harned, and Horace L. Traubel, with additional bibliographical and critical material by Oscar Lowell Triggs. 10 vols. New York and London: Putnam's Sons, 1907.

DN

Daybooks and Notebooks. Ed. William White. 3 vols. New York: New York University Press, 1978.

EPF

Early Poetry and Fiction. Ed. Thomas L. Brasher. New York: New York University Press, 1963.

LGF

Leaves of Grass. A Facsimile of the First Edition. With an introduction, a note on the text, and a bibliography by Richard Bridgman. San Francisco: Chandler Printing Company, 1968.

NUPM

Notebooks and Unpublished Prose Manuscripts. Ed. Edward F. Grier. 6 vols. New York: New York University Press, 1984.

PW

Prose Works, 1892. Ed. Floyd Stovall. 2 vols. New York: New York University Press, 1963–1964.

UPP

The Uncollected Poetry and Prose of Walt Whitman. Ed. Emory Holloway. 2 vols. Garden City, N.Y.: Doubleday, Page, 1921.

WWC

With Walt Whitman in Camden. Horace Traubel.

Vols. 1–3, 1905–1914; reprint, Rownan and Littlefield 1961. Vol. 4, Philadelphia: University of Pennsylvania Press, 1953. Vols. 5–7, Carbondale: Southern Illinois Press, 1964, 1982, 1992. Vols. 8–9, Oregon House, Calif.: W. C. Bentley, 1996.

A Whitman Chronology

CHAPTER ONE

1819-1854

You ask for . . . details of my early life
— *Specimen Days*, 1882

Walter Whitman Jr. (later Walt) is born on 31 May 1819 in West Hills, in Huntington Township on Long Island, New York, in a farmhouse reputedly built by his father. His parents, Walter and Louisa (Van Velsor), are of families whose ancestors — his English, hers Dutch and Welsh — had settled in the region two centuries earlier. There is already one boy in the family, Jesse, born the year before. Walter Sr. is a carpenter and at times a farmer. He will find it a great burden to provide for his large family of nine children, two of whom have disabilities. He is literate and interested in politics, most often leaning toward radicalism. Louisa is the primary caregiver in the family (Walt considered her "a perfect mother"), who often finds herself the peacemaker. The strong bond of love between her and her second son will be a continuing influence in both their lives. Just four days before young Walter's fourth birthday the Whitmans leave West Hills for Brooklyn.

When he is twelve Walter begins work in the printing trade but completes his apprenticeship in the same year (1835) that a disastrous fire wipes out most of New York's printing businesses. As a result, he is forced to seek employment as a teacher in one-room schoolrooms on Long Island. For one year, 1838–1839, he produces his own newspaper near the place he was born before returning to teaching and eventually to the newspaper business closer to New York. He begins to publish his first poems, which give little indication of what is to come. Politics becomes an interest, and in 1840 Walter campaigns for the Democratic Party nominee, Martin Van Buren. This leads to jobs on newspapers that espouse the party's principles and to editorships of respected newspapers, most notably the *Brooklyn Daily Eagle* in 1846. In addition, he writes short fiction pieces and sees them published in such prominent journals as the *Democratic Review* and the *American Review*. In 1842 he produces a temperance novel, *Franklin Evans, or the Inebriate*. The political scene intensifies as the issue of slavery and whether slavery should extend into new western territories become matters of national debate. Walter sides with the Free-Soil movement (those who oppose the extension) and eventually withdraws from the Democratic Party. In 1848 he loses the *Eagle* editorship and heads south to New Orleans to work on a paper there, taking his young brother, Jeff, with him. They do not remain long. When he returns three months later, Walter picks up what work he can find in printing and in writing for newspapers and periodicals, becoming very much "a man about town" in both New York and Brooklyn. His father becomes seriously ill, and in 1853 or 1854 Walter accompanies him on a final visit to West Hills.

1819

31 MAY. Walter Whitman Jr. is born to Louisa (Van Velsor) Whitman and Walter Whitman Sr. He is their second child; the first, Jesse, is fourteen months old. The Whitmans were among the earliest settlers of the West Hills, Huntington Township, area (NUPM, 1:6).

1820

The federal census taken in this year includes in its records of Huntington Township, Suffolk County, New York, the family of Walter Whitman, with ten members listed as follows: "Free White Males, 2 under ten years of age, 3 between 26 and 45 years of age; Free White Females, 1 under ten years of age, 2 between sixteen and twenty-five, 2 forty-five years and older; three of the individuals are said to be employed in agriculture." According to Whitman family records, included among these are Louisa (Van Velsor) Whitman, Walter Whitman Sr., Jesse Whitman, Walter Whitman Jr., and possibly Hannah (Brush) Whitman, mother of Walter Whitman Sr.

1821

3 FEBRUARY. Mary Elizabeth Whitman is born.

1823

27 MAY. The Whitman family moves to Brooklyn and settles into a rented house on Front Street near the Brooklyn Navy Yard.

28 NOVEMBER. Hannah Louisa Whitman is born.

1824

1 SEPTEMBER. Walter Whitman Sr. buys property at the corner of Washington and Johnson Streets on which he builds a house; the family lives in it for a short time before moving again.

1825

1 MARCH. Walter Whitman Sr. buys a lot at the corner of Tillary and Adams Streets in Brooklyn, where he builds a house. Whitman later claimed that the lots purchased in 1824 and 1825 "were mortgaged and we lost them" (PW 1:13).

2 MARCH. A child is born to the Whitmans but remains unnamed.

JULY. Walter is one of a number of schoolchildren who join in the welcome given the Revolutionary War hero General Lafayette, who is touring the country. The general lifts little Walter over an embankment to a safe viewing place for the honoring ceremony, a gesture Whitman always remembers (NUPM 1:32–35).

14 SEPTEMBER. The unnamed Whitman infant dies.

AROUND THIS TIME. Young Walter attends Sunday school at St. Ann's Episcopal Church at Sands and Washington Streets (DN, 3:614).

1826

FEBRUARY. Naomi (Williams) Van Velsor, mother of Louisa Whitman, dies. Whitman had great love and admiration for his "Quaker" grandmother, some of whose family had been of the Society of Quakers, though she herself was not a member (Binns, 347–348). The family is living on Van Dyke Street in Brooklyn.

1827

7 APRIL. Andrew Jackson Whitman is born. The Whitmans live on Adams Street until November, when they move to Tillary Street, where they remain until November 1831.

1829

4 JUNE. The steam-frigate *Fulton*, moored at the Brooklyn Navy Yard, explodes, killing forty people; Walter is at school and hears "the rumble, which jarred half the city" (DN, 3:615). A few days later Walter observes the military funeral for the dead officers and men killed by the explosion and is much impressed by the ceremony and the music (UPP, 2:265–266).

SUMMER. In what is the last year of his childhood before beginning work, Walter spends summer days on Long Island visiting his grandparents and enjoying the island's beaches, as he will continue to do for many years. In old age he recalled the Long Island of his boyhood days: "the soothing rustle of the waves, and the saline smell — boyhood's times, the clam-digging, barefoot, and with trowsers roll'd up" (PW, 1:12).

28 NOVEMBER. George Washington Whitman is born.

NOVEMBER. Young Walter accompanies his parents to hear the famed Quaker preacher Elias Hicks of Jericho, Long Island, at Morrison's Hotel in Brooklyn Heights. Though he does not understand the sermon, Walter is greatly impressed by the oratory and later remains a Hicks admirer, eventually writing a biographical sketch of the preacher (PW, 2:636−637).

1830

SUMMER. Walter begins work as an office boy in the law office of James B. Clark and his son, Edward, on Fulton Street in Brooklyn; Edward gives the boy a subscription to a circulating library so that he may continue his education, and Walter is soon reading adventure books (PW, 1:13). Later in the year he works in a doctor's office.

1831

Walter finds employment in the Brooklyn printing office of Samuel E. Clements, editor of the *Long Island Patriot*, where he becomes interested in printing and journalism. Brooklyn is still a village located on Long Island and will remain so until 1834 when it becomes a city; in 1899 it becomes part of metropolitan New York. He boards out, sharing quarters with other apprentices, though his family lives nearby.

1832

SUMMER. Walter begins working for another Brooklyn printer, Erastus Worthington.

FALL. Walter goes to work for Alden Spooner on the *Long Island Star*. The *Star* is a Whig paper, much in opposition to the Democratic *Patriot*, so the youngster becomes aware of newspaper politics.

WINTER. On one of his visits to Manhattan, Walter sees the aged millionaire John Jacob Astor carried from his stately home and, swathed in the furs that were the means of his fortune, placed in an impressively teamed sleigh (PW, 1:17).

1833

MAY. The Whitman family moves back to Long Island. Young Walter remains in Brooklyn to work on the *Star*. On his own in the city, he begins to attend theater productions and develops a great liking for them. He also belongs to a circulating library and a debating society, both of which become a form of education for him.

JUNE. Walter joins a crowd on a Brooklyn street cheering President Andrew Jackson on a tour of northern cities (UPP, 1:118).

18 JULY. Thomas Jefferson Whitman is born.

1834

The Whitmans are living in Norwich, near Oyster Bay, on Long Island. Walter is working in New York.

1835

12 MAY. Walter leaves the *Star* to become a compositor in Manhattan.

9 AUGUST. Edward Whitman is born; he has physical and mental disabilities.

SUMMER. Walter completes his printing apprenticeship and becomes a journeyman printer. In August a fire wipes out most of the establishments on Paternoster Row, the printing center of New York, with a resulting loss of printing work.

IN THIS YEAR. Whitman acquires Sir Walter Scott's *Complete Poems* and reads them all but reads "the ballads of the Border Minstrelsy over and over again" (PW, 2:723); the work remains a life-long favorite.

1836

MAY. Walter joins his family, now living in Hempstead, Long Island, and a month later begins teaching in Norwich, near his grandfather Van Velsor's farm in Cold Spring.

FALL. The Whitmans move to Babylon, and Walter teaches a three-month term there, either living at home or boarding at the homes of students. His brother George, now seven, is one of his pupils.

IN THIS YEAR. Walter writes a story, "My Boys and Girls," about his younger siblings but omits Edward.

1837

SPRING. Walter is still on Long Island, teaching at Long Swamp.

FALL. He teaches a term at Smithtown, where he becomes active in a debating society, engaging in numerous debates on serious subjects (Molinoff, *Smithtown*).

1838

JUNE. Walter begins a weekly newspaper in Huntington, the *Long Islander*, for which he does all the writing and printing; with his horse, Nina, he delivers the papers. George is his assistant, and the two live together in rooms above the printing shop.

8 AUGUST. "Effects of Lightning" is reprinted from the *Long Islander* in the *Long Island Democrat*. No copies remain of the 1838–39 *Long Islander*, but this piece had to have been originally published prior to 8 August and is the earliest known piece of published Whitman prose.

31 OCTOBER. "Our Future Lot," Whitman's earliest known poem, appears in the *Long Island Democrat*; reprinted from the *Long Islander*, it will reappear as "Time to Come" in 1842 in the *Democratic Review* and in the *New York Aurora* (Loving, "A Newly Discovered").

1839

SPRING. Walter gives up the *Long Islander* and leaves Huntington for New York, where he hopes to find work in the printing field. He is not successful. While it is not known for how much of his life he read the *Long Islander*, which continued publication, in his final years he read it weekly (WWC, 6:281).

AUGUST. Walter finds newspaper work in the Jamaica, Long Island, office of James J. Brenton, editor of the *Long Island Democrat*, who has already reprinted some of Whitman's *Long Islander* poems and essays. Walter writes a series of articles, "The Sun-Down Papers," for the *Democrat*. Employment includes living quarters at the Brenton home, and while Walter gets on well with his employer (who finds him a literary asset to the paper), Mrs. Brenton believes him slovenly and lazy and may be the reason for his leaving the *Democrat* (Allen, *Solitary Singer*, 35).

23 OCTOBER. "Fame's Vanity," a didactic poem, is published in the *Long Island Democrat*.

27 NOVEMBER. "My Departure," a poem about the death of a nature lover, appears in the *Long Island Democrat*.

FALL. With no immediate prospects in the newspaper field, Walter is teaching again, at Jamaica Academy in Flushing Hill.

DECEMBER. He begins teaching at Little Bay Side, near Jamaica. This post provides the first report of his teaching methods. Charles A. Roe, a ten-year-old when he was taught by Whitman, later reports that his teacher used such games as "Twenty Questions" to convey facts, did not depend upon corporal punishment for discipline, and played games with his students at recess (Myerson, 111).

1840

1 JANUARY. "Young Grimes," a poem, is published in the *Long Island Democrat*. It is an imitation of "Old Grimes," which was published in Providence, Rhode Island, in 1822 by Albert G. Greene, a popular but undistinguished poet.

2 JANUARY. Mary Elizabeth, Whitman's sister, marries Ansel Van Nostrand and moves to Greenport, Long Island.

5 MAY. "The Inca's Daughter," a poem, is published in the *Long Island Democrat*. It tells of the death of a proud Inca woman captured and tortured by the Spanish.

19 MAY. "The Love That Is Hereafter," a poem about death, is published in the *Long Island Democrat*.

MAY. The Whitman family moves to Dix Hills.

SPRING. Walter teaches at Trimming Square, Long Island.

14 JULY. "We All Shall Rest at Last," another poem on death, possibly inspired by William Cullen Bryant's "Thanatopsis" (1817), is published in the *Long Island Democrat*.

4 AUGUST. "The Spanish Lady," a poem about the tragic death of Inez de Castro of the royal family of Castile, is published in the *Long Island Democrat*.

SUMMER. Walter is teaching in Woodbury, near West Hills where he was born, and begins a correspondence with a friend, Abraham Leech, of Jamaica. The letters extend into the following year and contain many comic descriptions of Long Islanders and of the schoolteacher's experiences while "boarding round" in the homes of pupils. "O, damnation, damnation!" he writes, "thy other name is school-teaching and thy residence Woodbury." (Eight extant letters, written between 30 July 1840 and late 1841, appear in Miller, "Correspondence.")

22 SEPTEMBER. "The End of All," a poetic meditation on death, is published in the *Long Island Democrat*.

17 OCTOBER. "The Columbian's Song," a patriotic poem, is published in the *Long Island Democrat*.

FALL. Walter is teaching in Whitestone, near Jamaica. He is appointed Democratic electioneer for Queens County, supporting Martin Van Buren against the Whig presidential candidate, William Henry Harrison, and engages in debates on issues of the 1840 election.

IN THIS YEAR. The first three installments of "The Sun-Down Papers" are reprinted in the Long Island *Hempstead Inquirer*. Whitman may have taught at Southold, Long Island, but there is no direct evidence of it (Reynolds, 70–73).

1841

MARCH. Whitman is teaching in Whitestone, Queens County, New York.

MAY. Whitman goes to work in the printing office of the *New York New World*. This weekly paper, whose owners include Rufus Griswold and Park Benjamin, will play an important role in the nation's journalistic history (see Hudson, 587–589).

22 JUNE. "The Winding-Up," a revised form of "The End of All," is published in the *Long Island Democrat*.

29 JULY. Walter gives a speech at a Democratic rally in City Hall Park, New York, which is praised in William Cullen

Bryant's paper, the *Evening Post*. "We are battling for great principles — for mighty and glorious truths," he assures his audience concerning the Democratic Party. "It is our creed — our doctrine; not a man or set of men, that we seek to build up" (UPP, 1:51).

9 AUGUST. "Death in the School-Room (A Fact)," a short story about the brutal beating of a pupil by a school-teacher, is published in the *United States Magazine and Democratic Review*. Whitman's entry into the pages of the *Democratic Review* is important in that the monthly magazine has high literary standards and includes such authors as Bryant, Whittier, Longfellow, and Hawthorne. Whitman's early fiction, like his early poetry, is conventional; in his late years he admits to a wish "to have all these crude and boyish pieces quietly dropp'd in oblivion" (PW, 2: Introduction to *Collect*).

20 NOVEMBER. "Each Has His Grief," a revision of "The End of All," is published in the *New World*. The same issue includes his story "The Child's Champion."

NOVEMBER. "Wild Frank's Return" appears in the *Democratic Review*. The story concerns a prodigal son who seeks to return to his Long Island family but is dragged to his death by a runaway horse.

18 DECEMBER. "The Punishment of Pride," an allegorical poem, appears in the *New World*. It was previously titled "The Fallen Angel" when, according to Charles Roe, Whitman taught it to his pupils at Little Bay Side in 1839 (EPF, 19, n1).

DECEMBER. "Bervance: or, Father and Son" is published in the *Democratic Review*. It is a tale of a father who cannot love his eccentric son and, following a violent quarrel, has him committed to an insane asylum.

1842

29 JANUARY. "Ambition," a revision of "Fame's Vanity," appears in *Brother Jonathan*, a New York weekly literary magazine edited by Park Benjamin.

JANUARY. "The Tomb Blossoms," a story of a poverty-stricken West Indian woman who lovingly tends two graves not knowing in which her husband is buried, is published in the *Democratic Review.*

FEBRUARY. Whitman begins to write for the *Aurora*, a New York daily. The *Aurora*, a two-penny paper with little interest in literature or national politics, concentrates on the social side of New York life. Whitman's first articles are probably in a series called "Walks in Broadway" and offer glimpses of the city.

5 MARCH. Whitman hears Ralph Waldo Emerson lecture at the New-York Historical Society Library on "Nature and the Powers of the Poet" and reports in the *Aurora* Emerson's claim that "the business of the poet is expression — the giving utterance to the emotions and sentiments of the soul" (Rubin and Brown, 105).

18 MARCH. "The Death and Burial of McDonald Clarke" is published in the *Aurora.* A parody of Charles Wolfe's popular "The Burial of Sir John Moore at Corunna," the poem memoralizes McDonald Clarke, an eccentric New York poet who died in New York's Tombs prison in early March. Signed only "W.," the poem is later identified as Whitman's (Rubin and Brown, 11).

28 MARCH. The publishers of the *Aurora* "respectfully announce to their friends and the public that they have secured the services of Mr. Walter Whitman." Whitman now becomes part of the rough-and-tumble world of New York editorial journalism and will move from one paper to another at the mercy of various publishers and of his own temperament. As editor of the *Aurora*, located just four doors from City Hall, he enters into the city's political battles by holding his own against the city's nativists and regularly writes on theatrical and musical presentations.

MARCH. "The Last of the Sacred Army," a story about one of George Washington's soldiers, appears in the *Democratic Review.*

9 APRIL. "Time to Come," a revision of the earlier poem

"Our Future Lot" (which appeared originally in the *Long Islander* and in the *Long Island Democrat* in 1838), is published in the *Aurora*.

21 MAY. "Reuben's Last Wish," another tale of a father's cruelty to his son, this time because of the father's alcoholism, is published in a New York temperance paper, the *Washingtonian*.

MAY. Walter leaves the *Aurora*, having quarreled with its publishers.

IN THE SAME MONTH. "The Last Loyalist," a story of a Long Island episode in the Revolution, is published in the *Democratic Review*.

MAY OR JUNE. Walter begins to write for a New York daily, the *Evening Tattler*, and uses its pages to attack the *Aurora*'s publishers by reprinting diatribes directed against them by a Connecticut newspaper (Rubin and Brown, 12).

SEPTEMBER. "The Angel of Tears," an allegorical tale of an angel who descends to earth to reform sinners, appears in the *Democratic Review*.

IN THE SAME MONTH. Whitman loses his place at the *Tattler*, probably because of a personal disagreement with its owner.

23 NOVEMBER. *Franklin Evans, or the Inebriate* is published in a special issue of the *New World*. A temperance novel written at the suggestion of Park Benjamin, the work is very popular and sells well. Late in life Whitman ridicules the book and claims he wrote it for the money (WWC, 1:93). The book is republished by the *New World* in 1843 as *Franklin Evans; or the Merchant's Clerk: A Tale of the Times*.

10 DECEMBER. "A Sketch," a poem bearing the signature "W.," appears in the *New World*; because of its resemblance to "The Punishment of Pride" and "Each Has His Grief," both published in the *New World* in 1841, the poem is now believed to be Whitman's (Loving, "A Newly Discovered").

IN THIS YEAR. Whitman sees Charles and Catherine Dickens in a New York theater (NUPM, 3:1087).

1843

28 JANUARY. "The Madman," chapter one and part of a second chapter of what is intended as another temperance work (never completed), appears in the *New York Washingtonian and Organ* (formerly the *Washingtonian*).

11 MARCH. "Death of the Nature-Lover," a revision of the earlier "My Departure," is published in *Brother Jonathan.*

SPRING. Perhaps because of his activities on behalf of the Democratic Party, Walter is offered the editorship of the *Statesman*, a Democratic newspaper. The post lasts but a short time, so his may be only a temporary appointment. He is living in various Manhattan boardinghouses, writing and publishing short fiction.

1844

MARCH. "The Love of Eris: A Spirit Record" is published in the *Columbian Magazine*. It is a strange tale of an angel's ill-fated love for a mortal.

20 APRIL. "My Boys and Girls," the autobiographical story written in 1835, is published in the *Rover*. The Whitman boys, George Washington, Andrew Jackson, and Thomas Jefferson, are identified by name, and Mary appears as "M" (see EPF, 248–250).

MAY. "Dumb Kate" appears in the *Columbian Magazine*. It is a character sketch of a gentle young woman who is unable to speak. Seduced and abandoned, she dies shortly thereafter.

SUMMER. Whitman becomes editor of the *New York Democrat* but leaves within a few months. In this post Whitman exercises considerable independence of thought, which brings him into dispute with the Hunkers, the conservative faction of the Democratic Party. The *Democrat* is a party paper, and when its young editor chooses to support Silas Wright, the party's liberal candidate for governor, the Hunkers, powerful in New York City, turn on the paper, and Whitman is forced out.

SEPTEMBER. "The Little Sleighers, A Sketch of a Winter Morning on the Battery" is published in the *Columbian Magazine*.

OCTOBER. For a few weeks Walter writes for the evening edition of the *New Mirror*.

1845

MARCH. "Arrow-Tip," a novella, appears in the literary periodical the *Aristidean*. Later renamed "The Half-Breed: A Tale of the Western Frontier," it is a wildly improbable story.

IN THE SAME MONTH. "Shirval: A Tale of Jerusalem" is published in the *Aristidean*. It is based on an incident in the Gospel of Luke, chapter 7, where Jesus restores the life of a widow's son.

APRIL. "Richard Parker's Widow" appears in the *Aristidean*. It is a story of the mutiny on British ships at Nore in 1797.

MAY. "The Boy Lover" is published in the *American Review*, a Whig journal. It is a tale of three young men all in love with the same young woman. The fact that Whitman allows his work to appear in a Whig publication indicates how much he needs the money.

JULY—AUGUST. After a two-year absence from the pages of the *Democratic Review*, Whitman's "Revenge and Requital; A Tale of a Murderer Escaped" appears in this prestigious publication. The story draws upon the cholera epidemic that swept New York in 1832, which allows an escaped criminal to redeem himself through caring for its victims.

AUGUST. Walter leaves New York to return to Brooklyn. Hard-pressed to support himself, he rejoins his family, who have moved from Dix Hills to Brooklyn. His father purchases a lot and prepares to build a house for them all to live in.

29 NOVEMBER. Walter publishes an essay on "Art-Music and Heart-Music" in the *Broadway Journal*, whose editor is Edgar Allan Poe. Whitman later remembers having met Poe in his office at the *Journal*: "Poe was very cordial, in a quiet way, appear'd well in person, dress, etc. I have a distinct and pleasing remembrance" (PW, 1:17).

DECEMBER. "Some Fact-Romances," a collection of five stories based on what their author claims as fact, is published in the *Aristidean*. One of these romances concerns "an aged black woman" in New York City who undertakes to raise $200, which will allow her to place in a private asylum a child of the streets, a deaf girl.

WINTER. Walter writes articles and theater and music reviews for the *Long Island Star*, a Brooklyn newspaper published by Edwin B. Spooner, son of Alden Spooner, one of Whitman's earliest employers. Interested in most forms of entertainment, as well as politics, Whitman is very much a "man about town," finding a great deal to attract him in both Brooklyn and Manhattan. In these years Whitman develops a taste for opera, especially Italian opera, and refines his earlier interests in drama. Art, literature, music, and sculpture now take his attention almost as much as the drivers of the city omnibuses (called "stages"), beside whom he loves to ride the length of Broadway (PW, 1:18−19).

1846

MARCH. Whitman becomes editor of the *Brooklyn Daily Eagle*. The *Eagle* is not one of the penny papers, such as the *Aurora*, but a more typical four-page newspaper with editorials, news stories, and advertisements. Brooklyn is a city of some forty thousand people, and the *Eagle* is its most important newspaper. Whitman expands its coverage of literary material, adding poems, tales, book reviews, and excerpts from published writings, including an anonymous abridgement of his own *Franklin Evans*, renamed "Fortunes of a Country Boy." The *Eagle* is a liberal Democratic paper, and his party connections no doubt help gain him what he later calls "one of the pleasantest sits of my life" (PW, 1:288). While with the *Eagle* Whitman writes a number of editorials against the expansion of slavery (Brasher, 161–165) and in support of war with Mexico. The *Eagle*'s pages include many of Whitman's reviews of music recitals, operas, and concerts. Henry Sutton, the paper's printer's devil whom Whitman calls "Hen," later remembers the young editor as a "nice, kind man" whose daily routine is to write his editorials and other materials in the mornings, visit Gray's bathhouse on Fulton Street for a twenty-minute swim, take a ferry to New York, and return in the afternoon to proof copy (Brasher, 19). Whitman and William Cullen Bryant become friends; they share a love of walking and often stroll the city streets while Bryant recounts his experience of foreign cities. They disagree as to matters of prosody, though Whitman later claims they "never quarreled over such things" (WWC, 3:515).

1 JUNE. "The Play-Ground," a poem about children at play, appears in the *Eagle*.

LATE JUNE. A day trip to visit his sister Mary in Greenport provides a welcome respite from the city. Traveling by Long Island Rail Road, Whitman finds the dining-car food most agreeable (Allen, *Solitary Singer*, 77).

2 JULY. "Ode.—By Walter Whitman" is published in the *Eagle* with instructions that it is to be sung to the tune of "The Star-Spangled Banner." The song is listed on the program for a Fourth of July celebration held at Fort Greene, Brooklyn.

SUMMER. Whitman visits the exhibit of Hiram Powers's statue, "The Greek Slave."

1847

24 FEBRUARY. An enthusiastic opera attendee, Whitman writes an overview of the Brooklyn opera season for his *Eagle* readers.

23 MARCH. Whitman writes his first opera review, of Rossini's *Il Barbiere di Siviglia*. Writing editorials for the *Eagle* requires Whitman to broaden his political interests beyond those of city and party to a consideration of such great national issues as slavery. Not able to join forces with either the conservative or radical liberal factions of the Democratic Party, he seeks a middle ground by opposing the extension of slavery into new territories in the West (the Free-Soil position). When he joins forces with supporters of the Wilmot Proviso, which sought to prohibit slavery in the territories gained from the Mexican War, he defies some members of the Democratic Party. Typical of his editorials in favor of the Wilmot Proviso is one on 21 December 1846:

> If there are any States to be formed out of territory
> lately annexed, or to be annexed, by any means to
> the United States, let the Democratic members of
> Congress (and Whigs too, if they like) plant them-
> selves quietly, without bluster, but fixedly and with-
> out compromise, on the requirements *Slavery be
> prohibited in them forever.* We wish we could have
> a universal straight-forward setting down of feet
> on this thing, in the Democratic Party. *We must.*
> (Brasher, 104)

IN THIS YEAR. In his notebook Whitman writes a kind of prose poetry far different from the poems he is publishing. He begins to assume the "I" persona of the later *Leaves of Grass*, to expand individual views to include attitudes of both slaves and masters, and to become the kind of "American bard" he will later describe (Reynolds, 119).

1848

JANUARY. Whitman loses his position as editor of the *Brooklyn Eagle*.

17 FEBRUARY. The *Eagle* responds to the gloating of the *Brooklyn Advertiser*, with whom Whitman has feuded as editor of the *Eagle*:

> It is true, as you say,
> We sent Whitman away,
> But that is a private affair;
> But since you have spoken
> Know by this token,
> You have no *wit, man*, to spare.
> (Rodgers and Black, xxxiv)

MID-FEBRUARY. In the lobby of a New York theater Walter meets J. E. McClure, a part owner of the *Daily Crescent*, a paper soon to begin publication in New Orleans, and accepts his offer of work on the paper. His younger brother Thomas Jefferson (Jeff) is also offered a position. With a $200 advance, the two leave New York and travel by train, overland stage, and boat — the *St. Cloud* — to New Orleans. Walter keeps a journal and later publishes portions of it in the *Crescent*.

25 FEBRUARY. Walter and Jeff arrive in New Orleans, going first to a boardinghouse, later staying at the Tremont House. Walter's job involves such varied duties as clipping stories from other newspapers, writing articles, and overseeing a small staff; Jeff is office boy. Fourteen years old, Jeff is soon homesick and writes his mother repeatedly, begging for letters. When only one is received, he writes: "Mother, Just think what you would think of us if we had written you only one letter since we came away. . . . If you do not write to us pretty soon we will do something but I don't know what" (Berthold and Price, 13). Walter writes a series of character sketches for the paper, including "A Dusky Grisette," descriptions of city

sights, some comic pieces, some theater reviews, and at
least one poem, "The Mississippi at Midnight" (UPP,
1:202–205).

14 MARCH. The *Brooklyn Eagle* takes note of the *Crescent*,
adding, "Mr. Whitman, recently principal editor of The
Eagle, went out to New Orleans to take part in the con-
duct of this paper, and we discern his handy work in several editorials. We trust that both will flourish 'like a
green bay tree'" (Rodgers and Black, xxxvi).

25 MAY. A coolness between him and his employer causes
Walter to resign from the *Crescent*, and he and Jeff pre-
pare to leave the city two days later.

27 MAY. The Whitman brothers leave New Orleans on the
Pride of the West. Having come there by way of the Ohio
and Mississippi Rivers, their return is via the Mississippi
to the Great Lakes, finally on the Hudson River. Walter
writes of the "Long monotonous stretch of the Mississippi — Planter's dwellings surrounded with their ham-
lets of negro huts — groves of negro men women and
children in the fields, hoeing the young cotton" (NUPM,
1:85). Walter has his first opportunity on this journey to
see some of the country that lay beyond Long Island and
Manhattan and is especially pleased to view Niagara
Falls. In 1887 he writes an article for the *New Orleans
Picayune* recounting his time there (PW, 2:604–610).

15 JUNE. Walter and Jeff arrive home in Brooklyn.

JUNE. "The Shadow and the Light of a Young Man's Soul,"
though probably written some years earlier, is published
in the *Union Magazine of Literature and Art*. Autobiographical in many of its details, it is a tale of young
Archibald Dean, who loses his job as a result of the Manhattan fire of 1835 and must take up teaching in a one-
room country schoolhouse.

16 JULY. Whitman has his head "read" by phrenologist
Lorenzo Fowler. The reading indicates he is high in self-
esteem, caution, amativeness (love for the opposite sex),
adhesiveness (capacity for same-sex love), and combat-
iveness (Gohdes and Silver, 233–236). Introduced to
phrenology in 1846 by a lecture on the subject by Orson

Fowler (brother of Lorenzo), Whitman followed its method of self-correction for many years.

5 AUGUST. Brooklyn supporters of the Free-Soil Party, which includes defectors from both the Democratic and Whig parties, meet to elect delegates to a convention in Buffalo; Whitman is among the fifteen delegates elected. The Buffalo convention nominates Whitman's candidate, Martin Van Buren, for president and Charles Francis Adams for vice president.

9 SEPTEMBER. Whitman publishes the first issue of the *Brooklyn Weekly Freeman.*

10 SEPTEMBER. A fire destroys the building where the *Freeman* is printed. The paper resumes publication two months later, after the Whig candidate for president, Zachary Taylor, is elected; by spring of 1849 it is a daily paper. It soon loses the support of the Free-Soilers, however, many of whom effect a compromise with their opponents and return to the Democratic Party.

30 OCTOBER. Walter pays $100 for a lot on Myrtle Avenue in Brooklyn on which a house is erected for him and his family, with a printing office and bookstore on the first floor.

1849

29 MAY. Two days before Walter's thirtieth birthday, Brooklyn's Plymouth Church, where the abolitionist Henry Ward Beecher is minister, buries a time capsule. Among the twenty-four newspapers included is the *Brooklyn Daily Freeman.*

11 SEPTEMBER. Whitman resigns the editorship of the *Freeman*, which ends the paper.

1850

2 MARCH. "Song for Certain Congressmen" is published in the *New York Evening Post*. With a deliberately insulting

lyric (later called "Dough-Face Song") aimed at those congressmen who sought some compromise over the slavery issue, the poem sneers:

> Principle — freedom! — fiddlesticks!
>   We know not where they're found.
> Rights of the masses — progress! — bah!
>   Words that tickle and sound;
> But claiming to rule o'er "practical men"
>   Is very different ground (EPF, 45)

22 MARCH. "Blood-Money" is published in the *New York Tribune Supplement*. The poem scathingly compares those who back passage of the proposed Fugitive Slave Law, such as Daniel Webster, to Judas Iscariot, who betrayed Jesus.

14 JUNE. "The House of Friends," a poem, appears in the *New York Tribune*. Like "Blood-Money," the poem (later "Wounded in the House of Friends") reveals Whitman's bitterness at the passage of the series of laws that come to be known as the Compromise of 1850.

17 JUNE. From 106 Myrtle Avenue, Brooklyn, Whitman writes to the editors of the *New York Sun* offering for serial publication "The Sleeptalker," his condensed version of an English translation of the Danish romantic novel *The Children of King Erik Menved*, by Bernhard Severin Ingemann (CORR, 5:282–283; 282, n2). Ingemann's novel, in the style of Sir Walter Scott, has been translated by J. Kesson in an 1846 London edition not published in the United States. Whitman's title is taken from "a singular trait of one of the principal actors in the narrative" and no doubt is drawn from Bellini's opera *La Sonnambula*, based on Scott's *The Bride of Lammermoor*.

21 JUNE. Another poem, "Resurgemus," is published in the *New York Tribune*. Carried over into the 1855 *Leaves of Grass*, the poem refers to the 1848 revolutions in Europe. Its closing lines suggest the poet equates the wait for full liberty in the "house" of the United States with the wait for its arrival in Europe (EPF, 40).

1851–1854

Little is known of Whitman's activities in these years. In 1851 he is still living with his family in the house on Myrtle Avenue, where he works in his first-floor shop. For a short time he prints a single-sheet advertising paper, the *Salesman*, and in 1851 issues *The Salesman and Traveller's Directory for Long Island*. William Cullen Bryant's newspaper, the *Evening Post*, helps keep Whitman's name before the public: the 1 February 1851 issue carries an article by Whitman describing the Brooklyn Art Union (on 31 March he lectures there on "Art and Artists" [reprinted in UPP, 1:241–247]); a letter to the editor dated 21 March 1851 is full of civic pride for the rapidly growing city of Brooklyn; and a series of letters-essays from Paumanok, written during visits to his sister in Greenport, appear that summer. (Whitman always prefers "Paumanok," the Native American name for Long Island, and later uses it poetically, as he does "Mannahatta" for New York City.) Concerned for the health of his fellow Brooklynites, especially in light of the return of cholera in 1849, Whitman writes an article in that city's daily *Advertiser* for 28 June 1851 on the need for pure water of the sort New York has secured its citizens by building the Croton reservoir. In December 1851 he sees Louis Kossuth, hero of the Hungarian revolution of 1848, parade up Broadway during his visit to the United States (NUPM, 3:1065).

In March 1852 Walter's sister Hannah marries Charles Heyde, an artist whom Walter has introduced to the family. In May 1852 he sells the Myrtle Avenue house and builds another on Cumberland Street (perhaps with the help of his father, though Walter Sr. is not well) into which the family moves in September. In March of the following year Walter sells the Cumberland Street house, and in April the family moves into a small house on the same street. By May 1854 they are living on Skillman Street and in May 1855 on Ryerson Street, where Whitman lives at the time *Leaves of Grass* is published. Though Whitman later remembers it as having been September 1850 when he and his ailing father visit West Hills, biographers claim the year to have been either 1853 or 1854 (Allen, *Solitary Singer*, 561). Whitman's account of the visit includes details of the transportation between Brooklyn and West Hills: "We went up in the LIRR [Long Island Rail Road], and so in the stage to Woodbury — then on foot, along the turnpike and 'across lots' to Colyer's [Hannah Colyer, his father's sister and widow of Richard Colyer]" (NUPM, 1:4). Another railroad trip, probably in 1853, is to East Chatham, New York, to visit the Shaker community at Mount Lebanon. Whitman takes copious notes, with drawings, probably for an article, which may not have been written. He mentions meeting Shaker Elder Frederick W. Evans, who before 1830 had been associated with Frances Wright in plans for an intentional community (Holloway, "Whitman's Visit").

"Poem of Apparitions in Boston, the 78th Year of These States," later known as "A Boston Ballad," may be written in June 1854 at the time of the arrest and trial in Boston of Anthony Burns, a fugitive slave. In July 1854 Whitman has his picture taken by Gabriel Harrison, a Brooklyn photographer; from this an engraving on steel is later made, and that image is used as the frontispiece of the first edition of *Leaves of Grass*. On 20 October 1854 the *Evening Star* publishes Whitman's letter to the city council of Brooklyn in which he denounces that body for enacting Sunday blue laws forbidding streetcars and railroads to operate on Sunday.

In this period Whitman's liking for Italian opera develops into a passion. One of the 1851 letters from Paumanok is entirely on the subject of opera, and in 1855 he publishes "A Visit to the Opera," an essay in the New York magazine *Life Illustrated*. During these years there are reviews and notebook references to specific performances and singers (including the famed Jenny Lind and singers Giulia Grisi and Giovanni Mario) and an enthusiasm unmatched by any shown for his various other interests. Much of this, as well as his attendance at plays, is recounted in an 1885 piece, "The Old Bowery" (reprinted in PW, 2:591–597). He also visits repeatedly the year-long Crystal Palace Exhibition that opens in New York in 1853 and probably as often the Egyptian Museum of Dr. Henry Abbott on Broadway (PW, 2:681, 696–697).

Still another interest in these years, and the one most clearly reflected in his work, is language. According to Horace Traubel, in the early 1850s Whitman worked on the material Traubel later published as *An American Primer* (reprinted in DN, 3:729–757). In this work Whitman is fashioning a dictionary of American words that to his mind reflect "the new world, the new times, the new peoples"; this interest in language carries over into *Leaves*, which, Traubel claims, Whitman sometimes believed was "only a language experiment" (DN, 3:729).

CHAPTER TWO

1855-1859

... a bard commensurate with a people
— Preface, 1855 *Leaves of Grass*

The year 1855 is pivotal in Whitman's life. With the publication of *Leaves of Grass*, the thirty-six-year-old Whitman bursts upon the local and national scene in a way no other writer in America had. In an unhappy coincidence, Walter Whitman Sr. dies within a week of the publication.

The first eminent literary figure to take notice of *Leaves* is Ralph Waldo Emerson, who, having received a copy from the author, responds with a congratulatory letter soon to be read by many. With a lack of modesty that begins with the reviews he himself writes to puff his work, Whitman releases Emerson's letter to a New York newspaper without having secured Emerson's consent. Whitman's new eminence brings visits from various New England transcendentalists, including Moncure Conway, Henry David Thoreau, Amos Bronson Alcott, and, greatest of all, the admiring Emerson.

Perhaps because of this new attention, Whitman begins an intensive course of self-education; his notebooks for the years 1856–1859 indicate a wide reading in literature, geography, and European history. Whitman is preparing himself for what he believes will be a prominent career as writer and lecturer, but the reading public, unlike the New England literati, is not interested in his work. Nevertheless, in September 1856 Whitman publishes a second edition of *Leaves,* in which he demonstrates a more nationalistic and a more sexual poetic intent. Sometime in 1856 he writes a political diatribe, "The Eighteenth Presidency!," which is not published in his lifetime, and lays plans, which never materialize, for a career as a traveling lecturer. Whitman is looking in many directions at once, trying to fashion a career that will serve his primary interest, to have an effect on the American public and on the future of the nation.

Friendships formed about this time include those with abolitionists, crusaders for women's rights, and bohemians, as well as influential people in the publishing world. Women figure in his life as friends: Abigail (Abby) Price, Sarah Tyndale, and Sara Parton, better known as Fanny Fern, a newspaper columnist and author of the popular *Fern Leaves from Fanny's Portfolio* (1853). In laying out his own book Whitman not only faintly echoes the title of Fern's but also its leafy cover design. Whitman later finds himself pressured by James Parton, Fern's husband, for repayment of a loan on which he cannot make good.

In May 1857 Whitman begins working for the *Brooklyn Daily Times*, perhaps as editor but at least as a contributor of articles on such issues as the Brooklyn water works. Not only is Whitman personally interested in the water works — his brother Jeff is employed there — but he also champions the engineering feat the water works is undertaking, bringing clean water to Brooklyn, as a matter of civic improvement. He finds himself caught between his desire to publish another edition of *Leaves of Grass* and his publisher's (Fowler & Wells) reluctance to do so. Whitman finds himself again without work, and, if judged by the sonnetlike sequence of poems produced around this time, suffers a severe setback in love. Evenings spent at Pfaff's, a bohemian bar and restaurant on Broadway near Bleecker Street in Manhattan (where William Dean Howells makes a point of being introduced), provide an escape, as does the continual creation of poems intended for the next edition of *Leaves*. Before that happens Whitman publishes "A Child's Reminiscence," which is harshly criticized by at least one reviewer.

1855

6 JULY. The *New York Tribune* announces that "Walt Whitman's Poems, 'Leaves of Grass,'" is for sale by two establishments, one in Brooklyn and one in New York; the price is $2.

Leaves of Grass is printed (795 copies) by the Rome Brothers in Brooklyn and is distributed by Fowler & Wells (the brothers Lorenzo and Orson S. Fowler and Samuel R. Wells), publishers of the *American Phrenological Journal* (Myerson, *Walt Whitman*, 19). The book is a thin volume of just ninety-five pages. Some issues are bound in paper, others in dark green cloth. The covers of some, back and front, bear scrolls of ornamental leaves, and the book's title appears to sprout leaves and roots. The title follows a popular publishing conceit of the time by punning on leaves of a plant and leaves of a book. No author's name is given (though the name Walt Whitman appears midway through the first poem), but the copyright holder is identified as Walter Whitman, and a frontispiece engraving of a daguerreotype shows a young man casually dressed in the attire of a working man. Both the laborer's dress and the familiar "Walt" are part of the poet's attempt to distinguish himself from the American poetic establishment (where three-part formal names are the rule) and to identify with the working-class segment of society, which he believes is not represented in American poetry.

A long preface, loosely punctuated, puts forth a theory of poetry for America that emphasizes the need for a new kind of poetry suited to the new nation, which is itself "essentially the greatest poem." The "American bard" who will most faithfully transcribe that poetry, which lies innate within the nation, will be no delineator of class or particular interests and will not be "for the eastern states more than the western or the northern states more than the southern" (LGF, vii).

The twelve poems that follow are untitled (though several are grouped together under the title "Leaves of Grass"); the first — and longest — later known as "Song of Myself," begins: "I celebrate myself, / And what I assume you shall assume, / For every atom belonging to me as good belongs to you" (LGF, 13). Of the remaining poems, with the exception of "Resurgemus," published earlier (1850), there are none that are like anything Whitman has published to this time, though in their length and proselike quality they resemble the poetic fragments that have begun to appear in his notebooks in the early 1850s. Critics have generally agreed on the particular importance of two of the twelve poems, those that came to be known as "Song of Myself" and "The Sleepers."

11 JULY. Walter Whitman Sr. dies and is buried in the Cemetery of the Evergreens, Brooklyn (Allen, *Solitary Singer*, 151).

21 JULY. Having received a complimentary copy of *Leaves* from Whitman, Ralph Waldo Emerson writes from Concord, Massachusetts, to congratulate its author:

> Dear Sir,
>
> I am not blind to the worth of the wonderful gift of "Leaves of Grass." I find it the most extraordinary piece of wit & wisdom that America has yet contributed. I am very happy in reading it, as great power makes us happy. It meets the demand I am always making of what seemed the sterile & stingy Nature, as if too much handiwork or too much lymph in the temperament were making our western wits fat & mean.
>
> I give you joy of your free & brave thought. I have great joy in it. I find incomparable things said incomparably well, as they must be. I find the courage of *treatment*, which so delights us, & which large perception only can inspire.
>
> I greet you at the beginning of a great career, which yet must have had a long foreground somewhere, for such a start. I rubbed my eyes a little to see if this sunbeam were no illusion; but the solid sense of the book is a sober certainty. It has the best merits, namely, of fortifying & encouraging.
>
> I did not know until I, last night, saw the book advertised in a newspaper, that I could trust the

name as real & available for a Post-office. I wish to
see my benefactor, & have felt much like striking
my tasks, & visiting New York to pay you my respects. (Bucke, *Walt Whitman*, 138–139)

23 JULY. The first review of *Leaves of Grass*, by Charles A.
Dana, appears in the *New York Daily Tribune*. Positive in
almost all aspects, it calls Whitman an "odd genius" of
the type Emerson had called for (Price, *Reviews*, 3–8).

28 JULY. An anonymous review of *Leaves* appears in *Life
Illustrated*, a New York weekly magazine published by
Fowler & Wells; it claims the book "might be called,
American Life, from a Poetical Loafer's Point of View"
(Price, *Reviews*, 8).

SUMMER. Walt spends some time in Greenport, Long Island, with his sister Mary and her husband.

17 SEPTEMBER. Moncure Conway, a young transcendental-
ist, writes to Emerson describing his visit with Whitman
at the Rome Brothers print shop and how he told Whitman of Emerson's enthusiasm for *Leaves*. He tells of
Whitman accompanying him back to New York on the
ferry and how Whitman was "hail fellow" to all of the la-
boring class he met (Myerson, *Time*, 192–193). In 1882 a
former employee of the East River steamboat line will re-
call how Whitman used his skills as a teacher to fill in
gaps in the education of the boatmen and provide them
with books from his own library. In return he learns
everything he can about the operation of the boats.
Known to all as Walt, his presence on deck is welcomed
by the boatmen (Bucke, *Walt Whitman*, 32–34).

29 SEPTEMBER. The *Brooklyn Times* publishes "Walt Whitman, A Brooklyn Boy," an anonymous review of *Leaves*
and an account of its author's life (Price, *Reviews*, 21–22).
This review is written by Whitman.

SEPTEMBER. Charles Eliot Norton anonymously reviews
Leaves of Grass for *Putnam's Magazine* and finds it a
puzzling mixture of "Yankee transcendentalism and New
York rowdyism": "The writer's scorn for the wonted us-

ages of good writing extends to the vocabulary he adopts; words usually banished from polite society are here employed without reserve" (Price, *Reviews*, 14–18). The monthly *United States Review* prints an unsigned, glowing ("An American bard at last!") review of *Leaves of Grass* (Price, *Reviews*, 8–14); this review, too, is written by Whitman.

10 OCTOBER. The *New York Daily Tribune* publishes, with Whitman's permission but not Emerson's, the text of Emerson's letter praising *Leaves of Grass*.

OCTOBER. The *American Phrenological Journal* carries an anonymous review of *Leaves* and Alfred, Lord Tennyson's *Maud, and Other Poems*. The review unfavorably compares England's poet laureate to the new American poet, who is hailed as the representative of a new age.

10 NOVEMBER. Rufus Griswold writes an unsigned review of *Leaves* in the *New York Criterion*, referring to it as "this gathering of muck" (Price, *Reviews*, 26–27).

11 DECEMBER. Emerson apparently first visits Whitman, at the Ryerson Street house in Brooklyn (Rusk, 374). Late in life Whitman tells Horace Traubel he remembers still Emerson's "gentle knock" at the door of the Whitman house, his "slow sweet voice," and the words, "I came to see Mr. Whitman" (WWC, 2:130). According to this account, Whitman and Emerson go by ferry to New York where they dine. Whitman takes his visitor to a social function at Fireman's Hall, which the staid Emerson little enjoys, while Whitman is in his element (Rusk, 374).

Between 1 November 1855 and 8 November 1856 Whitman publishes articles on a variety of subjects in *Life Illustrated*. Some appear as part of a series titled "New York Dissected" (reprinted in Holloway and Adimari; the final article is reprinted in Loving, "Broadway"). These help keep his name before the public, no doubt with a view to increasing sales of his book. Despite Whitman's claim in the open letter addressed to Emerson in the 1856 edition of *Leaves*, it is very doubtful that all copies of the first edition are sold.

1856

JANUARY. Edward Everett Hale reviews *Leaves of Grass* for the *North American Review* (see Price, *Reviews*, 34–36). This is a positive review in the country's most influential literary journal. In later years Whitman will claim to have been roundly rejected by the critics, but scholars, noting the impressive number of approving or semi-approving reviews, conclude that the poet's major disappointment over the years was his failure to reach the masses for whom he wrote.

1 MAY. The Whitmans move to a house on Classon Avenue, far from the center of Brooklyn. It is a brownstone with five floors. Louisa Whitman takes in boarders while she and her family live in just part of the house. Walt shares an attic bedroom with his brother Eddie.

10 MAY. Fanny Fern (Sarah Payson Willis Parton), the highest-paid newspaper columnist of the time and a popular writer of prose and poetry, reviews *Leaves of Grass* in the *New York Ledger* and refers to Whitman as "this glorious Native American." She is the first woman to publish a positive review of *Leaves of Grass* (Joyce Warren, 160, 165–166; Price, *Reviews*, 46–48).

17 JUNE. Samuel R. Wells of Fowler & Wells writes to Walt that the poet must omit certain passages of *Leaves of Grass* or they will not publish it (CORR, 1:44, n10).

2 AUGUST. "The Slave Trade," an exposé of the use of New York's harbor by a slave ship providing slaves to Cuban sugar plantations, is published in *Life Illustrated*. It marks Whitman's return to the subject of slavery.

16 AUGUST. *Life Illustrated* announces that a new edition of *Leaves of Grass* will be published by 1 September.

SUMMER. Probably in this summer Whitman writes an essay titled "The Eighteenth Presidency!," which he subtitles "Voice of Walt Whitman to Each Young Man in the Nation, North, South, East and West." This essay, never published in his lifetime and found only in proof sheets, is intended to register Whitman's disgust with the presidencies of Zachary Taylor and Franklin Pierce and his desire to see as president someone who is independent of political parties. Addressed to the workingmen of the nation, the essay is crude and volatile in its language and naive in its belief that any honest workman could undertake national leadership.

SEPTEMBER. The second edition of *Leaves* appears. It contains a total of thirty-two poems but is smaller in overall size and omits the Preface of the previous year, though some of the same sentiments appear as prose poems. The volume contains a number of new poems, including "Sun-Down Poem" (later "Crossing Brooklyn Ferry"), where Whitman reaches a new height in poetic achievement. Poems now have titles (many of them ludicrously lengthy), and each is labeled "poem," as in "Poem of Walt Whitman, an American" (later "Song of Myself") and — one of the longest — "Poem for Asia, Africa, Europe, America, Australia, Cuba, and the Archipelagoes of the Sea." Punctuation, noticeably absent in the 1855 edition, is here regularized. Emblazoned in gold stamp on the spine of the 1856 edition is a passage from Emerson's letter of praise, "I Greet You at the Beginning of a Great Career," and the entire letter is reproduced (again without prior notification or permission) at the end of the poetical text, along with reviews — favorable and unfavorable — of the first edition. Appended to the Emerson letter is a response from Whitman offering Emerson (addressed as "dear Friend and Master") the new poems. Boasting untruthfully of a rapid sale of the entire 1855 edition, Whitman declares to Emerson his intention of printing several thousand copies of this second edition and of continuing to write "perhaps a thousand" poems. He concludes, with a flourish, that in a few years there will be an annual call for his poems of some "ten or twenty thousand." (For an analysis of this letter, see Price, *Whitman and Tradition.*) Whitman's unauthorized publication of Emerson's letter scandalizes many, and Emerson himself claims it to have been "very wrong indeed" (Rusk, 317) but does not retract his praise. In

1867 Whitman will approve John Burroughs's statement in *Notes on Walt Whitman, as Poet and Person* that he had not read Emerson until 1856, but he probably comes closer to the truth when he allegedly tells John Townsend Trowbridge in 1860, "I was simmering, simmering; Emerson brought me to a boil" (Myerson, *Time*, 173). (On the question of the Emerson and Whitman relationship, see Loving, *Emerson, Whitman*.)

4 OCTOBER. Amos Bronson Alcott, having come from Concord in the company of Henry David Thoreau, visits Whitman in his Brooklyn home. Alcott and Thoreau have traveled to New York at the urging of Emerson and because both are impressed by the 1855 *Leaves*. Alcott finds Whitman a man of "brute power," one "not so easily described." Nonetheless he provides one of the most detailed physical descriptions ever offered of Whitman at the outset of his poetic career:

> Broad-shouldered, rouge-fleshed, Bacchus-browed, bearded like a satyr, and rank, he wears his man-Bloomer in defiance of everybody, having these as everything else after his own fashion, and for example to all men hereafter. Red flannel undershirt, open-breasted, exposing his brawny neck; striped calico jacket over this, the collar Byroneal, with coarse cloth overalls buttoned to it; cowhide boots; a heavy round-about, with huge outside pockets and buttons to match; and a slouched hat, for house and street alike. Eyes gray, un-imaginative, cautious yet sagacious; his voice deep, sharp, tender sometimes and almost melting. When talking will recline upon the couch at length, pillowing his head upon his bended arm, and informing you naively how lazy he is, and slow. (Shepard, 286–287)

8 NOVEMBER. "Broadway, the Magnificent!" appears in *Life Illustrated*.

9 NOVEMBER. Alcott and Thoreau call on Whitman but fail

to find him at home. Louisa Whitman visits with them, offering much praise of her son (Shepard, 289).

10 NOVEMBER. Alcott and Thoreau return, bringing Sarah Tyndale, Philadelphia abolitionist and women's rights advocate; all three visit with Walt.

19 NOVEMBER. Thoreau writes to his friend Harrison Blake that Whitman is "apparently the greatest democrat the world has seen," adding, "I am still somewhat in a quandary about him,—feel that he is essentially strange to me, at any rate" (Thoreau, 142). They are "strange" to each other; both men are very strong-minded, and though Whitman admires the New Englander, he finds him disdainful of the working class (WWC, 1:212).

20 NOVEMBER. Alcott, Thoreau, and John Swinton, a printer and Free-Soil advocate, dine with Whitman in Brooklyn.

7 DECEMBER. Thoreau writes again to Blake that, having read the second edition of *Leaves*, he finds the poems "exhilarating, encouraging," though it seems to him that Whitman "does not celebrate love at all. It is as if the beasts spoke" (Thoreau, 144).

12 DECEMBER. Alcott and Whitman meet again in New York and dine at Taylor's Saloon, where they talk of the general condition of the country and Walt declares "the growing of Emerson" the "best" thing it has achieved (Shepard, 293).

28 DECEMBER. Alcott writes in his journal that he and Thoreau paid a visit to the home of Samuel Longfellow, brother of Henry Wadsworth Longfellow; Whitman, also invited, came in his "Bloomers and behaving very becomingly, though not at home, very plainly, in parlours" (Shepard, 294). "Bloomers" refers to a style of very full and loose-fitting pants that Whitman wears tucked into his boots. They are the male equivalent of the loose pants worn by such women's rights advocates as Amelia Bloomer, after whom they are named, and Whitman's friend Abby Price.

1857

25 FEBRUARY. Whitman dines with Hector Tyndale, son of Sarah Tyndale, and seeks advice of this well-traveled importer and businessman for the improvement of his poems. Tyndale suggests "breath" without concern for details (NUPM, 1:351).

MAY. Whitman goes to work on the *Brooklyn Daily Times*, perhaps as its editor. It is located at 145 Grand Street but a year later moves to a location on South Seventh Street (now Broadway) near the ferry depot. The subject of Whitman's connection to the *Times* is still unclear. The assumption that he was the *Times*'s editor is based on identifications by Emory Holloway of more than two hundred *Times* editorials and numerous reviews as Whitman's (Holloway, *Uncollected Poetry*; see also Holloway and Schwarz). In 1885 Whitman is queried by a letter writer about his employment at the *Brooklyn Times*, and his response does not imply an editorship (see chapter 7).

16 JUNE. A police riot occurs in New York City, requiring the army to intervene; Whitman records the event in his notebook (NUPM, 1:272).

17 JUNE. Oliver Dyer, an attorney representing James Parton, arrives at the Whitman home to collect money owed by Walt. Parton, a successful biographer, is the husband of Fanny Fern (Sara Parton). In a 21 April 1856 letter to Whitman, Fern had written admiringly of *Leaves of Grass* and invited him to call. A friendship then developed between the Partons and the poet. When Whitman was eager to buy the plates of *Leaves* from Fowler & Wells, Parton had offered a loan of $200, which Whitman accepted, giving a note in exchange. When the note was due, Whitman was unable to pay. In lieu of payment, several of Walt's books and an oil painting are removed from the Whitman house; Dyer fails to deliver these to Parton, who thereafter considers Whitman a defaulter (WWC, 3:237–238).

20 JUNE. Whitman writes to Sarah Tyndale that he has a hundred poems ready for publication but that Fowler & Wells "retard" the book; he intends to purchase the plates from them and bring out a third edition of *Leaves* (CORR, 1:44).

24 JULY. Tyndale offers a loan of $50 toward purchase of the plates.

IN THIS YEAR. Whitman has plans to publish in two years' time a book of 365 poems that will be "a new Bible," but it is not to be. Instead, he continues writing articles for the *Times* and lives at home with his mother and brothers George, Jeff, and Eddie.

1858

SUMMER. Walt has a warning of the strokes that are to come, for he claims to have had a "sunstroke" that causes dizziness and weakness.

1859

FEBRUARY. Jeff marries Martha Emma Mitchell (Mattie) and brings her to live with his family in a house on Portland Avenue when the Whitmans move there in May.

SPRING. Walt reads Dante's "Inferno," which he values greatly for its economy of words and its "simplicity — like the Bible's." Twelve poems written in 1859 (probably in spring or early summer) are collectively titled "Live Oak with Moss" and evolve into the "Calamus" poems of the 1860 *Leaves*. Evidently intended as a sonnet sequence, the poems recount a love affair with a man that ends unhappily.

AROUND THIS TIME. Whitman spends time at Pfaff's. Owned by Charles Pfaff, this bar and restaurant is the gathering place for most of the city's bohemians. Here the poet meets theater people (including the notorious

Ada Clare — actually Jane McElheney — mistress of American composer Louis Moreau Gottschalk), musicians, freethinkers of all kinds, critics, newspaper writers, and even other poets and writers. Here, too, he meets Henry Clapp, editor of the *Saturday Press*, a literary periodical founded in 1858, and, in 1860, William Dean Howells. An 1863 letter from John Swinton describes Whitman's activities at Pfaff's: "to sit by Pfaff's privy and eat sweet-breads and drink coffee, and listen to the intolerable wit of the crack-brains" (WWC, 1:416). Whitman later claims his greatest pleasure in Pfaff's was "to look on — to see, talk little, absorb" (WWC, 1:417). A draft of a poem on the subject of Pfaff's never goes beyond the notebook version (see NUPM, 1:454).

26 JUNE. Walt cautions himself in his notebook: "It is now time to <u>Stir</u> first for <u>Money</u> enough <u>to live</u> and provide for <u>M</u> . <u>To Stir</u> — first write Stories and get out of this Slough" (NUPM, 1:405). "M" may be his mother, his sister Mary, or a lover (Holloway and Schwarz, 16).

SUMMER. Whitman is out of work and has no publishing prospects for a new edition of *Leaves*. Nevertheless, his notebooks are filled with proposals for new poems; one, "Pictures," appears to be a completed version (NUPM, 4:1295 ff). While poetry is still his primary interest, it does not pay, and so he turns his thoughts to writing fiction.

24 DECEMBER. "A Child's Reminiscence" (later "Out of the Cradle Endlessly Rocking") appears on the front page of the *Saturday Press* Christmas issue. The poem is in two parts, the "Pre-Verse," a twenty-one-line opening statement that establishes both setting and mood, and the remaining stanzas, called "Reminiscence." Perhaps a recollection of an incident from childhood (Whitman tells Abby Price it is based on fact), the reminiscence is of a child's discovery of a pair of mockingbirds on a Long Island beach.

28 DECEMBER. A review in the *Cincinnati Daily Commercial* calls "A Child's Reminiscence" "inexplicable non-

sense" and its author "a person of coarse nature and strong, rude passions" (Consolo, 21).

IN THIS YEAR. Whitman may write parts of *Rambles Among Words*, a book on English etymology published in this year by his friend and instructor in French, William Swinton (see James Perrin Warren).

CHAPTER THREE

1860-1863

Quicksand years . . .
—*Drum-Taps*, 1865

"Quicksand years that whirl me I know not whither," Whitman writes in the opening line of an 1861 poem. The term "quicksand" aptly describes the turbulence of these years, which begin with the unexpected appearance of a publisher for *Leaves of Grass*. The Boston firm of Thayer & Eldridge allows Whitman a free hand in the book's production, and the 1860 edition is, in his eyes, "first rate." Mutually delighted with their partnership, Whitman and his publishers immediately plan another book, but the 1861 bankruptcy of the Boston firm ends all such hopes.

While Whitman is in Boston, Emerson urges the poet to eliminate some of the more sexual poems, but Whitman refuses. In Boston Whitman meets William Douglas O'Connor who, with his wife, Ellen (Nellie), enters the first rank of Whitman admirers. Another admirer appears as well, John Townsend Trowbridge, to whom, it is alleged, Whitman professes Emerson's defining influence.

In April 1861, as he is coming from the opera, Whitman learns of the firing on Fort Sumter. Not long after, his brothers George and Andrew enlist. Whitman is caught up in the war fever that overtakes the North in the wake of its overwhelming defeat at the battle of First Bull Run and sounds his own alarum, "Beat! Beat! Drums!," his first poetic effort of the war.

In 1862 George is wounded slightly at Fredericksburg, Virginia. Having gone to be with him, Walt remains in Washington in hopes of securing employment with a government agency. The only work available to him is as a copyist in the Army Paymaster's Office, but proximity to the army hospitals allows Whitman to undertake an important role as hospital visitor, bringing solace and cheer to the wounded and dying. Throughout 1863 he maintains a steady correspondence with family members in Brooklyn, with friends there and in New York, and with some recovered soldiers who have returned to their regiments. In his letters he tells of seeing President Lincoln almost daily, as well as captured Southern troops being marched up Pennsylvania Avenue and of his July Fourth celebration with the wounded. Whitman plans a book of war memoranda to be based on his experiences and on those related to him by soldiers.

At home, his family falls into considerable disarray, principally because Andrew, having completed his three-month enlistment, is afflicted with a serious throat ailment. At Jeff's urging, Walt obtains a leave of absence from his work and returns to Brooklyn late in 1863; the day after he arrives back in Washington Andrew dies. While his brother is still lying dead in the house, another brother, the emotionally troubled Jesse, exhibits threatening behavior toward family members, and Jeff solicits Walt's help in effecting his institutionalization.

1860

7 JANUARY. "All About a Mocking-Bird" appears in the *Saturday Press*; obviously written by Whitman, it responds to the *Cincinnati Daily Commercial*'s ridicule of "A Child's Reminiscence." Whitman defends the poem and takes the opportunity to announce that "there will also soon crop out the true 'Leaves of Grass,' the fuller-grown work of which the former two issues were the inchoates" (Consolo, 25).

14 JANUARY. "You and Me and To-Day" (later "With Antecedents") appears in the *Saturday Press*. Henry Clapp, owner of the *Saturday Press*, allows Walt access to the pages of his newspaper in order to keep the poet's name before the public. He is also helpful in marketing the 1860 edition of *Leaves*. In 1888 Whitman tells Horace Traubel that Clapp, through his newspaper, was a "much

needed ally" in 1860 "when almost the whole press of America when it mentioned me at all treated me with derision or worse" (see WWC, 1:236). In the pages of the *Saturday Press*, a number of women defend Whitman and the 1860 edition of *Leaves* (Ceniza, 110–134).

JANUARY. Whitman becomes more aggressive in seeking publication of his poems. He offers *Harper's Magazine* a new poem, "A Chant of National Feuillage," asking payment of $40, offers "Thoughts" to the *New York Sunday Courier* for $10, and writes to James Russell Lowell, editor of the *Boston Courier*, regarding "Bardic Symbols," which has already been accepted. In all cases he reserves the right to republish the poems in a future collection (CORR, 1:46–48).

10 FEBRUARY. The Boston publishers William Thayer and Charles Eldridge write to Whitman claiming, "We want to be the publishers of Walt Whitman's poems" (Allen, *Solitary Singer*, 236–237).

15 MARCH. Whitman arrives in Boston.

MARCH–APRIL. The *Boston Saturday Evening Gazette* carries a notice: "WALT WHITMAN IN BOSTON.—The poet of *Leaves of Grass* (who hails from New York) has been spending the last four weeks in Boston, busy in the overseeing of a much larger and superior collection of his tantalizing *Leaves*" (*Leaves of Grass Imprints*, 65). Radical in their political and social interests, Thayer and Eldridge are young men who seek to publish that which will advance their ideas. Impressed by *Leaves*, they are more than eager to add Whitman to their list of authors and offer him a free hand in the publication process. A series of letters in February and March establishes the agreement, and by mid-March Whitman is in Boston. By 29 March about 120 pages have been set up, and by 10 May the book is essentially complete. The new *Leaves* is electrotyped, with various typefaces adding an elegance to the finished work. Whitman is thoroughly pleased and declares the book "first rate."

Almost as soon as Whitman has settled in his boardinghouse in Boston, Emerson calls upon him. The two spend a day together, and as they walk the Boston Common Emerson advises against including the "Enfans d'Adam" poems in the new edition (PW, 1:281). Whitman will not consider this, believing expurgation "apology," "surrender," and "an admission that something or other was wrong" (WWC, 1:224). The matter settled, the two proceed to a friendly dinner at the American Hotel.

In Boston Whitman goes several times to services at the Methodist Seamen's Bethel Chapel to hear the famous preacher Father Edward Taylor (Father Mapple in Melville's *Moby Dick*), who has been a sailor and whose sermons are couched in sailor's terms. Whitman describes him as superior to Daniel Webster, Henry Clay, and other such celebrated speakers, the "one essentially perfect orator" he has heard (PW, 2:549).

Whitman's notebook kept during his Boston stay contains many references to places and people seen. One of the most interesting is his account of "black persons in Boston," whose status he finds very different from that of blacks in New York. In Boston, they hold good jobs, eat in whatever restaurants they please, and even serve on juries (NUPM, 1:422). The comment is significant because his Boston stay brings Whitman into immediate contact with abolitionists, a group he has long viewed as fanatical disunionists. Among them are William Douglas O'Connor, author of the abolitionist novel *Harrington* (1860) published by Thayer & Eldridge, and his wife, Ellen Tarr O'Connor. (For Ellen O'Connor's [later Ellen Calder] impressions of Whitman, see Myerson, *Time*, 194–212.) Another is the journalist John Townsend Trowbridge, to whom Whitman is said to have made his avowal of Emerson's empowering influence (see chapter 2). Trowbridge says of Whitman at this time: "He was not a loud laugher, and rarely made a joke, but he greatly enjoyed the pleasantries of others. He liked especially any allusion, serious or jocular, to his poems" (Trowbridge, 367).

The 1860 edition of *Leaves of Grass* is a thick volume of 456 pages, bound in cloth with various symbols of Whitman's choosing stamped on the cover. Still no author's name appears on the title page, and the frontispiece is a steel engraving of a photograph taken in New York by Charles Hine showing a very different (and much heavier) Whitman from the 1855 edition. This edition carries no prose preface and no reviews or letters, nothing but the poems, some of which are revised from the earlier two editions. There are 124 new poems, all titled ("Sun-Down Poem" is now and will remain "Crossing Brooklyn Ferry"), with numbered stanzas. A new poem, "Proto-Leaf," leads off the 1860 edition and presents the poet's intention in the way the 1855 prose preface does.

The most important addition is the "Calamus" group of poems. A cluster of forty-five poems named for a phallic-shaped plant found in swamp regions of the eastern United States, it celebrates the love of men for men. Scattered throughout the group are the twelve "Live Oak with Moss" love poems written in 1859, the best known of which is "I Saw in Louisiana a Live-Oak Growing." As a complement to "Calamus," the edition includes fifteen poems celebrating heterosexual love, "Enfans d'Adam" (later "Children of Adam"), among which is the often-anthologized poem later known as "I Sing the Body Electric." "A Child's Reminiscence" appears as "A Word Out of the Sea" and announces the theme of love and death that pervades this edition, viewed by many critics as Whitman's greatest. A facsimile of Whitman's working copy of this edition offers a glimpse of the poet at work, since Whitman used the 1860 edition for revision purposes in preparing the 1867 edition (see Golden).

APRIL. "Bardic Symbols" (later "As I Ebb'd with the Ocean of Life") appears in the *Atlantic Monthly*.

19 MAY. The *Saturday Press* announces the publication of the new *Leaves of Grass* and praises it.

24 MAY. Whitman arrives home from Boston (CORR, 1:54).

2 JUNE. A *Saturday Press* reviewer finds the new *Leaves* offensive and suggests that the author should commit suicide. This is surprising because the *Press* has been

Whitman's ally to this point, but the review may be designed to promote sales. The *Press* also publishes a number of Whitman parodies in this month.

16 JUNE. Whitman joins the New York crowds who turn out for a great parade on Broadway to welcome the first Japanese envoys to the United States. Following Commodore Matthew C. Perry's visit to Japan in 1853, Japan and the United States are about to embark on a trade agreement.

27 JUNE. The *New York Times* publishes "The Errand-Bearers" (later "A Broadway Pageant"), a poem about the parade of 16 June, and the "Princes of Asia."

JUNE. Numerous reviews of the new *Leaves* appear in the United States and in England; although they are mixed in their overall assessments, many are positive (Reynolds, 403–404).

10 OCTOBER. A defense of *Leaves* (now generally believed to have been written by the poet) appears in the *Brooklyn City News*.

11 OCTOBER. Edward, Prince of Wales, visits New York, and Whitman is in the crowd that gathers to see the future King Edward VII.

15 NOVEMBER. A meteor over New York later moves Whitman to write of 1859 as the "Year of Meteors," and he questions if he is not himself one of the meteors.

AROUND THIS TIME. Thayer & Eldridge advertise another book by Whitman said to be in preparation, *Banner At Day-Break*, to include "The Errand-Bearers" and other poems. The book never materializes, mainly because the publishers experience financial difficulties.

1861

10 JANUARY. The firm of Thayer & Eldridge declares bankruptcy; Whitman has received only $250 in royalties (Reynolds, 405). The plates of the 1860 edition of *Leaves* become the property of a Boston publisher, Richard Worthington, who issues a pirated edition (Golden, 2:xxxiv).

19 FEBRUARY. In New York Whitman sees Abraham Lincoln, who is on his way to Washington for the inauguration. Whitman is not a supporter of Lincoln, but with the outbreak of the Civil War he will come to fiercely admire the president's determination to maintain the union of states.

13 APRIL. Whitman attends a performance of Gaetano Donizetti's opera *Linda di Chamounix* at the New York Academy of Music; on his way home about midnight he buys a newspaper and reads of the firing on Fort Sumter in South Carolina on 12 April by Southern forces (Schmidgall, 59).

19 APRIL. George Whitman enlists in the Brooklyn Thirteenth Regiment for a hundred-day period. He goes to Washington for training and remains posted there for a time as part of the guard protecting the city against attack by Southern troops.

31 MAY. On his forty-second birthday, Whitman writes in his notebook that he has done well so far but that the best of his poem (*Leaves of Grass*) "remains unwritten" and is yet to be done (Furness, 135).

12 JULY. George Whitman's enlistment is almost over, and Walt writes him that the family is pleased because they suspect that, despite George's denials, there must be "*something*" to the newspaper accounts of mismanagement of the Thirteenth Regiment (CORR, 1:56). Army mismanagement later becomes a major complaint of Whitman's, part of the war which he claims is never reported.

15 JULY. "Longings for Home" (later "O Magnet-South") appears in the *Southern Literary Messenger.*

28 SEPTEMBER. "Beat! Beat! Drums!" appears in *Harper's Weekly* and in the *New York Leader.* This is Whitman's contribution to the effort, undertaken by most newspapers and periodicals in New York, to arouse readers to the Union cause following the defeat at Bull Run in July. Quite unlike the poems he will later write about the fateful consequences of war, this has all the emotion of war fever.

1 OCTOBER. Whitman offers the *Atlantic Monthly* three poems. They are rejected because of their contemporary nature, an indication that all three may have been as war specific as was one of them, "Eighteen Sixty-One," later part of the 1865 *Drum-Taps* (CORR, 1:57).

12 OCTOBER. The *New York Leader* publishes "Little Bells Last Night" (later "I Heard You Solemn-Sweet Pipes of the Organ"). The poem is a strange mixture of war and love in which the pulse of a loved one's embracing arm is imaged as "little bells" that seem to outsound the trumpets of war.

30 OCTOBER. Having reenlisted for three years or the war's duration (this time in New York's Fifty-first Volunteers), George Whitman leaves for camp.

2 NOVEMBER. "Old Ireland" appears in the *New York Leader*. During this period Whitman is unemployed except for the freelance writing he does for various newspapers and weekly magazines. Between 2 June 1861 and 1 November 1862 he contributes twenty-five articles to the *Brooklyn Daily Standard* under the running title "Brooklynania." These consist mainly of a loosely chronicled history of Brooklyn but also include accounts of trips to Long Island in the summer and fall of 1861 and sketches of New York scenes. He publishes another series of articles in the *New York Leader* under the title "City Photographs." The first four of these articles are reports of his visits to Broadway Hospital, located on Broadway near Pearl Street. Originally, the visits are an outgrowth of his interest in the city's stage drivers — often the victims of accidents — and Whitman comes to the hospital regularly. In 1861 he extends his attention to include the war wounded sent north. Filled with details of ward maintenance and information on the hospital's medical staff and patients, the articles forecast the work Whitman will soon undertake in Washington (see Glicksberg).

NOVEMBER. "Walt Whitman, poète, philosophe et 'rowdy'" appears in *La Revue Européenne*. An essay by Louis Etienne, it includes translations of some poems, the first translation of Whitman into French.

1862

Little documentation exists for events in Whitman's life for most of this year. He continues to supply articles and essays to newspapers and to visit Pfaff's for evening entertainment. Perhaps it is there Whitman meets someone called Ellen Eyre. A letter dated 25 March is from someone with (or using) that name who appears to have enjoyed at least one night's "pleasure" with him (Allen, *Solitary Singer*, 279).

28 MAY. Andrew Whitman enlists for a three-month term with the Union forces. Mustered in on 16 June, Andrew will be discharged in Brooklyn at the end of his term on 12 September (Murray).

16 DECEMBER. The *New York Herald* lists the wounded of the Fifty-first Regiment following the battle at Fredericksburg, Virginia, three days earlier; included is the name of First Lieutenant G. W. Whitmore (a misspelling), and Walt leaves the same day to find his brother.

In June 1861 the U.S. Sanitary Commission came into existence as a branch of the Army Medical Department, but the battle of First Bull Run (21 July 1861) had proven the inadequacy of that department to meet the needs of the wounded; hence civilians often went to tend their kin. Walt's journey is hectic: his money is stolen in Philadelphia, and he is unable to find George when he searches for him in the hospitals in Washington. Help comes when he encounters William D. O'Connor, now a clerk in a government office, and Charles Eldridge, his former publisher now assistant to the Army Paymaster. On 17 December he is in Falmouth, Virginia, where George, with a facial wound that is already healing, is preparing to return to active duty. George has been promoted twice and is promoted again, to captain, while Walt is still with him (CORR, 1:58−60).

25 DECEMBER. Walt spends Christmas in a large deserted campground under a clear sky in Virginia near the Rappahannock Army of the Potomac (NUPM, 2:508).

29 DECEMBER. Walt writes his mother detailed news of George and provides a firsthand report of her captain-son's life: "Every captain has a tent, in which he lives, transacts company business, etc., has a cook . . . and in the same tent mess and sleep his Lieutenants, and perhaps the first sergeant" (CORR, 1:60). In the same letter Walt describes one of his first sights on arriving at Falmouth, a "heap" of amputated limbs piled under a tree in front of the hospital. It is his first exposure to the grim fact of the thousands of amputations that occur in this war, some of which he describes in *Drum-Taps* and in *Specimen Days & Collect*. At the end of the letter he breaks the news that he will not return to Brooklyn immediately but will remain in Washington long enough to see if he can find employment.

ON THE SAME DATE. Whitman prepares to seek government employment in Washington and writes to Emerson requesting letters of recommendation to Secretary of State William H. Seward and Secretary of the Treasury Salmon P. Chase and an introductory letter to Senator Charles Sumner. He intends, he tells Emerson, to apply on literary, not political, grounds (CORR, 1:61).

Though Whitman is a New Yorker and Sumner a Massachusetts senator, Sumner is one of the most powerful men in the Senate, since the Republican Party (of which he is a co-founder) had come to power in 1861; Whitman hopes to gain Sumner's help through Emerson.

AROUND THIS TIME. Whitman hears of a soldier's experience, which he uses in one of his finest *Drum-Taps* poems, "A Sight in Camp in the Day-Break Gray and Dim," where he tells of uncovering the face of a dead soldier: "Young man, I think I know you — I think this face is the face of the Christ himself, / Dead and divine and brother of all, and here again he lies."

Louisa Whitman may receive the news of Walt's decision to remain in the Washington area with mixed feelings. While she is in need of the money his employment will provide, she also is heavily dependent upon this son for emotional support in dealing with her troubled and troublesome family. Crowded into the family quarters of the Portland Avenue house with her are Jesse (unstable and abusive), Edward (with several disabilities), and Jeff, his wife, and daughter Mannahatta (all three of whom frequently eat at Louisa's table). Andrew and Nancy, with their two sons, live nearby; Andrew is very ill, and Nancy, a heavy drinker and probably a prostitute, neglects her home and children. From a distance (Vermont) another daughter, Hannah, complains constantly of her husband's abuse, and he of her worthlessness. The extent to which Whitman feels these things and his mother's anxiety are both hinted at in a letter to Emerson of this time where he claims to be "excellent well, (my only torment, family matters)" (CORR, 1:61).

1863

2 JANUARY. Walt returns to Washington.

2–4 JANUARY. Walt writes a three-part letter to his sister-in-law Martha Whitman. The first part (2 January) describes the office, located in a house on Fifteenth and F Streets, of Major Lyman S. Hapgood, Army Paymaster, where he is a copyist — work obtained with the aid of Charles Eldridge (see entry for 16 December 1862). On 3 January he writes from the boardinghouse at 394 L Street where William D. and Ellen (Nellie) O'Connor live and where he is also staying. He describes his visits to Campbell Hospital (one of the recently constructed army hospitals) and some of the wounded he encounters there. The final part, added on 4 January, refers to the loss of the *Monitor*, the Union's ironclad vessel lost at sea 30 December 1862 (CORR, 1:62–64).

5 JANUARY. An article praising George's regiment appears in the *Brooklyn Daily Eagle* under the title "Our Brooklyn Boys in the War." Portions of this and similar newspaper articles published between 1863 and 1865 are later used in writing *Memoranda During the War* (1875) and *Specimen Days & Collect* (1882).

17 JANUARY. Whitman writes a long letter to Emerson describing the conditions at Campbell Hospital and mentioning his intention to write "a little book" on the war (CORR, 1:68–70; PW, 1:41–42). This is his first reference to *Drum-Taps*, to be published after the war's end.

JANUARY. Whitman writes a number of thank-you letters for funds sent to purchase items for the wounded in Washington hospitals. These items typically consist of fresh fruit, biscuits, tobacco, milk, paper to write letters home, and stamps to post them. Though in *Specimen Days* Whitman will speak highly of many of the female nurses, he is critical of the U.S. Sanitary Commission's agents; he refers to himself not as a nurse but as a "hospital visitor."

11 FEBRUARY. Whitman sees New York's Senator Preston King, who refuses to help him obtain work. Later he and Ellen O'Connor visit the Senate gallery and the Supreme Court, where Chief Justice Roger B. Taney and other justices appear to him as "a lot of old mummies" (NUPM, 2:553).

20 FEBRUARY. Whitman has an appointment with Senator Charles Sumner and asks if Sumner will give him "a boost" if by 4 March he has not yet obtained government employment (NUPM, 1:564). Later Whitman will learn of the prejudice against him that prevented him from obtaining the job he sought (see entry for 10 December 1863).

26 FEBRUARY. "The Great Army of the Sick: Military Hospitals in Washington," another letter-article, appears in the *New York Times* (PW, 1:296–300). Whitman discusses the newly constructed army hospitals, such as Armory Square (built in summer 1862), and their superiority to those set up in public buildings, such as the Patent Office hospital.

7 MARCH. George Whitman arrives in Brooklyn on furlough.

19 MARCH. Another of Whitman's letters, "The Great Washington Hospital," appears in the *Brooklyn Daily Eagle*. Like the *Times* piece, it is critical of hospital bureaucracy, which extends military discipline into the wards.

ON THE SAME DATE. Whitman writes a letter to two male friends in New York in which he tells of "a tremendous friendship" he has struck up with a young Mississippi captain about nineteen years old: "our affection is quite an affair, quite romantic — sometimes when I lean over to say I am going, he puts his arm round my neck, draws my face down, etc., quite a scene for the New Bowery" (CORR, 1:81).

21 APRIL. Walt writes to Thomas P. Sawyer, a sergeant from Massachusetts. It is a long letter filled with news of other soldiers he and Sawyer knew while the latter was in the hospital and of Walt's current activities. It is highly emotional, largely because Whitman is not sure he will ever see Sawyer again and is eager to convey the fullness of his affection: "My love you have in life or death forever" (CORR, 1:90–93). Sawyer, wounded at Bull Run on 29 August 1862, has recovered at the Armory Square Hospital where Whitman visits. Both during and after the war, Whitman writes many letters to Sawyer but hears from him infrequently.

26 APRIL. Whitman writes to Sawyer again; while he has heard nothing from Sawyer, others have. Whitman gently reproves him for not coming to pick up some clothing he held ready for him to take when he left Washington. Though ready to supply Sawyer with clothing, Whitman writes to his mother on 28 April that since leaving Brooklyn he has not yet bought any new clothes; in May she sends him some shirts. As in the earlier letter, he assures Sawyer of his continuing love and prays God will allow Sawyer to feel "a little at least of the feeling I have about you" (CORR, 1:94).

ON THE SAME DATE. Whitman receives a letter from "dear comrade & brother" Thomas Sawyer and makes a note of it, without further comment, in his notebook (NUPM, 2:531).

2 MAY. Whitman sees a procession of about a hundred Confederate soldiers pass down Pennsylvania Avenue on their way to prison. Filled with compassion for their

plight, he feels they are all his "brothers . . . Americans, silent proud young fellows" (NUPM, 2:533).

20 JUNE. Walt notes that his sister-in-law Martha, Jeff's wife, has had a baby girl (NUPM, 2:536). Jessie Louisa, born 17 June, is their second daughter (Mannahatta is the first), and on 22 June Walt writes his mother this is "all the better. (I am not sure but the Whitman breed gives better women than men)" (CORR, 1:110).

30 JUNE. Whitman writes to his mother and tells her how every evening the heavily guarded president passes along Fourteenth Street (where Whitman works in the Army Paymaster's Office) on his way to Soldier's Home outside Washington where he spends the hot summer nights: "he looks more careworn even than usual — his face with deep cut lines . . . very sad" (CORR, 1:113).

4 JULY. Whitman views a parade on Pennsylvania Avenue and learns of General George Meade's victory over General Robert E. Lee at Gettysburg on 4 July. He continues to go to the Armory Square Hospital with bottles of blackberry and cherry syrup, "good and strong, but innocent," which he mixes with ice water and distributes in the wards (PW, 1:54–55).

11 JULY. Whitman accompanies Major Hapgood to Analostan Island, off Georgetown, to issue payments to the First Regiment U.S. Colored Troops. The men look as though they have "the soldierstuff" in them and their officers enough of a military air to bring up some "'abolition' thoughts" (PW, 2:587–589).

JULY. Nothing is recorded in his diary for the month of July, and his correspondence falls off considerably, with fewer letters to his mother than usual. When he does write he speaks of hot and humid weather, which seems to take a toll on him. On 7 July he describes for his mother a kind of triage system he has devised for allocating attention to the wounded so that he conserves some of his energy by concentrating on "the few where the investment seems to tell best" (CORR, 1:115).

1 AUGUST. Though he has said nothing of it in existing

letters to his mother, Whitman writes to a beloved soldier, Lewis K. Brown, that he has been unwell for the last three weeks in a way he has never been ill before. His affection for Brown is deep, and he speaks of what he admits is "probably a dream," that they and an unidentified third party could live and work together after the war (CORR, 1:121).

To this point Whitman has been in good health. A contemporary description of him provides the picture: "Mr. Whitman, when in full health, was physically slow of movement, and walked with a peculiarly heavy drag. I saw him many times at Washington, in the sixties. At that time he used no cane, and his walk was almost lazy, swaggery, and his response to questions was very deliberate" (Donaldson, 34–35).

10 AUGUST. Whitman writes to Mr. and Mrs. S. B. Haskell of Breseport, New York, to tell them of the final days of their son's life in the Armory Square Hospital. The letter is one of many such letters that Whitman writes and summarizes his feelings for all the war dead: "He is one of the thousands of our unknown American young men in the ranks about whom there is no record or fame, no fuss made about their dying so unknown. . . . Poor dear son, though you were not my son, I felt to love you as a son" (CORR, 1:129).

16 AUGUST. "Washington in the Hot Season" is published in the *New York Times* (see PW, 1:301–302).

SUMMER. Whitman brings to the attention of James Redpath, the Boston publisher, his need for funds to support his hospital work. Redpath begins a chain of contributors, including the Bostonians Ralph Waldo Emerson, Dr. L. B. Russell, Mrs. C. P. Curtis, Henry Lewis, and others, who continue their aid in 1864 and 1865 (Donaldson, 142–152).

3 SEPTEMBER. Louisa Whitman writes to Walt; this time her worries are for son Jesse, whose mental instability is causing him to miss work (Allen, *Solitary Singer*, 304). Jesse's emotional problems appear to have worsened about this time. Varying explanations of his illness

include his brother Jeff's belief that he has syphilis (Berthold and Price, 85), his mother's belief that he is "deranged" but manageable (Allen, *Solitary Singer*, 308), his niece's (Jessie Louisa Whitman) belief that he had been the victim of a street attack (Molinoff, *Notes*, 19, 22), and Walt's belief that he had suffered a head injury in a fall from a mast when working at the Brooklyn Navy Yard (Allen, *Solitary Singer*, 318).

22 SEPTEMBER. Whitman's communication, titled "From Washington," appears in the *Brooklyn Daily Union* (see UPP, 2:26–29).

1 OCTOBER. "Letter from Washington" appears in the *New York Times* (see UPP, 2:29–36).

4 OCTOBER. Walt dines with the O'Connors. The O'Connors continue to be, as Walt tells his mother, "truly friends," and he visits them regularly (CORR, 1:157).

6 OCTOBER. Walt has cut his hair and beard, making him the main subject of conversation among his acquaintances (CORR, 1:160). Photographs by Alexander Gardner in 1863 or 1864 show Whitman with short hair and beard.

21 OCTOBER. Whitman writes to James Redpath, the publisher of Louisa May Alcott's *Hospital Sketches* (1863), in which she recounts her experiences as a nurse in the Union Hotel Hospital in Washington. Whitman proposes a book to be called *Memoranda of a Year (1863)*, which would not only tell of similar experiences but make the case for needed reforms of the national hospitals and of the military which, he claims, is wanting in "democratic spirit" (CORR, 1:160). The book, which he hopes to see published by mid or late November, is too costly a project for Redpath (WWC, 4:418). Though *Drum-Taps* is eloquent on the subject of the wounded and dead of the Civil War, *Memoranda During the War* (1875) is the fullest account of Whitman's war experiences and is later incorporated into *Specimen Days* (1882). James Redpath thinks highly of Whitman and his poetry but had run into some puritanical objections earlier in the year when trying to raise money to help Whitman's war efforts.

ON THE SAME DATE. Whitman writes in his notebook of a delegation of Maryland slaveholders who have called on the president to object to having slaves taken into the army. He adds Lincoln's retort that he would take them not only from Maryland "but from all the border and slave states" since the need of the country demanded it (NUPM, 2:539).

22 OCTOBER. Jeff Whitman writes from Brooklyn that Andrew's condition has worsened so that "he cannot last long" and urges Walt to come home (Berthold and Price, 81).

Like his mother, Jeff is a faithful correspondent, keeping Walt informed of family matters, especially Andrew's decline. With a family of his own to care for, Jeff misses having George and Walt to help in dealing with their mother and their other siblings. As early as February he had begun pressuring Walt to prod George into leaving the army in whatever "honorable" way possible. He supports Walt's hospital work but believes Walt should come home, at least for a time, to help with Andrew. Jeff's and Walt's letters of this year also touch on the draft riots of 13−16 July in New York City and on their differing opinions of Lincoln: Jeff believes Lincoln lacks the necessary "force [to] do as he thinks best" (Berthold and Price, 59).

31 OCTOBER. Whitman is at the White House to see John Hay, the president's secretary, hoping to obtain leave that will enable him to return home. He catches a glimpse of the president talking with a friend and comments in his notebook on Lincoln's "inexpressibly sweet" face, adding "I love the President personally (NUPM, 2:539).

LATE OCTOBER. Whitman meets John Burroughs, a young New York naturalist and writer who has wished to know the poet since his first reading of the 1855 *Leaves*. Burroughs describes the poet at this time as "large and tall, above six feet, with a breezy, open-air look" and as one who "always had the look of a man who had just taken a bath" (Burroughs, *Whitman, a Study*, 52). Burroughs joins the circle of friends who regularly meet at the O'Connor home and remains close to Whitman the rest of his life.

2 NOVEMBER. Walt arrives home about 8 P.M. The trip home has proven somewhat dislocating for the contrast between the war he has left and the "wondrously prosperous" cities and towns he passes through (NUPM, 2:540).

3 NOVEMBER. On this election day, Whitman votes Republican along with the majority of voters in the state (CORR, 1:176).

4 NOVEMBER. Walt hears Gaetano Donizetti's opera *Lucrezia Borgia* at the New York Academy of Music; in his notebook he pronounces the singers, soprano Giuseppina Medora, tenor Francesco Mazzoleni, and bass Hannibal Biachi, "very fine" (NUPM, 2:540). Whitman's New York friends see that he has a good time while away from his self-imposed hospital duties. By his own accounts he spends almost every night with them at the opera, at the theater, or at supper parties "(men only)" where there is much partaking of food and drink (CORR, 1:183).

8–9 NOVEMBER. Though enjoying his New York holiday, Whitman does not forget those he has left in the Armory Square Hospital; he writes a long letter to Lewis K. Brown "and all my dear comrades in the hospital," recounting his recent activities (including a detailed description of the opera) and, inquiring after his comrades by name, sending his love to each (CORR, 1:175–182).

13 NOVEMBER. Whitman probably attends the opera *La Somnambula*, which features Clara Louise Kellogg in the title role (CORR, 1:183).

16 NOVEMBER. Whitman is at the opera again, this time to hear Giuseppi Verdi's *Il Trovatore*; Whitman describes it in a letter to Charles Eldridge but then seems almost to be admonishing himself to return to work by saying he "*must*" be continually bringing out poems (CORR, 1:185).

25 NOVEMBER. A regiment of black soldiers marching up Broadway in uniform and with muskets attracts Whitman's attention (NUPM, 2:540).

1 DECEMBER. Walt says farewell to Andrew as he prepares to return to Washington.

2 DECEMBER. He arrives in Washington.

3 DECEMBER. A telegram from Jeff brings word of Andrew's death; Walt does not go home for the funeral. The return to Washington is mandated by the terms of the work release, issued to allow him to vote in his home state. To George he writes (5 December) that he is very sorry not to have remained at home longer (CORR, 1:189). His leavetaking of Andrew will have been with full knowledge that he is not likely to see his brother alive again.

10 DECEMBER. John T. Trowbridge, Walt's friend from Boston, is in Washington staying at the home of Secretary of the Treasury Salmon P. Chase. On this date he presents Whitman's request for government employment and offers Emerson's letter of recommendation. Chase would like to oblige but considers *Leaves of Grass* "a very bad book," and he cannot possibly bring its author (whom he considers a disreputable person) into government service. Even the mention of Whitman's work in the hospitals fails to impress him (NUPM, 2:663).

AROUND THIS TIME. Major Hapgood moves his office from the house on Fifteenth Street, and Whitman is now doing his copy work in his room at 456 Sixth Street (CORR, 1:189). When he moves to Sixth Street in October, he describes his room to his mother as on the third floor, in the back, with a window that looks out on a yard with grass and trees, a good big bed, gaslight, and water brought by a young black girl. The cost is $10 a month, including gaslight but not fuel, which would account for the lack of heat Trowbridge later remembers (CORR, 1:168−69; Myerson, *Time*, 169−191). Trowbridge says of the poet's appearance at this time that he was "trimly attired, wearing a loosely fitting but quite elegant suit of black" (Myerson, *Time*, 175).

15 DECEMBER. Jeff Whitman writes Walt a lengthy account of an incident at the house in Brooklyn on 6 December, the day after Andrew's death, when the emotionally un-

stable Jesse has threatened harm to Jeff's daughter, Hattie, while verbally abusing Martha. Still incensed, Jeff has forbidden Jesse access to their rooms. In turn, Louisa Whitman refuses to visit them. Since their mother is often the object of Jesse's threats, Jeff is determined to place him in an institution and seeks Walt's help in winning their mother over to this solution.

28 DECEMBER. Jeff writes again from Brooklyn another long letter, mostly about Jesse, suggesting a private hospital rather than the municipal asylum, with the cost of about $15 per month to be shared by the brothers. Walt has urged their mother to hospitalize Jesse, but she has been unwilling; it now seems there is no recourse.

IN THIS YEAR. A steady correspondence with his mother throughout 1863 reveals Whitman's major concerns to be his family and the wretched suffering of the war wounded. The welfare of his sister Hannah is frequently mentioned, as is his strong desire to build a "ranch," as he calls it, for his mother and family somewhere on Long Island. Walt cautions his mother to save as much money as she can toward this end, but on hearing from Jeff that their mother is economizing too much and denying herself, Jesse, and Eddie proper meals, he begs her to "have a steak of beef or mutton, or something substantial for dinner" (CORR, 1:144). In July when New York's attempts to comply with the Conscription Act set off the worst riots in Manhattan's history, Walt fears Jeff will be taken and sees no remedy but to borrow the amount necessary to buy his way out under the terms of the draft law (CORR, 1:117). To his great relief, Jeff is not drafted. As the summer turns to autumn and Andrew's illness progresses, fears for this brother's life intensify (CORR, 1:144). Walt and his mother continually exchange news of George, for whom he has nothing but the highest praise at all times. Though he seeks to allay his mother's fears for George's safety, Walt cannot forebear writing of the horrors he encounters in the hospital wards: "O the sad, sad things I see, the noble young men with legs &

arms taken off" (CORR, 1:105). At times an individual soldier so impresses him that Whitman tells his story in detail, as in the case of the twenty-six-year-old from Pennsylvania who does not survive amputation of his wounded leg (CORR, 1:100).

1864-1867

Bathed in war's perfume . . .
— *Drum-Taps*, 1865

Despite the demands of family and his hospital service, Whitman has not forgotten his poetry: in November 1863 he returns to Washington with the manuscript of *Drum-Taps*, which earlier he had left behind in Brooklyn. In 1864 Whitman visits Virginia battlefields, and by winter's end his physical and emotional condition is such that he longs for a rest. In June 1864 he is so ill that the doctors tell him not to visit the hospitals for a time, and he returns home. In October George is taken prisoner, and the early part of 1865 is devoted to trying to obtain his freedom, achieved finally through a general exchange of prisoners. Walt is working now for the Department of the Interior and attends Lincoln's second inauguration. Around this time he probably meets Peter Doyle, who becomes his loving companion. In spring the war ends, Lincoln is assassinated, and *Drum-Taps* is published. In June Whitman is fired from his job on charges of indecency and moves to the Attorney General's Office. In October he publishes *Sequel to Drum-Taps*. William O'Connor rushes to Whitman's defense with *The Good Gray Poet*, published early in 1866. With the publication of the more somber 1867 edition of *Leaves* (the fourth), there develops a new image of Whitman, furthered by his friends O'Connor and John Burroughs. Through them England becomes interested in Whitman.

1864

5 JANUARY. Lewis K. Brown, Whitman's beloved soldier friend, having returned to the hospital because of an unhealed leg wound, has his left leg amputated below the

knee at the Armory Square Hospital; Whitman observes the surgery through an open door (NUPM, 2:669).

29 JANUARY. Whitman writes his mother that Brown is recovering well under his watchful eye; in the same letter he mentions having become acquainted with Congressman James A. Garfield of Ohio (CORR, 1:193). Garfield remains friendly even after becoming president, and at his assassination in 1881 Whitman writes "The Sobbing of the Bells" (see chapter 7).

JANUARY. Before re-enlisting, George Whitman goes home on a thirty-day furlough, making Walt long to be there. Walt also has a great desire to be present at "a first class battle" and is later allowed to join the army at Culpepper, Virginia, for a few weeks.

IN THE SAME MONTH. John Burroughs arranges for Whitman to give lectures in Washington, to be followed by a lecture tour of New York, Brooklyn, and Boston, but the plans fall through (CORR, 1:200−201, n23).

6 FEBRUARY. Whitman leaves for Virginia, where he visits the division field hospitals. He finds no wounded, as they are evacuated to Washington as quickly as possible, and decides to return to Washington where he feels he is needed (CORR, 1:197).

29 MARCH. Walt writes his mother that, though he feels well enough, he needs some "intermission" from the war because of the steady assault on his emotions (CORR, 1:205).

31 MARCH. Whitman and a friend go to see the famous New England spiritualist Charles H. Foster, and on 5 April he pronounces such practices "humbug" (CORR, 1:206, 208).

25 APRIL. General Ambrose Burnside's army moves through Washington, and Walt waits three hours as the procession of troops passes before he sees his brother George. George is tanned and looks "hardy"; the two are able to walk a distance together in the ranks, long enough for Walt to give George news of home (CORR, 1:212).

21 MAY. Whitman moves from his garret room to a boarding-house at 502 Pennsylvania Avenue, near Third Street (CORR, 1:226).

Whitman's letters in April and May recount both rumors and facts of the army's movements, most of the time with some reference to George's regiment, involved around this time in the battle at Spotsylvania, Virginia. Walt repeatedly asserts his faith in General Grant, and to Jeff he writes that had it been his lot to fall in battle he would feel it a noble and manly death (CORR, 1:225).

7 JUNE. Walt writes his mother that he has been ill for a week with weakness, sore throat, and a "bad feeling" in his head. He longs to be home for just a few days, able then to return refreshed to the "sad scenes" of his hospital work (CORR, 1:230−232).

Whitman's need of a rest from the suffering and death that consumes his strength is shared by the soldiers he visits. As he writes to his mother, two years or more of war, with bad food and bad water, the fighting, and the terror of it all, have impaired the physical and mental health of large numbers of soldiers and caused many of those who care for them to become "callous."

14 JUNE. The doctors have told Whitman not to come inside the hospitals for a time until he is better. He feels that the boardinghouse air is bad, that he has been working too long in the hospitals, and that if only he could see his family he would be better (CORR, 1:233).

17 JUNE. Having been told by the doctors to go north for a time (CORR, 1:237), Walt plans to leave for home in a day or two but is fearful of not being in Washington "if anything should happen to George" (CORR, 1:234).

22 JUNE. Whitman leaves Washington for home.

5 JULY. Whitman writes to William O'Connor of his intention to "move heaven and earth" to publish *Drum-Taps* as soon as he is well enough (CORR, 1:235−236).

24 JULY. In a letter to O'Connor, Whitman tells of his hopes of publishing *Drum-Taps* himself, of stereotyping and printing an edition of five hundred, which he could sell by his own efforts (CORR, 1:239).

SUMMER. Walt visits various local hospitals where the war wounded are tended; he and his mother attend the funerals of two of George's friends killed in battle.

29 OCTOBER. "Fifty-First New York City Veterans," a brief

history of George Whitman's regiment, appears in the *New York Times* (UPP, 1:37–41).

5 DECEMBER. Walt commits his brother Jesse to the Kings County Lunatic Asylum, citing as the reason for his condition a fall from the mast of a sailing ship some sixteen years earlier (Allen, *Solitary Singer*, 318). The choice of the Kings County hospital, despite the family's earlier plans to place Jesse in a private institution, may be because of Walt's favorable impression of the hospital, formed during visits at this time to various New York and Brooklyn institutions.

11 DECEMBER. Whitman's *New York Times* article "Our Wounded and Sick Soldiers — Visits Among the Hospitals" describes the field hospitals in Virginia and local hospitals in the cities of New York and Brooklyn, with the Kings County hospital where Jesse is committed singled out for praise (CW, 7:101–127).

26 DECEMBER. George's trunk containing his uniform, revolver, and personal items, including his war diary, arrives at the Whitman home. The family has no idea of George's whereabouts; Walt has been unable to find any trace of the officers of the Fifty-first Regiment (NUPM, 2:744–746).

27 DECEMBER. A letter from Whitman appears in the *Brooklyn Eagle* and in the *New York Times* urging a general exchange of prisoners. Secretary of War Edwin Stanton has refused an exchange because it would provide fresh troops for the Confederate army and has rejected terms that would not include all black soldiers captured by the South, a policy Whitman calls "cold-blooded" (Glicksberg, 179).

1865

6 JANUARY. Walt writes to William O'Connor of his hopes for early publication of *Drum-Taps* and describes his feelings about the work. He believes it superior to *Leaves*

for its controlled passion; it has none of the "perturbations" of *Leaves*, and every word is essential to its meaning. As to *Leaves*, his "first born," it contains some things he would not now write, but he shall let them stand as proof "of phases passed away" (CORR, 1: 246–248). The letter is the first indication of Whitman's intention to stylistically alter future editions of *Leaves of Grass*, a change of attitude that appears directly related to his sobering war experiences.

19 JANUARY. From an exchanged prisoner of war the Whitmans hear their first news of George in more than three months, that he is well but a prisoner. The news of his capture on 30 September 1864 at Poplar Grove Church, Virginia, is conveyed in a letter from George dated 2 October and delivered to Louisa Whitman by the exchanged prisoner; George writes, "I am in tip top health and Spirits, and am as tough as a mule and shall get along first rate" (Loving, *Letters*, 132). He becomes seriously ill in the prison camp, however, and is a long while recovering.

20 JANUARY. A letter arrives from George dated 27 November 1864; he is a prisoner at Danville, Virginia, one of 350 officers being held in a tobacco warehouse (NUPM, 2:747–748).

23 JANUARY. Walt is back in Washington, in a room at 468 M Street, with a "secesh" landlady (Mrs. Newton Benedict) who provides him room, fuel, and food for $32.50 per week (CORR, 1:266). Whitman can afford this because — thanks to the intercession of William O'Connor — he is working as a copyist in the Office of Indian Affairs of the Department of the Interior, located in the basement of the Patent Office. Though impressed by the physical appearance of the Native Americans who come to the office, he thinks of them as recipients of the nation's "bounty" (NUPM, 2:786; see also "An Indian Bureau Reminiscence," PW, 2:577–580; and Folsom, *Representations*, 55–98). He visits the hospitals as before but, for health reasons, not so often or for such long pe-

riods, and he arranges for packages of food and clothing to be sent to George (CORR, 1:249, 250).

EARLY FEBRUARY. Whitman devotes himself to the effort to obtain George's release. He receives help from his friend John Swinton, an editor of the *New York Times*, in pursuing a possible special exchange, but this proves unnecessary when George is included in a general exchange of prisoners later in the month.

19 FEBRUARY. George Whitman is released from prison camp.

23, 27, 28 FEBRUARY. Whitman sees large numbers of Southern soldiers who have surrendered and interviews some of them. Though called by their army "deserters," Whitman points out that the word does not truly apply to them (PW, 1:89–91).

AROUND THIS TIME. Whitman probably meets Peter Doyle, the former Confederate soldier who becomes his close companion and remains so for many years (Murray, 1). Doyle, a twenty-one-year-old streetcar conductor at the time, describes their meeting, though with what is believed to be an incorrect memory of the year:

> You ask where I first met him? It is a curious story. We felt to each other at once. I was a conductor. The night was very stormy,— he had been over to see [John] Burroughs before he came down to take the car — the storm was awful. Walt had his blanket — it was thrown round his shoulders — he seemed like an old sea-captain. He was the only passenger, it was a lonely night, so I thought I would go in and talk with him. Something in me made me do it and something in him drew me that way. He used to say there was something in me had the same effect on him. Anyway, I went into the car. We were familiar at once — I put my hand on his knee — we understood. He did not get out at the end of the trip — in fact went all the way back with me. I think the year of this was 1866. From that time on

we were the biggest sort of friends. (Bucke,
Calamus, 23)

EARLY MARCH. George arrives home in Brooklyn and remains on furlough recuperating from illness contracted
in the prison camp.

4 MARCH. In Washington, Walt attends the second inauguration of Abraham Lincoln, applies for and receives a
two-week leave of absence from work, and heads home.
He decides to remain in Brooklyn long enough to bring
out his book and receives a two-week extension of his
leave. George, too, is granted an extension of his furlough because of his continued ill health (CORR, 1:258).

12 MARCH. Another of the Washington "Letters" appears
in the *New York Times.* A composite of three items relating to the inauguration, it includes a description of the
crowds along Pennsylvania Avenue which Whitman did
not carry over into *Memoranda During the War* or *Specimen Days:*

> Mud, (and such mud!) amid and upon which
> streaming crowds of citizens; lots of blue-dressed
> soldiers; any quantity of male and female Africans,
> (especially female;) . . . clattering groups of cavalry-
> men out there on a gallop . . . processions of firemen,
> with their engines, evidently from the north; a regi-
> ment of blacks, in full uniform, with guns on their
> shoulders; the splendor overhead; the oceanic crowd,
> equal almost to Broadway. (Bandy, 24)

1 APRIL. Walt signs a contract with Peter Eckler, a New York
printer, for five hundred stereotyped copies of *Drum-
Taps,* which are bound and delivered to the printer at the
end of May (CORR, 1:261, n39).

9 APRIL. General Lee surrenders at Appomattox, ending
the war.

14 APRIL. President Lincoln is shot at Ford's Theater. Peter
Doyle is present in the theater and later recounts the

events, which Whitman will use in fashioning his Lincoln lectures:

> There was nothing extraordinary in the performance. I saw everything on the stage and was in a good position to see the President's box. I heard the pistol shot. I had no idea what it was, what it meant — it was sort of muffled. I really knew nothing of what had occurred until Mrs. Lincoln leaned out of the box and cried, "The President is shot!" . . . I saw Booth on the cushion of the box, saw him jump over, saw him catch his foot, which turned, saw him fall on the stage. He got up on his feet, cried out something which I could not hear for the hub-bub and disappeared. I suppose I lingered almost the last person. A soldier came into the gallery, saw me still there, called to me: "Get out of here! we're going to burn this damned building down!" I said: "If that is so I'll get out!" (Bucke, *Calamus*, 25–26)

15 APRIL. In Brooklyn the Whitmans hear the news of the president's death. Walt later remembers that though his mother prepared breakfast as usual for the two of them, neither ate, not then nor later in the day, satisfying themselves with but half a cup of coffee and reading all the newspapers of the day (Perry, 154). Walt roams the streets of New York and Brooklyn observing the mournful atmosphere, the all-pervasive black bunting, lowering clouds, flags at half staff, shops closed, and streets deserted; at 11:00 A.M. the new president, Andrew Johnson, is sworn in (NUPM, 2:763).

THE WEEK OF 17 APRIL. Whitman returns to Washington.

1 MAY. Whitman is promoted to clerk, second class, in the Department of the Interior (Reynolds, 455).

13 MAY. George, returned to his regiment, is promoted to major (CORR, 1:262, n43).

20 MAY. A letter to the editor of the "Armory Square Hospital Gazette," signed "W.W.," comments on the capture of Jefferson Davis and the death of President Lincoln

(Holloway, "Finale"). This publication is issued by and for soldiers in the Washington hospitals, and Whitman is a contributor (PW, 1:288).

23–24 MAY. Walt sees the two-day grand review of the Union armies: "the long and glittering wide ranks — will they never stop? For two whole days commencing early in the morning and continuing long into the night" (NUPM, 2:779). He writes to his mother that he has seen President Johnson; Generals Grant, Sherman, and Meade; Secretary Stanton; and George, who marched with the Fifty-first Regiment (CORR, 1:260–263).

31 MAY. Whitman celebrates his forty-sixth birthday. The *New York Herald* carries the following notice: "The Secretary of the Interior has issued a circular to the heads of bureaus in the department, to report as to the loyalty of each of the employees under him, and also whether there are any whose fidelity to duty or moral character is such as to justify an immediate dispensation of their services."

MAY. The printing of *Drum-Taps* is completed. It is a seventy-two-page volume with a brown cover; some of its fifty-three poems (all new) have been written between the outbreak of the war and the time of Whitman's arrival in Fredericksburg (Allen, *Solitary Singer*, 577, n55); the rest reflect his months of nursing service. In this collection Whitman portrays himself in "The Dresser" (later "The Wound-Dresser"). The appearance of "Pioneers! O Pioneers!" in this volume reflects Whitman's belief, born of his days as a Free-Soiler, that in large part the Civil War has been fought to insure that the settling of the West would be by free Americans, with no slave labor involved.

4 JUNE. Jeff writes to Walt of their mother's troubles with Eddie; with Jesse out of the household, Jeff would now like to make other arrangements for Edward as well (Berthold and Price, 111).

30 JUNE. "The services of Walter Whitman of New York as a clerk in the Indian Office will be dispensed with from and after this date" (WWC, 3:471). With these words Whitman is dismissed from his clerkship by the new

Secretary of the Interior, James Harlan, who attempts to impose his high sense of morality on others. He is said to have found in Whitman's desk a copy of the 1860 *Leaves of Grass* and deemed it immoral. Though many are dismissed at this same time for economic reasons, Whitman's case receives wide attention because of the indignation of William O'Connor.

1 JULY. On the strength of O'Connor's appeal to Assistant Attorney General J. Hubley Ashton (one of those who gathered often at O'Connor's home), Whitman is transferred to the office of the Attorney General (NUPM, 2:797−799). He finds the office interesting, for it is here that wealthy Southeners must come for special pardons before they can enter into any kind of business dealings. Though the pardons are issued, Whitman says they await the president's signature, when he "gets good and ready" (CORR, 1:265).

25 AUGUST. Whitman may be present at the baseball game that, he reports, was played between the Philadelphia Athletics and the Washington Nationals (CORR, 1:266). The Nationals are a team made up of government clerks; their games are played on a field behind the White House (Folsom, *Representations*, 40).

EARLY OCTOBER. Whitman returns to Brooklyn on a month's furlough to see to the collating of *Sequel to Drum-Taps*, which he has been working on while revising the 1860 edition of *Leaves of Grass*. His mother is in Burlington, Vermont, visiting Hannah; George has returned to working as a carpenter (CORR, 1:267−268). The *Sequel*, printed in Washington and only twenty-four pages, contains poems in memory of Lincoln, and for this reason Whitman wishes to have it bound into the larger *Drum-Taps*. It includes the metered (atypical for Whitman) "O Captain! My Captain!" and the elegy "When Lilacs Last in the Dooryard Bloom'd."

28 OCTOBER. The *New York Tribune* carries an announcement by the New York firm of Bunce & Huntington of the publication of *Drum-Taps*, bound with *Sequel to Drum-Taps* (CORR, 1:270, n64).

4 NOVEMBER. "O Captain! My Captain!" appears in the *Saturday Press*.

16 NOVEMBER. In an unsigned review of *Drum-Taps* in the *Nation*, Henry James attacks *Leaves of Grass* and implies that in *Drum-Taps* Whitman is trading on the nation's experience of war (Miller, *Century*, 13–18).

NOVEMBER. William Dean Howells reviews *Drum-Taps* in the *Round Table*, finding it more to his liking than *Leaves* (of which he says, "You had at times to hold your nose") but lacking in "art" (Price, *Reviews*, 112–114).

1866

JANUARY. *The Good Gray Poet*, William O'Connor's pamphlet defending Whitman against the accusations of James Harlan, is published in New York by Bunce & Huntington. Written in the summer of 1865, the pamphlet, though ostensibly aimed at Harlan for his ignorance in condemning Whitman's poetry and for abridging freedom of literature, really attempts to rehabilitate the poet's reputation and make his work more acceptable to the general public. O'Connor's main arguments are that all great literature contains some material that might be deemed offensive, though this material was intended to uplift, "never to degrade," and that it is not innocence but "guilty thought" that attaches "shame, secrecy, baseness" to the human body (Bucke, *Walt Whitman*, 116). To these are added pages of encomia hailing Whitman's patriotism, simplicity of life, and service to the war wounded. The title of the piece enters the Whitmanian lexicon, so that Whitman in his late years comments, "William's other name for me, has stuck — stuck" (WWC, 1:4).

20 JANUARY. Richard Henry Stoddard's review of *The Good Gray Poet* in the *Round Table* ridicules it and Whitman. The *Saturday Press* carries a review of *Drum-Taps* that finds the poems beautiful but unrefined.

24 JANUARY. Franklin B. Sanborn, the Boston journalist

and abolitionist who has helped to support Whitman's hospital work, offers a complimentary view of *Drum-Taps* in *Commonwealth* magazine.

1 MAY. The Whitman family moves to 840 Pacific Street, Brooklyn. From Washington Walt writes that he continues to visit the remaining hospitalized soldiers every Sunday and often one day in mid-week (CORR, 1:275).

3 MAY. Whitman visits the home of George Washington at Mount Vernon and finds it a pleasant spot (CORR, 1:275).

6 MAY. Whitman probably attends the funeral of Count Adam Gurowski, a Polish exile, eccentric, and Whitman admirer, who had been in the circle of friends meeting at the O'Connor home (CORR, 1:275).

13 MAY. Walt visits the Quarter Master's Hospital, where he finds some with old wounds, some "brokendown sick," and some discharged soldiers who have no place else to go; in a letter to Louisa Whitman he deplores the government's lack of help and the mere $8 monthly pension it provides (CORR, 1:276).

SUMMER. Whitman continues another habit, acquired during the war when Congress often held night sessions, of visiting the Capitol to hear the speeches. For the first time in years he has half a dozen new shirts made (CORR, 1:277). As the summer wears on he begins to worry about reports of cholera in New York (the last of the city's three epidemic outbreaks in the century) and warns his mother not to exert herself unduly (CORR, 1:279). His own health is affected by the heat, and he carries an umbrella for shade and moves slowly but goes to baseball games and to marine band concerts (CORR, 1:279–280, 281).

23 JULY. Whitman has found his position in the Attorney General's Office "agreeable," though he believes the pay not good (CORR, 1:282). His work consists of copying, from drafts, letters and legal opinions being sent to the president, Cabinet members, and other high officials — "only the big men," as he writes to his friend Abby Price (CORR, 1:283).

6 AUGUST. Having obtained a leave from his job, Walt goes

to New York to bring out a new edition of *Leaves of Grass*, "that *unkillable* work!" (CORR, 1:282). In New York he takes a room in Abby Price's home and, while the book is being printed by William Chapin, makes trips to Long Island and to upper Manhattan, enjoying Central Park and boat rides on the river as well as his usual Broadway jaunts and streetcar rides (CORR, 1:283, 285). He has problems with the printers, who make "ridiculous" errors, and for this reason he stays longer than planned to supervise the work (CORR, 1:286).

25 SEPTEMBER. Whitman returns to Washington (CORR, 1:287).

26 OCTOBER. On behalf of his friends, Abby and Edmund Price, Whitman petitions Attorney General Henry Stanbery for a pardon for Erastus O. Parker, former postmaster of Monument, Massachusetts, who had been convicted in 1862 for embezzlement. The Prices are friends of Parker's niece, hence their request to Whitman to seek a reinvestigation of the case. His petition is carefully researched and well written, and the pardon is granted immediately (CORR, 1:289–291).

OCTOBER. An article by Moncure Conway, titled "Walt Whitman," is published in the London, England, *Fortnightly Review*. Though it is supportive of the poet, a good deal of it Whitman finds "ridiculous," even "impudent" (CORR, 1:294, 297). Not long after, William O'Connor writes to Conway in England suggesting a British publication of Whitman's poems (Reynolds, 462).

14 NOVEMBER. Whitman is promoted to third-class clerk and is given a pay increase to $1,600 annually and a permanent appointment (CORR, 1:294).

1 DECEMBER. The New York periodical *Galaxy* contains John Burroughs's essay, "Walt Whitman and His 'Drum-Taps.'" The *Galaxy*, owned by Francis P. and William C. Church, began in 1866 as a New York rival to Boston's *Atlantic Monthly* and Philadelphia's *Lippincott's Magazine*. Unlike O'Connor's overwrought pamphlet, this is a seriously considered piece of work that raises the level of Whitman criticism (Allen, *Solitary Singer*, 375) by

noting such things as the intricately dramatic structure of "When Lilacs Last in the Dooryard Bloom'd": "It is dramatic, yet there is no procession of events or development of plot, but a constant interplay — a turning and re-turning of images and sentiments, so that the section in which is narrated how the great shadow fell upon the land occurs far along in the piece" (Burroughs, "Drum-Taps"). As the essay is partly Whitman's own construction, however, it is also important for what it reveals about the image of himself that he wishes to create, the image of an original poet mocked and neglected.

AROUND THIS TIME. The newly printed edition of *Leaves of Grass* appears. Though referred to as the 1867 edition because that date appears on the title page, the book is printed in New York in 1866. Its publication history is complicated by the fact that it is variously bound, with some issues containing *Drum-Taps* and *Sequel to Drum-Taps*. Its publication history is further complicated by the financial problems and bankruptcies among printing and book distribution firms around this time, which interfere with the production (WWC, 2:257). The edition is poorly presented in a dull brown cover, with no photograph of Whitman (nor an author's name), and printed in a common typeface.

2 DECEMBER. The *New York Times* publishes a six thousand–word review by William O'Connor of the new *Leaves of Grass*, along with *Times* owner Henry J. Raymond's qualified endorsement, his reservations being based on a perceived indecency in the poems (Allen, *Solitary Singer*, 376).

3 DECEMBER. Whitman witnesses a parade held in honor of the incoming Fortieth Congress and reports to his mother that two-thirds of the paraders are "darkies" (CORR, 1:299).

18 DECEMBER. Whitman writes his mother that he has sent her a copy of the new *Leaves of Grass* (CORR, 1:302). This is his first documented reference to the new edition, which verifies its existence in print prior to 1867.

25 DECEMBER. Walt has paid (partly with money Jeff

raised) for a Christmas dinner to be served at one of the hospitals he still visits regularly (CORR, 1: 303).

29 DECEMBER. With the New Year holiday and his "soldier boys" in mind, Whitman writes to a Washington friend soliciting $2 toward some festivities (CORR, 1: 304).

1867

The fourth edition of *Leaves of Grass* marks a significant change in the book's evolution. Whitman has worked long and hard at revising the 1860 edition, and almost every poem carried over in 1867 shows evidence of this. Except for the annexed *Drum-Taps* and *Sequel to Drum-Taps*, there are only six new poems, but the rest have been individually reworked, most line by line, and the whole reordered, with some cluster titles eliminated and their constituent poems scattered or dropped. Despite this critical activity, the work reveals some disorganization in its groupings, a fault critics have laid to the war's influence on Whitman. New is "Inscriptions" (later "One's-Self I Sing") at the head of all, a position it retains in subsequent editions. "Enfans d'Adam" is now "Children of Adam" and remains in essentially the same order, but "Calamus" has lost three of its more revealing poems. This and other changes in the sexual aspect of the work suggest that Whitman is censoring himself to fit the image of the "Good Gray Poet" (Asselineau, 1:282; Killingsworth, 147–151), though it has been argued that the textual evidence for this is weak (Golden, 2:lvii).

1 JANUARY. Whitman visits soldiers in a Washington hospital, bringing them tobacco, and then goes to the O'Connor home for turkey dinner (CORR, 1:305).

7 JANUARY. Whitman goes alone to the opera to hear Verdi's *Ernani* at the National Theatre (CORR, 1:306). Years earlier, Whitman had described the opening scene of this opera, a favorite of his, in the essay "The Opera" (Holloway and Adimari, 21).

FEBRUARY. Whitman moves to 472 M Street; Jeff spends a

few days with his brother and meets the O'Connors, who are "much pleased" with him (CORR, 1:314).

5 MARCH. Clerks in the Attorney General's Office are granted a 20 percent pay increase, retroactive to 1 January (CORR, 1:316). A week later Whitman writes his mother about how comfortable he is at his job, especially since he is able to come back to the heated office with its library for evenings of reading and work using the gaslight at office expense (CORR, 1:318).

27 MARCH. Whitman reports to Abby Price on his thus far unsuccessful efforts to lobby members of Congress who are set to consider a tax bill that she fears will include a tax on ruffles on clothing (CORR, 1:321–322). Price is a part-time dressmaker and has offered Whitman $1,000 if he is successful in deflecting this item from taxation (CORR, 1:321, n59). The following year he learns that there had been no intention to tax ruffles (Allen, *Solitary Singer*, 381). Whitman has also been asked, but declined, to seek government assistance for Henry St. Marie, who reported the whereabouts of John H. Surratt, wanted in connection with the conspiracy to murder Lincoln (CORR, 1:320). Surratt's mother, Mary Surratt, was hanged for her part in the conspiracy, and in July Whitman attends John Surratt's trial (CORR, 1:334).

15 APRIL. Whitman attends a concert at Metzerott Hall given by Pasquale Brignoli, tenor, and Euphrosyne Parepa-Rosa, soprano (CORR, 1:324). When Brignoli dies in 1884, Whitman writes a memorial poem, "The Dead Tenor."

23 APRIL. William O'Connor returns from New York, where he has gone to seek an editorial position with the *New York Times*. He brings Walt news of an offer made to Jeff to work in St. Louis, Missouri, on the construction of a water works. Louisa Whitman, knowing that Eddie is not welcome in Jeff's home, has written to Walt of her worries about a place to live; on this date he writes to reassure her and on 29 April to encourage Jeff to accept the offer (CORR, 1:325–336).

4 MAY. Walt arrives at his mother's home to assist in caring for George, who is very ill with erysipelas (an infectious

skin disease). Martha has sold most of her and Jeff's furniture even before their plans are finalized (Jeff leaves on 5 May for St. Louis; Martha and the children are to follow later), and Louisa is emotionally overwrought (CORR, 1:327–328).

6 MAY. In England, an essay in the *Chronicle* by the poet William M. Rossetti hails Whitman as a poet of great originality whose writings are "both poetic and rhythmical" (Blodgett, 21). Having read the 1855 and 1867 *Leaves*, Rossetti greatly admires the work. He is also much influenced by O'Connor's *Good Gray Poet* and Burroughs's *Notes* (which he reads in manuscript). Moncure Conway has praised Whitman to him personally as well as in an 1866 essay in the London *Fortnightly Review*. Rossetti's appraisal has a great impact on American critics and is reprinted in a number of American periodicals. William's brother, Dante Gabriel, does not share his enthusiasm and though he contributes to funds raised on Whitman's behalf, cannot accept the sexual frankness of *Leaves* (Barrus, 220).

12 MAY. While still in Brooklyn Whitman receives word that George W. Carleton, the New York publisher approached by O'Connor, has declined (in what O'Connor calls a "Pecksniffian" manner) to have anything to do with *Leaves* (CORR, 1:329, n78).

AROUND THIS TIME. John Burroughs publishes his *Notes on Walt Whitman, as Poet and Person*. Written with the help of Whitman and O'Connor, it further enhances Whitman's claim to originality by insisting that, prior to publishing the 1855 *Leaves*, Whitman "had never read the Essays or Poems of Mr. Emerson at all" (Burroughs, *Notes*, 16). Burroughs continues the Whitman/Emerson controversy in his 1896 biography, *Walt Whitman, a Study*, where he says, "Emerson's prayer was for the absolutely self-reliant man, but when Whitman refused to follow his advice with regard to certain passages in the 'Leaves,' the sage withheld further approval of the work" (231). Burroughs is as convinced of Whitman's genius as O'Connor but writes the latter (4 January 1867), "I do not think that either you or I or both, are the guardians of Walt's fame, or that we can make or unmake it" (Perry, 189).

24 JULY. Whitman sends Moncure Conway in London a facsimile of the 1867 *Leaves* prepared for publication and with an introduction written, he tells him, by William O'Connor. He gives Conway "full power" in obtaining publication of this in England (CORR, 1:332–333). (Despite his claim, it has been established that Whitman wrote the introduction to the London edition [Furness, 141–149].) William Rossetti is interested in publishing *Leaves* in England, but problems arise when publishers fear prosecution on obscenity charges; the history of the London edition continues throughout this year.

7 AUGUST. Whitman sends a new poem in praise of the Civil War victors, "A Carol of Harvest, for 1867" (later "The Return of the Heroes"), to the *Galaxy* at the publisher's request; he is paid $60 for it (CORR, 1:337), and it is published in the September issue. It is William O'Connor's urging that has led to the editors' request for a poem.

7 SEPTEMBER. Whitman sends the *Galaxy* another new poem with a Civil War theme, "Ethiopia Commenting" (later "Ethiopia Saluting the Colors"), which is accepted but never published. He tells Francis P. Church he is writing a prose piece of some length, which he proposes to call "Democracy," and asks if Church would be interested in publishing it (CORR, 1:338). "Democracy" (later *Democratic Vistas*) is Whitman's response to "Shooting Niagara: And After?," Thomas Carlyle's bitter attack on democracy in general and American democracy in particular, issued in the wake of England's 1867 Reform Bill, which redefined and broadened suffrage. Carlyle's essay appeared in the *New York Tribune* on 16 August 1867.

15 SEPTEMBER. Having obtained a leave of absence, Whitman visits Brooklyn; the family now lives at 1194 Atlantic Street. Whitman goes to many of the places he frequented earlier in New York and Brooklyn, but in his new postwar mood, as he writes Ellen O'Connor, he does not enjoy them as before (CORR, 1:342).

1 NOVEMBER. Whitman writes Conway that his feelings are "passive" with regard to a publication of selections from *Leaves*, rather than the entire volume, to be edited by William Rossetti. He "empowers" Rossetti to substitute words for any the English poet finds unacceptable in poems chosen for the volume (CORR, 1:346–347).

10 NOVEMBER. Whitman writes a letter regarding the London edition, which is to be sent to Moncure Conway by William O'Connor, thus obscuring Whitman's authorship. The main points intended for Rossetti are: that Whitman is not unconventional but worthy of representing American democracy; that *Leaves* is not to be judged by literary standards since it derives from a "universal law" of cosmic proportions; and that a totality of the individual, as represented by the poetic personality in *Leaves*, is its ultimate meaning, along with the "modernness" of the work (CORR, 1:348–349). Since Conway's October 1866 *Fortnightly Review* article, Whitman cannot rely upon him to present the book and its author in the light he wishes, hence this letter. Late in life he tells Traubel the letter gives his own idea of his book and therefore is not to be "despised" (WWC, 1:383).

17 NOVEMBER. Rossetti writes that there is nothing to prevent publication in England of the entire 1867 *Leaves*, but with "modification or excision here and there" (WWC, 3:300).

22 NOVEMBER. Without having received Rossetti's most recent letter, Whitman writes to him that, while he has agreed to word substitutions, he wishes to avoid any "expressed or implied" expurgation; the London edition is to be presented as a selection of poems drawn from the various American editions (CORR, 1:350). Evidently as a means of preventing expurgation, Whitman states that he wishes all the original numbering of stanzas and clusters to be followed and included.

3 DECEMBER. Whitman responds to Rossetti's suggestion of 17 November for a modified version of *Leaves*. He states that he will not consent to an expurgated edition of his poems, pointing out that he has "steadily" refused to do

so in America, but that if such an edition has already been sent for printing, he would not expect its abandonment at the editor's loss; in that event, however, he directs that there should be no suggestion of his having authorized an expurgation (CORR, 1:352–353). Rossetti informs Whitman that printing is too far advanced to admit of a complete edition and that selections for the London edition have been made on the following bases: poems with objectionable words are eliminated in their entirety and Rossetti has included his favorite poems (CORR, 1:352, n45). The question of exclusion versus expurgation of poems in the London edition has been variously interpreted, even by Whitman, as can be seen in his 1871 comment on "the horrible dismemberment" of *Leaves* (CORR, 2:133) and in later comments to Traubel (e.g., WWC, 1:224). Early commentators, such as Binns and Perry, defend Rossetti's exclusions; more recently, Kaplan and Reynolds fault Whitman for consenting to expurgation.

DECEMBER. The *Galaxy* publishes "Democracy," in which Whitman acknowledges the faults of the democratic system but insists on the ideal of democracy as the means by which individuals, and eventually society, are made better. A recently discovered manuscript, probably dating to late 1867, may have been planned as part of this essay. Titled "Of the black question," it includes the then-current argument of ethnological science that blacks would disappear from human history through the workings of evolution (Sill, 73).

CHAPTER FIVE

1868-1875

the lights and shades
—Preface, *As a Strong Bird on Pinions Free*, 1872

The years 1868–1875 include some of Whitman's best and, undoubtedly, some of the worst times. Though discouraged by Reconstruction politics and the practice of democracy in the United States, he takes up the defense of democratic principles, first in "Democracy" and later in *Democratic Vistas* (1871). Appreciation of his work continues to grow in England, where in 1868 William M. Rossetti edits a volume of selections from *Leaves of Grass*, titled *Poems of Walt Whitman*. Poet Algernon Charles Swinburne honors him by linking him to William Blake, and he is noted by a number of literary critics. A friendly correspondence begins with Alfred, Lord Tennyson, and, unexpectedly, with the Englishwoman Anne Gilchrist, widow of the Blake biographer Alexander Gilchrist, who declares her love for Whitman and proposes marriage. On the Continent some of his poems are translated into German and some into Danish, while at home he receives invitations to read at an exhibition of American industry, at the Dartmouth College commencement, and at a meeting of mathematicians at Tufts College. *Passage to India* distinguishes his 1871 edition of *Leaves of Grass*, and some minor poems, widely circulated, keep his name before the public.

It is in his personal life that things go awry in this period. Changes in Whitman's family include Jeff's move to St. Louis and his wife's subsequent illness and death; the accidental death of one of Andrew's sons; Jesse's death in the Brooklyn asylum; George's marriage to Louisa Haslam and move to New Jersey, leaving his mother to deal with Edward; and his mother's illness, leading to the breakup of her home and her death in 1873. Just months before his mother's death Whitman suffers a paralyzing stroke, which

[81]

leaves him "A batter'd, wreck'd old man," as he describes
the hero of his "Prayer of Columbus" later in the year. Sep-
arated from his beloved Peter Doyle by distance (after Walt
goes to live with George and Louisa in Camden, New Jersey) and from William O'Connor by anger (the result of a
bitter argument), Whitman almost succumbs to loneliness
and despair. But while slowly adjusting to his physical limi-
tations, he is able to print a small number of *Memoranda
During the War* and begins to plan another edition of *Leaves*
and a book of prose and poetry to be called *Two Rivulets*.

1868

17 JANUARY. Jeff Whitman writes to Walt that he and his
family arrived safely in Pittsburgh on their way to St.
Louis. Jeff, Mattie, and the children settle in St. Louis
late in January, but because of the pressure of work Jeff
does not resume correspondence with Walt until July,
when he begins to express fears at his wife's persistent
throat ailment (Berthold and Price, 124, 125). By September the doctors in St. Louis are recommending a trip
East, and Mattie returns to Brooklyn.

24 JANUARY. Whitman attends a lecture by zoologist Alexander Agassiz at the E Street Baptist Church, Washington (CORR, 2:14, n10).

JANUARY. *Putnam's Magazine* carries a story by William
O'Connor titled "The Carpenter." An allegory present-
ing Whitman as a Christ figure, it appears to be part of
the attempt to create an ideal image of the poet.

5 FEBRUARY. *Poems of Walt Whitman*, edited by William M.
Rossetti, is published in London.

17 FEBRUARY. Whitman writes to Moncure Conway that
having his book and his cause fall into William Rossetti's
hands was a piece of the greatest "good fortune" (CORR,
2:16).

18 FEBRUARY. In a letter to the publisher of the London edition of selections from *Leaves*, John Camden Hotten,
Whitman accepts the proposed terms for sale of the vol-

ume in England and the United States. Sales in the United States are to bring an author's royalty of twenty-five cents per copy, with Whitman retaining full copyright (CORR, 2:16–17).

19 FEBRUARY. Whitman arranges for the binding of ninety copies of the 1867 *Leaves* (CORR, 2:18).

FEBRUARY. Copies of Algernon Charles Swinburne's study of William Blake reach America; Swinburne argues that there is a spiritual connection between the poetry of Blake and Whitman, which further enhances the latter's European reputation.

9 MARCH. Whitman receives from London his copy of *Poems of Walt Whitman*. He writes to the publisher, John Camden Hotten, offering (at a price of $40 gold) the original plate of the frontispiece for the 1855 *Leaves* to replace the "marked blemish" portrait included in the first printing (CORR, 2:21–22).

24 APRIL. Hotten has agreed to Whitman's suggestion of 9 March and plans to use the photograph from the 1855 *Leaves* as the frontispiece, so Whitman writes detailed instructions for cropping the photo (CORR, 2:28).

ON THE SAME DATE. An essay on "Walt Whitman" by Ferdinand Freiligrath appears in the *Augsburg Allgemeine Zeitung*; it begins by asking "Who is Walt Whitman?" and answers by declaring him nothing less than "mankind and the world" (Miller, *Century*, 31). A translation of this appears in the *New Eclectic Magazine* in July, and Whitman and O'Connor are immediately eager to contact Freiligrath about a translation of *Leaves* into German. Later in the year they send him a copy of the 1867 edition, *The Good Gray Poet*, and Burroughs's *Notes*. Though the German poet will publish ten of the poems in translation later in this year, the hoped-for translation of *Leaves* is not forthcoming.

26 APRIL. Whitman sends Amos Bronson Alcott a copy of "Personalism," which Alcott so admires that he later uses the term to define his own philosophy (CORR, 2:29).

14 AUGUST. Whitman enjoys a trip to Alexandria, Virginia, by steamer; it provides welcome relief from the heat in

Washington, of which he repeatedly complains in letters to his mother.

15 AUGUST. John Addington Symonds writes to William Rossetti asking why certain poems from *Leaves* are not included in the London edition: "Is it because you would not submit them to the necessary purgation for English readers?" (*Rossetti Papers*, 363).

2 SEPTEMBER. "A CHILD RUN OVER AND KILLED." The *Brooklyn Eagle* reports the death of "a little boy, named Andrew Whitman" (Walt's nephew), who was run over by a cart while playing in Hudson Avenue. In May Whitman's mother had sought Walt's help in having the children removed from Nancy Whitman's care because they were neglected, but Walt ignored her (Allen, *Solitary Singer*, 395).

7 SEPTEMBER. No doubt with the vices — alcoholism and, perhaps, prostitution — of little Andrew's mother in mind, Walt writes his mother that the child is out of this world of "sin and trouble" and is not to be mourned (CORR, 2:42).

15 SEPTEMBER. Whitman arrives in New York on his annual vacation. He stays with Abby Price in New York and takes one meal a day with his mother in Brooklyn, finding the daily trip by ferry a large part of the pleasure of his visit (CORR, 2:48).

18 SEPTEMBER. Peter Doyle writes Walt that it "seems more than a week" since they last saw each other. This initiates a six-month correspondence between Whitman and Doyle (CORR, 2:4). Doyle writes of his daily activities at work, of his evening entertainment, and often of mutual friends; Whitman does the same but is more affectionate, addressing Doyle as "dearest boy," "son," and "dear comrade" and referring to himself as Doyle's "father" or the "old man."

25 SEPTEMBER. Whitman writes Doyle that he is having a small number of the 1867 *Leaves* printed. He tells him he is able to think of him "with more calmness" than when they were together and that he doesn't know what

he should do if he did not have Pete in his thoughts (CORR, 2:47).

27 SEPTEMBER. Whitman visits the infamous Five Points district of New York City and spends two hours observing; he finds the visit "instructive but disgusting" (CORR, 2:53). Five Points, in lower Manhattan, east of Broadway, is a crime-ridden slum often visited by writers (Charles Dickens in 1842) and reformers. In 1866 Bayard Taylor published an account of a Five Points visit in the *Nation* and may have spoken of it to Whitman when he called on him late in the same year (CORR, 1:305).

5 OCTOBER. New York Democrats hold a torchlight parade. The following day Whitman writes Peter Doyle a description of the parade, expressing his pleasure (CORR, 2:55–56).

MID-OCTOBER. Whitman visits Providence, Rhode Island, where he stays in the homes of former Congressman Thomas Davis and Dr. William Channing; he writes to Doyle of dinner parties with flirtatious women, of carriage rides, and of being generally "in clover" (CORR, 2:60).

25 OCTOBER. Whitman writes to Jeff from New York with a report of Mattie's examination by Dr. A. D. Wilson of Brooklyn: one of her lungs is affected, but there is no imminent danger (CORR, 2:68). Mattie's condition does not improve substantially, but she will return to St. Louis in December.

OCTOBER. The London *Broadway Magazine* publishes "Whispers of Heavenly Death," a collection of five short poems — "Whispers of Heavenly Death," "Darest Thou Now O Soul," "A Noiseless Patient Spider," "The Last Invocation," and "Pensive and Faltering."

2 NOVEMBER. Back in Washington, Whitman writes to the *Galaxy* editor withdrawing "Ethiopia Commenting," which has not been published since its submission on 7 September 1867 (CORR, 2:69).

30 NOVEMBER. Whitman sends Ralph Waldo Emerson a new poem, "Proud Music of the Sea-Storm," asking him

to place it with the *Atlantic Monthly*. James T. Fields, editor of the *Monthly*, accepts the poem (later "Proud Music of the Storm") and publishes it in the February 1869 issue.

8 DECEMBER. Whitman writes to Dr. Samuel Thayer of the University of Vermont Medical School asking for information on the condition of his sister Hannah. Dr. Thayer has amputated Hannah's left thumb after it failed to respond to treatment of an infection (CORR, 2:73–74).

17 DECEMBER. Whitman offers a poem, "Thou Vast Rondure, Swimming in Space," to the London *Fortnightly Review*; it is accepted but never appears. Whitman later incorporates the poem into "Passage to India."

1869

In the first half of this year conditions are unsettled in the office of the Attorney General until President Grant appoints Ebenezer R. Hoor as Attorney General.

18 JANUARY. The *Washington Star* notes the appearance of "Proud Music" in the February *Atlantic Monthly*, seeing it as a recognition of the poet by the Boston literary group to match that accorded him in England; the blurb has been placed with the paper by Whitman (Holloway, "Press Agent," 483).

20 JANUARY. Whitman offers "Thou Vast Rondure" to James T. Fields, hoping for simultaneous publication in the *Atlantic Monthly* and in the London *Fortnightly Review*; neither magazine publishes the poem.

15 MARCH. Louisa Whitman writes to Walt asking him to lend George $600 until May (Allen, *Solitary Singer*, 407). George has moved to Camden, New Jersey, but is building houses in Brooklyn. Jeff has already loaned George $3,000, payable in monthly installments of $200, for which he holds mortgages; Walt provides the sum requested by his mother (Berthold and Price, 136). Louisa Whitman and Eddie move into one of the houses, on Portland Avenue, on 1 May.

7 APRIL. Louisa Whitman writes Walt that Eddie has met an escapee from the asylum where Jesse is confined who reports terrible conditions at the hospital (Allen, *Solitary Singer*, 408).

9 MAY. The *Washington Sunday Chronicle* carries another of Whitman's self-placed notices; this one comments on his good health on nearing fifty and indicates his intention to publish another edition of *Leaves* later in the year (Holloway, "Press Agent," 484).

18 AUGUST. Whitman returns to Brooklyn, probably to see his poems through the printing process. Shortly after arriving he suffers a sick spell (perhaps a slight stroke) and consults a doctor, who believes it still the result of an illness contracted in the army hospitals (CORR, 2:86).

21 AUGUST. Walt writes to Peter Doyle chastising him for what was probably suicidal talk at their last meeting. The talk of suicide is prompted by skin eruptions on his face, which Pete interprets as a sign of serious illness (CORR, 2:84). Whitman promises to take care of Pete should his fear be realized. The two correspond throughout the summer.

9 SEPTEMBER. Whitman marvels at the display, all along Broadway in New York City, of flags and streamers at half-mast to mark the funeral of General John Rawlins, the deceased Secretary of War (CORR, 2:88).

28 SEPTEMBER. Whitman writes William O'Connor details of the 1857 loan of $200 from James Parton and the manner of repayment (CORR, 2:89–90; see chapter 2).

9 DECEMBER. Whitman sends two photographs of himself to William Rossetti, one of which is for the Englishwoman, as yet unknown to him, who has expressed such deep appreciation of his poetry. The woman, Anne Gilchrist, is the widow of William Blake's biographer, Alexander Gilchrist, and a critic highly regarded by England's leading literary figures. Encouraged by her enthusiasm for the selected *Leaves*, Rossetti has loaned her Whitman's own corrected copy of the complete volume to which she responds, in letters to Rossetti, with unbounded emotion and intelligent understanding.

Rossetti has sent copies of her letters to O'Connor, who has shown them to Whitman, and the photographs are the result. By this time Gilchrist has reworked her letters into an essay on Whitman, sent in late November to O'Connor.

Whitman's frequent gifts of photographs in these years reflect his growing preoccupation with his own image as both the product of a camera lens (as in his instructions to his English publisher regarding the *Leaves* frontispiece) and of his own making via newspaper blurbs and the writings of friends. In the late 1860s his photographs are on sale in Washington, and he is sometimes asked to autograph copies (CORR, 2:79). Two photographs of this period are with Peter Doyle (see Folsom, *Representations*, 167–170).

25 DECEMBER. The *Washington Saturday Evening Visitor* publishes "The Singer in the Prison."

1870

JANUARY. "Brother of All, with Outstretched Hand" (later "Outlines for a Tomb"), written at the death of Massachusetts merchant and philanthropist George Peabody, appears in the *Galaxy*.

21 MARCH. Whitman learns of the death of his brother Jesse at Kings County Lunatic Asylum. Jesse dies of a ruptured aneuryism and is buried by hospital authorities in a pauper's grave (Allen, *Solitary Singer*, 419).

4 APRIL. Whitman offers a new poem, "Passage to India," to the editor of San Francisco's *Overland Monthly*, Bret Harte, who declines it (CORR, 2:94); the poem becomes the title piece of the seventy-five-poem *Passage to India* appended to the next edition of *Leaves*.

MAY. "Warble for Lilac-Time" appears in the *Galaxy*.

IN THE SAME MONTH. Boston's the *Radical* publishes Anne Gilchrist's essay, "A Woman's Estimate of Walt Whitman," in which she writes:

And I know that poetry must do one of two
things,— either own this man as equal with her
highest, completest manifestors, or stand aside, and
admit that there is something come into the world
nobler, diviner than herself, one that is free of the
universe, and can tell its secrets as none before.
(Traubel, Bucke, and Harned, 42)

ALSO IN MAY. Whitman cuts his right thumb and when
it becomes infected is unable to work, so he returns
to Brooklyn for a two-week stay, taking Peter Doyle
with him (Murray, 24). Later, in describing the trip to
Dr. Bucke, Doyle says they stayed in Jersey City and
took dinner with Whitman's mother; he also remembers
Whitman taking him to see the opera *Poliuto* (Donizetti's opera was performed at the Brooklyn Academy of
Music on 26 May with tenor Charles Lefrane and soprano Clara Kellogg) (Murray, 24).

15 JULY. Writing in his notebook, Whitman admonishes
himself:

TO GIVE UP ABSOLUTELY and for good, from the
present hour, this FEVERISH, FLUCTUATING, useless
UNDIGNIFIED PURSUIT of 16.4 — too long, (much
too long) persevered in, — so humiliating — — It
must come at last and had better come now . . . —
avoid seeing her, or meeting her, or any talk or explanations — or ANY MEETING WHATEVER, FROM
THIS HOUR FORTH, FOR LIFE. (NUPM, 2:888)

This entry has been interpreted as a coded reference to
the sixteenth letter of the alphabet, P, and the fourth, D,
for Peter Doyle (Cargill, 25), and the substitution of fem-
inine for masculine pronouns has been detected (Asselineau, 187, 329, n57).

SUMMER. Whitman arranges for a substitute clerk to cover
his duties in the Attorney General's Office and takes
leave from 27 July to 15 October. During this time he

oversees the printing of the fifth edition of *Leaves of Grass*, *Passage to India*, and *Democratic Vistas*. While in Brooklyn he writes a series of letters to Peter Doyle in which he describes his New York activities and, because of Doyle's job insecurity, offers encouragement and a promise of financial aid. In the first of these letters, dated 30 July, Whitman refers to the hour of their parting, between 10 and 11 p.m. on a street corner in Washington, when he realizes for the first time that his deep feelings for Pete are returned, and he reveals the "pleasure and comfort" this brings him (CORR, 2:101).

30 SEPTEMBER. Whitman sees some of the military parade that accompanies the burial in New York of Admiral David G. Farragut (CORR, 2:114).

14 OCTOBER. Having given up his room on M Street prior to going to New York, Whitman writes to William O'Connor and asks him to engage a room for him at the St. Cloud Hotel in Washington (CORR, 2:116).

1871

The fifth edition of *Leaves of Grass* encompasses two printings, one in 1871 and one in 1872, each with two issues. The first issue of the initial printing is 384 pages, while the second issue of the 1871 printing, with "Passage to India" and seventy-four more poems (twenty-four of them new), totals 504 pages. Both are published by J. S. Redfield of New York, as are the two issues of the second printing in 1872 (Myerson, *Walt Whitman*, 49–59). The 1871–1872 edition includes "Drum-Taps" (formerly a separate publication) and two new poems, "The Singer in the Prison" and "Brother of All with Generous Hand," and shows a general regrouping of poems. "Proud Music of the Storm" and "Whispers of Heavenly Death" are important new additions. The supplement, *Passage to India*, contains the title poem, which Whitman describes as his attempt to celebrate modern engineering and its accomplishments — notably, the completion of the Suez Canal, the Union Pacific Railroad, and the international Atlantic cable — by lifting them to spiritual heights (CORR, 2:96–97). This is followed by poems drawn from earlier editions of *Leaves*, which, together with *Passage to India*, appear to be the basis of the new volume of poems Whitman promises in the preface to the 1872 *Leaves*. In 1871 Whitman also publishes the prose work *Democratic Vistas*, an expansion of his essays "Democracy," "Personalism," and the heretofore unpublished "Orbic Literature."

9 JANUARY. Whitman applies for the position of pardon clerk in the Department of Justice (CORR, 2:117). He is not granted the post.

JANUARY. "A Study of Walt Whitman, The Poet of Modern Democracy" by Roden Noel appears in *Dark Blue*, an English periodical. Burroughs sends Whitman a copy in October (CORR, 2:162, n55).

MID-FEBRUARY. Whitman enjoys Washington's carnival, complete with horse races and parades of people in fancy dress and masks (CORR, 2:118).

MARCH. A Danish periodical, *For Ide og Virkelighed*, includes an article on Whitman by Rudolf Schmidt. Whitman prints excerpts from this in his 1872 pamphlet *As a Strong Bird on Pinions Free* (the entire article appears in Traubel, Bucke, and Harned, 231–248).

IN THE SAME MONTH. Whitman attends the opera twice in New York, both times to hear the Swedish soprano Christine Nilsson, first in Verdi's *Il Trovatore* and then in Meyerbeer's *Robert le Diable*; Pasquale Brignoli, who is in the latter opera, is his favorite tenor (CORR, 2:169, n80).

14 APRIL. George Whitman marries Louisa Orr Haslam, and the couple takes up residence in Camden, New Jersey.

27 APRIL. Whitman writes to Tennyson expressing the hope that the English poet will visit America (CORR, 2:174–175). The letter refers to a prior correspondence (now missing) between the two poets in 1871.

MAY. Whitman prepares an editorial (never published) defending Peter Doyle's brother, police officer Francis M. Doyle, against newspaper claims of police brutality re-

lated to Doyle's arrest of a young boy on theft charges
(NUPM, 2:783).

SPRING. Whitman receives a copy of Swinburne's *Songs Before Sunrise* with its laudatory "To Walt Whitman in
America." Such praise from European poets is great
comfort to Whitman, but Swinburne will later change
his mind (see chapter 7).

20 JUNE. Whitman returns to Brooklyn on his annual vacation. He writes to Peter Doyle regularly while away and,
because of his recent poor health, assures him that he is
doing very little work and is spending most of his time at
home caring for his mother (who is not well), riding the
ferry, and visiting Coney Island (on 16 July he writes to
Doyle while on the sands of that beach). On 14 July he
writes Doyle (originally an Irish immigrant) about the
murderous riot in New York City at the annual parade by
New York's Irish commemorating the 1609 Battle of the
Boyne.

LATE JUNE. The newspapers report Whitman's death in a
train accident, and his attempts to correct the story are
not printed (CORR, 2:123).

JUNE. "O Star of France," a poem on the defeat of France in
the Franco-Prussian War, appears in the *Galaxy*.

27 JULY. Whitman leaves Brooklyn for New Haven, Connecticut, to visit his friend, artist Charles Hine, who is
dying of tuberculosis (CORR, 2:130). Hine dies on 4 August; a painting he had done of Whitman is among the
possessions Whitman bequeaths to his brother George.

28 JULY. In a letter to William Rossetti, Whitman says he
considers his *Leaves* "substantially finished" but that he
plans to add to *Democratic Vistas* in future years (CORR,
2:131).

JULY. An anonymously published essay titled "The Poetry
of Democracy: Walt Whitman" appears in London's *Westminster Review*, which has earlier (October 1860) taken
a hostile position toward Whitman. Its author, Edward
Dowden, professor of literature at the University of Dublin, examines Whitman's poetry for what it reveals of
"the characteristics of democratic art" as distinguished

from the art of an aristocracy (Hindus, 146). Dowden identifies himself to Whitman as the author, and on 22 August Whitman writes his thanks (CORR, 2:133–134); this begins a correspondence between the two that lasts until Whitman's death.

1 AUGUST. The Committee on Invitations of the American Institute invites Whitman to deliver an original poem at the opening of their fortieth annual exhibition on 7 September in New York. Whitman accepts the offer on 5 August (CORR, 2:132). The National Industrial Exhibition, an annual exhibition devoted to American industry, displays American-made machinery and manufactured products.

AUGUST. Whitman writes to a London publisher, F. S. Ellis, proposing a moderately priced edition of the 1871 *Leaves of Grass*; Whitman is eager to have his poems come to the attention of the English public and is unhappy at the "dismemberment" of his book in the Rossetti selections (CORR, 2:133). The proposal is rejected because it is not possible under English law to publish all of Whitman's poems.

3 SEPTEMBER. Responding to Whitman's gift of his latest three books and most recent photograph (sent via William Rossetti on 28 July), Anne Gilchrist writes Whitman a long letter in which she describes the emotions she feels for the *Leaves* poet: "nothing in life or death can tear out of my heart the passionate belief that one day I shall hear that voice say to me, 'My Mate. The one I so much want. Bride, Wife, indissoluble eternal!'" (Harned, 60). Gilchrist writes two other letters in this year, on 3 November and 27 November, both expressing similar sentiments.

7 SEPTEMBER. Whitman delivers his poem "After All, Not to Create Only" at the National Industrial Exhibition. Press coverage of the event is mixed, and Whitman responds aggressively to the negative criticism by placing favorable articles with friendly newspapers (CORR, 2:138–139; NUPM, 2:897–899, 900). The poem extols American industry but calls for a spiritual dimension

to be added to its creativity. Whitman publishes the poem as a pamphlet later in the year and as part of the 1872 *Leaves of Grass*. In 1876 the title is changed to "Song of the Exposition" to honor the Centennial Exposition.

OCTOBER. Robert Buchanan, an English admirer who in 1868 had lauded the 1867 edition of *Leaves* in the *Broadway Magazine*, writes an article (using the pseudonym Thomas Maitland) in the *Contemporary Review* on "The Fleshly School of Poetry" in which he attacks Dante Gabriel Rossetti (among others) for immorality. Swinburne then charges Buchanan with inconsistency for upholding Whitman while denouncing Rossetti; Buchanan responds in 1872 by admitting there are at most fifty lines of Whitman's poetry that he finds indecent but forgivable because the poet is "a spiritual person" (Hindus, 150).

26 DECEMBER. Whitman writes a short, formal letter to Anne Gilchrist to acknowledge receipt of all three of her letters (CORR, 2:145).

28 DECEMBER. Whitman sees President Grant on "the avenue" (probably Pennsylvania Avenue) and salutes him, as is his habit; Grant, as will become his habit, returns the salute by calling out, "After all, not to create only!" (CORR, 2:147).

29 DECEMBER. Peter Doyle's brother, police officer Francis M. Doyle, is shot and killed in the line of duty; Walt attends the funeral held on New Year's Eve (CORR, 2:148–149).

1872

1 JANUARY. Whitman receives notice of transfer to the Solicitor's Office, Treasury Building, still within the Department of Justice; he plans to request leave as of 1 February (CORR, 2:148, 157).

27 JANUARY. Whitman writes to John Addington Symonds

acknowledging receipt of his poem "Love and Death" (CORR, 2:158–159).

30 JANUARY. Whitman sends William Rossetti a copy of "The Mystic Trumpeter" (CORR, 2:159–162). His letter to Rossetti is a long recital of neglect on the part of his American audience, a frequent complaint made to his European admirers.

JANUARY. Ralph Waldo Emerson lectures in Baltimore and Washington; Whitman hears him in Baltimore, finds nothing new in Emerson's message since its initial genius, and is not interested (CORR, 2:150, 155).

7 FEBRUARY. John Addington Symonds writes from England identifying himself as a scholar of Greek and Roman forms of male friendship and asking for an elaboration of Whitman's meaning in "Calamus" (WWC, 1:74–76). Whitman does not respond. Symonds writes again in 1875 and again in 1890, still seeking an answer. Whitman finally responds in 1890 with a shocked denial of the inference Symonds has drawn (see chapter 8).

10 FEBRUARY. Whitman arrives at his mother's house on Portland Avenue, Brooklyn, for an extended visit (CORR, 2:165). This is the first of three visits to Brooklyn in this year; during each of them he writes regularly to Peter Doyle in Washington.

FEBRUARY. "The Mystic Trumpeter" appears in the *Kansas Magazine*.

20 MARCH. Whitman writes to Anne Gilchrist and warns her not to construct an "imaginary ideal Figure" when the real Whitman is "a very plain personage" (CORR, 2:170).

MARCH. "Virginia—The West" appears in the *Kansas Magazine*.

EARLY APRIL. Whitman returns to Washington.

27 APRIL. Whitman sends Tennyson a copy of the most recent *Leaves* and *Democratic Vistas* (CORR, 2:174).

31 MAY. On his fifty-third birthday Whitman concludes the preface to *As a Strong Bird on Pinions Free*.

LATE SPRING. Martha Whitman, with husband Jeff, comes

east from St. Louis for medical consultation and is diagnosed with cancer (CORR, 2:156, n36; Waldron, 77–78).

10 JUNE. Whitman is in Brooklyn.

26 JUNE. Having been invited by the graduating students of Dartmouth College in New Hampshire to read a poem, Whitman delivers "As a Strong Bird on Pinions Free" (later "Thou Mother with Thy Equal Brood"), in which the bird is an image of America. After the address, Whitman issues the poem, along with six others, in pamphlet form. From New Hampshire he visits his sister Hannah in Vermont, journeying on 24 and 25 June up the Connecticut River valley, then spending 28 and 29 June in Hanover, New Hampshire. He stays a week in the Burlington, Lake Champlain, region of Vermont, returning by way of Albany, New York, where he makes an overnight stop, and then down the Hudson River. Once back in Brooklyn he is ill and extends his work leave for two weeks starting 11 July. About this time Whitman complains of ill health in many of his letters and commits frequent errors in dating, indications, perhaps, of his increasing hypertension.

18 JULY. As Whitman is riding a Fifth Avenue stage in New York City, a man rushes out and mounts the stage to greet him; it is the California poet Joaquin Miller, who introduces himself and asks permission to call. The following day he spends three hours with Whitman, who finds him more satisfying than his poetry (CORR, 2:182).

EARLY AUGUST. Louisa Whitman and Eddie move to Camden to live with George and Louisa. Mattie Whitman, in St. Louis, repeatedly writes to Walt and his mother begging for a visit from her mother-in-law, but to no avail (Waldron, 81–89).

Whitman and William O'Connor quarrel, which leads to a separation not ended until 1882. The quarrel occurs in the O'Connor home and is believed to have stemmed from Whitman's belief that, despite the passage of the Fifteenth Amendment two years earlier, blacks are not capable of voting judiciously (Barrus, 96; see also Freedman; and Loving, *Whitman's Champion*).

2 SEPTEMBER. Whitman sends Tennyson a copy of the pamphlet *As a Strong Bird on Pinions Free* (CORR, 2:184).

23 OCTOBER. Whitman makes a will and sends it to his brother George for safekeeping (CORR, 2:187). The will leaves everything to his mother and, after her, to George for the care of Edward.

17 NOVEMBER. Whitman drafts a letter to the postmaster in Washington seeking a change of the postal law to allow manuscripts and proofs passing between authors and publishers to be posted at book rates; he argues for an expanded definition of "books" by drawing an analogy to Jefferson's use (in the Declaration of Independence) of "man" in a generic sense (CORR, 2:188−189). No change is effected.

IN THIS YEAR. The Russian poet Ivan Turgenev discovers *Leaves of Grass* and begins to translate the poems into Russian. Only one of these translations, a manuscript of "Beat! Beat! Drums!," has survived (see Chistova).

1873

14 JANUARY. Whitman attends a farewell concert at Lincoln Hall given by opera tenor Giovanni Mario and soprano Carlotta Patti (CORR, 2:191). Though Whitman comments to his mother that he heard Mario sing thirty years ago, his earliest hearing was in October 1854 when Mario and Giulia Grisi opened the New York Academy of Music in *Norma*.

22 JANUARY. Whitman has a stroke during the night and loses the use of his left arm and leg.

26 JANUARY. Whitman writes the news of his stroke to his mother (CORR, 2:192). Dr. William B. Drinkard attends him, and some of Whitman's friends — Peter Doyle, Ellen O'Connor, John Burroughs and his wife, Ursula, Charles Eldridge, and Mrs. J. Hubley Ashton (wife of the Assistant Attorney General) — care for him. Burroughs has decided to move to New York but is seeing to the sale of his Washington home and stays on.

17 FEBRUARY. Whitman makes his first venture into the street following his stroke and finds it "more exertion than [he] could bear" (CORR, 2:199). His left leg is almost useless, and his room at 535 Fifteenth Street is on the fourth floor. The winter drags on with little progress toward a return to work. He manages to write four short poems, which are published in the *New York Daily Graphic* in March and April. A fifth poem, "Warble for Lilac-Time," which appears on 12 May, had been previously published in the *Galaxy* in 1870.

19 FEBRUARY. Mattie Whitman dies in St. Louis. Jeff writes to his mother (24 February) describing Mattie's final hours, when she could no longer speak but held the hands of her children and husband until lapsing into unconsciousness (Waldron, 4).

5 MARCH. The *Graphic* publishes "Nay, Tell Me Not To-day the Publish'd Shame," a poem referring to government scandals.

6 MARCH. "With All Thy Gifts" appears in the *Graphic*.

15 MARCH. "The Singing Thrush" (later "Wandering at Morn") is published in the *Graphic*.

24 MARCH. "Spain, 1873–74," a poem on the failure to establish a republic in Spain, appears in the *Graphic*.

1 APRIL. Whitman returns to work on a part-time basis but continues to feel weak and complains of dizziness and head pain.

4 APRIL. "Sea Captains, Young or Old" (later "Song for All Seas, All Ships"), inspired by two 1873 marine disasters, appears in the *Graphic*.

19 APRIL. Whitman has a second application of electricity to his left leg (CORR, 2:215). Dr. Drinkard applies electric shock on a number of occasions but with little improvement to the leg.

15 MAY. Whitman makes a new will leaving all his property to his mother in trust for Edward; he leaves Peter Doyle $89 owed to him and a silver watch (NUPM, 2:917–919).

20 MAY. Whitman arrives in Camden, having been summoned because of his mother's illness.

23 MAY. Louisa Whitman dies. Her final written words to her children close with "farewell my dear beloved Walter" (WWC, 4:514). His mother's death is, in Whitman's words, "the great dark cloud of my life" (CORR, 2:242). A friend describes Whitman at the side of his mother's coffin:

> He was bent over his cane, both hands clasped upon it, and from time to time he would lift it and bring it down with a heavy thud on the floor. . . . he had sat there all through the previous night. (Myerson, *Time*, 282)

2 JUNE. Whitman returns to Washington and goes to the home of the Ashtons for a short stay (CORR, 2:221, n87).

18 JUNE. Whitman writes to Peter Doyle for the first time from 322 Stevens Street, Camden, where he has gone to stay with George and Louisa after obtaining a two-month leave of absence. He lives in the same two rooms his mother occupied before her death and keeps them as she left them (CORR, 2:222, 223).

26 JUNE. John Burroughs writes to Charles Eldridge expressing his concern for their friend Walt:

> The fact is, I begin to doubt whether Walt is going to recover, and I am very apprehensive of another attack. . . . He is a mere physical wreck to what he was. . . . It is a terrible misfortune, one of the saddest spectacles I have ever seen. His mental powers seem to be as vigorous as ever, which is the brightest part of his case, but to be stricken with such physical weakness that he cannot walk a block without resting — it is very pitiful. (Barrus, 83)

7 JULY. Whitman reads in the *New York Herald* of the appointment of William O'Connor to the government position of chief clerk of the Lighthouse Board and writes to Eldridge that he is "*truly pleased.*" In March of the

following year Whitman writes to Peter Doyle that O'Connor is no longer in this position but is clerk in the Library of the Treasury Department (CORR, 2:226, 286).

24 JULY. Whitman writes to Pete giving him a word of "caution" that he may not recover (CORR, 2:229).

14 AUGUST. Whitman writes to his superior requesting official acceptance of the substitute clerk he has hired to perform his duties (CORR, 2:232).

8 SEPTEMBER. Jeff Whitman visits Walt in Camden while on his way to New York for a week's yachting vacation (CORR, 2:241).

29 SEPTEMBER. George and Louisa Whitman move to 431 Stevens Street, Camden, a pleasant corner house to which George has added a large second-floor room, with bay window, intended for Walt, who chooses instead a small room on the third floor (CORR, 2:248).

SEPTEMBER. John Burroughs's article "The Birds of the Poet," with lengthy quotations from "Out of the Cradle Endlessly Rocking," appears in *Scribner's Monthly*.

3–4 OCTOBER. Whitman writes Peter Doyle that he has re-made his will leaving everything to his brother Edward, except for $200 and a gold watch, which are left to Doyle (CORR, 2:248).

13 OCTOBER. Whitman writes to Charles Eldridge and to Peter Doyle with instructions to remove some items of winter clothing from the room he still rents on Fifteenth Street in Washington and send them to him in Camden, an indication that he has given up hope of an early return to Washington (CORR, 2:250–252).

24 AND 29 NOVEMBER. "Halls of Gold and Lilac," a two-part article describing Washington scenes, is published in the *Graphic* (see UPP, 2:42–49).

25 DECEMBER. Whitman spends Christmas — a cold, snowy day — alone, as George and Louisa have gone to Delaware for a visit; his hopes that Pete would spend a day or two with him have been dashed by Pete's failure to respond to the invitation (CORR, 2:262).

This is perhaps the darkest year of Whitman's life.

The deaths of his mother and sister-in-law and his own paralysis are complicated by the absence of his friend John Burroughs and the estrangement of William O'Connor. The move to Camden, while an improvement so far as his daily care is concerned, has brought further isolation, especially from Peter Doyle. His letters to Doyle and to Charles Eldridge reveal his depression and a fixation on disasters of all types, including railroad wrecks, accidents involving personal injury and death, and deaths of others who have had strokes. Late in the year he produces two important poems, "Song of the Redwood-Tree" and "Prayer of Columbus"; in each he identifies with his central image, first with a dying California sequoia and then with the ailing Columbus, imprisoned in old age.

1874

24 JANUARY. A series of articles relating to the Civil War, titled " 'Tis But Ten Years Since," begins in the *Graphic* and concludes on 7 March. These are later included in *Memoranda During the War* (1875).

11 FEBRUARY. In a letter to Ellen O'Connor, Whitman refers to having twice recently destroyed large numbers of letters and manuscripts as preparation "for what might happen," meaning his death (CORR, 2:276).

27 FEBRUARY. Whitman sends President Grant the articles on the Civil War from the *New York Daily Graphic* (CORR, 2:280). The president's secretary writes a note of appreciation on Grant's behalf (CORR, 2:280, n51).

FEBRUARY. "Song of the Redwood-Tree" appears in *Harper's Monthly*.

4 MARCH. Whitman receives a copy of *Demokratiske Fremblik*, the Danish edition of *Democratic Vistas* translated by Rudolf Schmidt (CORR, 2:282).

20 MARCH. An invitation arrives from the Mathematician Society of Tufts College, Massachusetts, to read at their

meeting on 17 June (CORR, 2:290). Whitman is not able to make the trip but sends a poem, "Song of the Universal," which is read on the occasion.

MARCH. "Prayer of Columbus" appears in *Harper's Magazine.*

MID-APRIL. John Burroughs visits Whitman for a Saturday and Sunday stay (CORR, 2:293).

5 MAY. Whitman writes to Ellen O'Connor of a new physical ailment, a severe and steady pain of the chest and left side (CORR, 2:297). At his death an autopsy will reveal a chest abcess of long-standing, which gave considerable pain and spread into the lung.

21 MAY. "A Kiss to the Bride," a poem on the marriage of the president's daughter, Nelly Grant, appears in the *New York Daily Graphic.*

24 MAY. Whitman writes to Tennyson acknowledging receipt of a recent letter and photograph (CORR, 2:301).

AROUND 25 MAY. Peter Doyle makes his first visit to Whitman in Camden (CORR, 2:304, n21).

17 JUNE. "Song of the Universal," the poem written for the Tufts College commencement, appears in two New York papers, the *Daily Graphic* and the *Evening Post*; the following day it appears in the *Springfield* (Mass.) *Republican* and on 20 June in the *Camden New Republic.*

22 JUNE. Whitman writes to President Grant asking to be retained in his position as clerk (CORR, 2:306).

AROUND 24 JUNE. Jeff arrives from St. Louis to spend a few days in Camden (CORR, 2:306).

1 JULY. Whitman acknowledges receipt of the notice of his termination from the Treasury Department (CORR, 2:307).

AROUND 8 JULY. Tennyson sends wishes for a speedy recovery (CORR, 2:307–308).

10 JULY. Whitman writes of his dismissal to Pete and says he has bought a "cheap lot" in Camden where he thinks of putting up a little house for himself, adding, "I hope and trust things may work so that we can yet be with each other, at least from time to time." (CORR, 2:308). The lot, at 460 Royden Street, costs him $450.

12 JULY. Edward Carpenter, the English author, writes a long letter to Whitman thanking him for providing "a ground for the love of men," thus making men feel unashamed of their "noblest" instincts. "Women are beautiful," he adds, "but, to some, there is that which passes the love of women" (WWC, 1:160).

10 OCTOBER. George Saintsbury, the English critic, publishes a critique of *Leaves of Grass* in the *Academy* (London), concentrating on Whitman's form (rather than formlessness) as reflected in such poetic conventions as his catalogs.

3 NOVEMBER. "An Old Man's Thought of School," a poem written for the dedication of a new public school in Camden, appears in the *Graphic*.

14 NOVEMBER. "Death of a Fireman" appears in the *Camden New Republic*; it is a tribute to William Alcott, a Camden firefighter and friend of Whitman's who has died unexpectedly (CORR, 2:315, n51; PW, 1:156–157).

16 DECEMBER. Whitman writes to the editor of the *Graphic* declining an offer to write on spiritualism, which he considers "crude humbug" (CORR, 2:318).

DECEMBER. The *Graphic* Christmas issue includes "A Christmas Garland," a mixture of new poems ("In the Wake Following" [later "After the Sea-Ship"] and "The Ox-Tamer") and assorted prose pieces (reprinted in UPP, 2:53–58).

1875

16 FEBRUARY. Whitman has another stroke, less severe than the first and on the right side (CORR, 2:323).

24 FEBRUARY. Whitman requests of the printer William J. Linton a thousand copies of a photograph of himself to be used in a book (CORR, 2:323). This is the earliest indication of his plans for another book.

1 APRIL. Whitman writes to John Burroughs about the latter's essays (in preparation) on Emerson, advising that his own name be brought into the discussion but with no

further elaboration on the relationship between him and Emerson (CORR, 2:327). Burroughs's essays, "A Word or Two on Emerson" and "A Final Word on Emerson," appear in the *Galaxy* in February and April 1876 and are reprinted in *Birds and Poets* (1877) (CORR, 2:326, n20). Whitman's suggestion, which Burroughs heeds, may result from the publication in 1874 of *Parnassus*, a collection of Emerson's favorite poems that does not include any of Whitman's poems.

30 APRIL. Whitman reads in the newspaper of a railroad accident involving the Baltimore and Potomac Railroad, for which Peter Doyle works, and writes Pete of his relief at not finding his name among the injured (CORR, 2:329).

APRIL. Whitman writes a note to William Rossetti mentioning his plans for a new volume of prose and verse (CORR, 2:327–328). In May he elaborates: the book is to be called *Two Rivulets*, two streams of prose and poetry reflecting the "real and ideal" (CORR, 2:320).

25 JUNE. Whitman writes to Doyle acknowledging for the first time that his full recovery is not probable and that he will set his mind to bringing his two books (*Leaves* and *Two Rivulets*) into shape (CORR, 2:335).

JUNE. The poet Joaquin Miller visits Whitman.

23 JULY. The *Springfield* (Mass.) *Republican* publishes an article, "Walt Whitman, His Life, His Poetry, Himself," by James Matlack Scovel, which Whitman has helped write; it is reprinted in a number of newspapers and magazines (CORR, 2:337, n54). Scovel, a Camden lawyer, is also coeditor, with Henry L. Bonsall, of the *Camden New Republic*; he later publishes "Walt Whitman as I Knew Him" in *Lippincott's Monthly Magazine* (May 1904).

24 JULY. Whitman writes to Tennyson and abandons all hope of visiting him in England: "I shall never see you & talk to you" (CORR, 2:335).

27 JULY. After a two-year silence, Whitman writes a brief letter to Anne Gilchrist (CORR, 2:336).

11 AUGUST. Tennyson, about to leave for a European holi-

day, sends Whitman wishes for a return to health (CORR, 2:339).

AUGUST. James B. Marvin, writer and clerk in the Internal Revenue Office, visits Whitman before leaving for England; Whitman later provides him a letter of introduction to Gilchrist (CORR, 2:341).

SUMMER. Whitman spends much of his time at the printing office of the *Camden New Republic* (whose coeditor, Harry Bonsall, encourages his use of the premises), where he has *Two Rivulets* and *Memoranda During the War* set in print. *Memoranda* is the Civil War book Whitman once proposed to James Redpath (21 October 1863) (see chapter 3). Sixty-eight pages long and designated "Author's Publication," about 1,000 copies are printed, 750 of which are bound (DN, 1:13–14); an additional 100 copies are bound into *Two Rivulets* (Myerson, *Walt Whitman*, 189).

4 NOVEMBER. Walter Orr Whitman is born to Louisa and George Whitman.

5 NOVEMBER. Whitman writes Peter Doyle that he plans to come to Washington on 8 November for a few days. This marks his return to the city. The visit is extended to three weeks, during which he stays at the home of friends from his Washington days, Mr. and Mrs. Michael Nash (CORR, 2:342, 344).

15 NOVEMBER. Sixteen of Whitman's Washington supporters sign a petition to the Secretary of the Treasury requesting Whitman's reinstatement to a post in the department. The secretary apparently accedes to the request, but nothing further comes of it (CORR, 2:342–343, n71).

17 NOVEMBER. Whitman attends the reburial of the remains of Edgar Allan Poe and the dedication of a Poe memorial in Baltimore; he is the only literary figure to appear.

18 NOVEMBER. Edwin Einstein, a friend from Whitman's days at Pfaff's in New York, writes to discover if Whitman is in financial need as is stated in a *New York Sun* article (CORR, 2:343, n72).

26 NOVEMBER. Whitman responds to Einstein with a recital of his physical and financial problems but claims no immediate need (CORR, 2:344–345).

NOVEMBER. Moncure Conway returns from England and visits Whitman; he publishes his account of the visit in the *Academy* (27 November 1875) and privately informs William Rossetti that Whitman is not in need (CORR, 2:344, n76).

20 DECEMBER. Whitman applies to the Library of Congress for the copyright to *Two Rivulets* (CORR, 2:345).

30 DECEMBER. Whitman writes to an unidentified correspondent telling of his health problems. He claims that no United States publisher will print his work and that booksellers have embezzled his proceeds (CORR, 2:345–346). The letter is a precursor to the 26 January 1876 article in the *West Jersey Press*, which stirs a great controversy.

DECEMBER. "Walt Whitman, The Poet of Joy" appears in the *Gentleman's Magazine* (London); written by Standish James O'Grady, it is published under the pseudonym Arthur Clive. Noting the almost total absence of joyfulness in contemporary literature, the critic praises Whitman for representing life "as a boon beyond price" (Miller, *Century*, 58).

IN THE SAME MONTH. Scottish author Peter Bayne attacks Whitman in the *Contemporary Review*, calling his poetry "atrociously bad" (Hindus, 157). Whitman has visits from Charles Eldridge, Moncure Conway, and Richard Monckton Milnes, Lord Houghton, a friend of Tennyson's (CORR, 2:344). In 1865 Milnes had hoped to see Whitman but had been dissuaded by the literary people of Boston (NUPM, 2:802).

1876-1880

the Indian Summer of my life?
— Notebook, 1880

The nation's centennial year brings a reprint of the 1871–1872 edition of *Leaves of Grass* accompanied by a second volume, *Two Rivulets.* The year begins, however, with Whitman stirring a controversy over his supposed neglect and impoverishment. Hottest in England, where his friends raise a wide subscription to the new edition, the controversy spills over into the United States press, even bringing William O'Connor to Whitman's defense though their estrangement continues. Correspondence and contact with Peter Doyle lessen in these years, especially after Walt begins the practice of regular stays at George and Susan Stafford's farm in southern New Jersey.

Whitman spends more and more time visiting with friends as a way of escaping the monotony of life in Camden. George and Louisa's home is not a cheerful place (their infant son, Walter, dies in 1876, and another is stillborn the following year), and the Staffords are welcoming. In 1876 Anne Gilchrist arrives in Philadelphia with three of her grown children, and Whitman is provided his own room when he visits her family. These years also bring into his life some of the men who will be among his closest friends from now until his death: John H. Johnston, Dr. Richard Maurice Bucke, and Robert Ingersoll. Edward Carpenter comes from England on his first visit in 1877. The following year Whitman has a bout of rheumatism and seeks the services of the renowned Dr. S. Weir Mitchell. In the same year, he attends the funeral of an old friend, William Cullen Bryant. By 1879 he is well enough to give a lecture in New York on Abraham Lincoln and to travel west for the first time, to a Kansas celebration and to visit Jeff in St. Louis. In

1880 he takes another journey, to Ontario, Canada, to visit
Dr. Bucke and his wife, Jessie.

1876

Although often referred to as an edition, the 1876 *Leaves of
Grass* is actually a reprint of the 1871–1872 edition but does
not include the *Passage to India* annex, which appeared in
the second issue of the first printing of that edition in 1871.
The annex, along with other works previously printed as
pamphlets (*Democratic Vistas, After All, Not to Create Only*,
and *As a Strong Bird on Pinions Free*), is now bound into a
separate volume, *Two Rivulets*, with separate pagination.
The title of this volume indicates its double flow, of poetry
and prose. The book includes some new prose pieces, most
notably "Memoranda During the War," previously offered
as a separate pamphlet. Poems in *Two Rivulets* appear with
prose commentary running beneath. "After All, Not to Create Only," written for the 1871 National Industrial Exhibition in New York and already in the *Leaves* volume, re-
appears here as "Song of the Exposition" with an added
subtitle: "The Muse Invited to Philadelphia." In the preface
to *Two Rivulets*, dated 31 May 1875, his fifty-sixth birthday,
Whitman relinquishes his earlier stated intention to write a
second volume of poetry to equal *Leaves of Grass*. The one
hundred copies of the 1876 reprint of *Leaves of Grass* are
produced on the presses of the *Camden New Republic*, with
Whitman still the publisher and copyright owner.

15 JANUARY. John Burroughs visits Whitman in Camden.

22 JANUARY. Whitman sends a postcard greeting to Peter
Doyle. Since 1875 he has begun the practice of regularly
sending Doyle postcards, often in lieu of letters.

26 JANUARY. "Walt Whitman's Actual American Position"
appears in the *West Jersey Press* of Camden. This article,
unmistakably by Whitman, may have been instigated by
Peter Bayne's December 1875 attack, which it pointedly
mentions. Complaining of a generalized neglect of the

poet in his own country, the article cites the upcoming two-volume edition as an undertaking necessary "to keep the wolf from the door" (Furness, 246).

ON THE SAME DATE. Whitman sends a copy of the *West Jersey Press* article to William Rossetti, suggesting he publish it in an English literary journal (CORR, 3:20).

27 JANUARY. Whitman reads a poem by Johann Schiller at a Camden event to benefit the local poor fund. Though Whitman is much given to private acts of charity, such public efforts are uncharacteristic and suggest a connection to the *West Jersey Press* article, with its reference to his own need "to keep the wolf from the door."

JANUARY. Whitman sends the *West Jersey Press* article to Edward Dowden in Ireland, suggesting its publication (CORR, 3:22).

11 FEBRUARY. Whitman sends William Rossetti an article, "The American War," and a poem, "The Man-of-War Bird," for publication in London (CORR, 3:23); the poem appears in the *Athenaeum* in April.

19 FEBRUARY. "Eidolons," "To a Locomotive in Winter," "When the Full-grown Poet Came," and "Out from Behind This Mask" appear in the *New York Tribune*. They are intended as a preview of the forthcoming reprint of *Leaves of Grass*.

4 MARCH. Whitman writes to Edward Dowden that he has learned to be "thankful" for critical attacks, as it brings to light unknown friends (CORR, 3:27).

6 MARCH. Whitman writes to Abraham (Bram) Stoker acknowledging his letter (CORR, 3:28). On 18 February 1872 Stoker, later the author of *Dracula*, had written Whitman a long confessional letter, concluding with "I thank you for all the love and sympathy you have given me in common with my kind" (WWC, 4:185); the letter (to which Whitman responds on this date) was not sent until 14 February 1876. Stoker will visit Whitman in 1884 (see chapter 7).

11 MARCH. Excerpts from the *West Jersey Press* article are published in the *Athenaeum*.

13 MARCH. A letter from the socialist reformer Robert Buchanan excoriating those in the United States for neglecting Whitman appears in the *London Daily News*. He suggests a subscription list be formed among English supporters for the forthcoming Whitman edition.

14 MARCH. A letter from William Rossetti supporting Buchanan's suggestion is published in the *Daily News*. This sets off a series of letters on the topic that appear throughout the month.

17 MARCH. Whitman writes to William Rossetti attempting to set the record straight: he accepts his English friends' concern and generosity; though poor, he is "not in want" and hopes to live on the sales of his works (CORR, 3:29–30).

ON THE SAME DATE. Whitman writes to Anne Gilchrist, attempting to dissuade her from her plan to come to live in America; Gilchrist has written on 25 February of this plan. Whitman tries to convince her that America is not the place for her and that he will visit her in England as soon as he is able (CORR, 3:31).

MID-MARCH. Moncure Conway visits Whitman before returning to England; he questions Whitman's sister-in-law about the poet's finances, and on 18 March Whitman writes him much the same thing he has told Rossetti (CORR, 3:31).

18 MARCH. The *Saturday Review* (London) publishes an article on Whitman. The author takes the position that, if Whitman is neglected and in need, it is his just deserts for his indecent poetry.

28 MARCH. Bayard Taylor writes an editorial, "In Re Walt Whitman," in the *New York Tribune* attacking Buchanan and Whitman's poetry. It is the first of three editorials he will write on the subject; the others appear on 30 March and 12 April. Taylor, a writer who enjoys considerable popularity as a poet, has been an admirer of Whitman but publicly ridiculed "After All, Not to Create Only," the poem Whitman read at the 1871 National Industrial Exhibition. From that point on the two are enemies. Letters of support for Whitman in the *Tribune*

are limited to those of two friends, John Swinton (1 April) and John Burroughs (13 April). Other newspapers take up the issue, expressing mostly negative attitudes toward Whitman (Allen, *Solitary Singer*, 471).

29 MARCH. Hoping to take advantage of the attention generated by the controversy, Whitman sends William Rossetti corrected copies of his two volumes for a possible London edition of the complete *Leaves*, which never materializes (CORR, 3:33).

30 MARCH. Whitman writes to Rossetti concerning orders from England for his new *Leaves* and again urging a London edition; he refers to the "row" about him in the American press, but not with displeasure (CORR, 3:34).

1 APRIL. Whitman visits the home of George and Susan Stafford in Kirkwood, New Jersey, for the first time (NUPM, 2:818).

4 APRIL. Whitman writes to Daniel Whittaker, a printer on the *Camden New Republic*, asking him to begin teaching the trade to the office boy, Harry Stafford, the son of George and Susan Stafford (CORR, 3:37).

7 APRIL. Whitman writes Rossetti his disapproval of a report in the *London Daily News* which says that Moncure Conway has a letter from Whitman stating he is in no financial need (CORR, 3:37; WWC, 1:345–346). On 17 April the *New York Tribune* reports this and on 26 April quotes Conway as denying Buchanan's claims of Whitman's poverty.

13 APRIL. Franklin B. Sanborn visits Whitman (CORR, 3:39).

19 APRIL. "Walt Whitman, A Visit to the Good Gray Poet" by Franklin B. Sanborn appears in the *Springfield* (Mass.) *Republican*; (reprinted in Myerson, *Time*, 3–13).

ON THE SAME DATE. Whitman writes for the first time to a new friend, John H. Johnston, a New York jeweler; Johnston quickly becomes part of the Whitman circle (CORR, 3:40).

22 APRIL. A letter from William O'Connor, headed "Walt Whitman: Is He Persecuted?," appears in the *Tribune*. Drawn into the fray because of the newspaper attacks on

Whitman, O'Connor displays none of his earlier fervor in this reasoned defense, which is criticized in the same issue by Bayard Taylor as having been written under British influence. O'Connor's letter does not signal a reconciliation with Whitman.

16 MAY. Whitman writes to Robert Buchanan assuring him that all of the points made in Buchanan's letter to the *London Daily News* (13 March) are essentially true; he insists, as he has to Rossetti and others, that he is not in "pinching" want and hopes through the sale of his books to be able to build a small place for himself to live on the lot he owns in Camden (CORR, 3:47).

2 JUNE. Henry Wadsworth Longfellow and the Philadelphia publisher George W. Childs come to Camden to visit Whitman. Not finding him at home, they catch up with Whitman at the ferry pier and spend a half hour in conversation (WWC, 1:129–130). It is later reported (by J. B. Marvin) that Whitman found Longfellow "dapper and dainty and effeminate . . . like the lord whose wife was advised to keep him dressed well but never let him open his mouth" (Peattie, 247).

MID-JUNE. Whitman makes his first extended visit with the Stafford family at their Kirkwood, New Jersey, farm, located about fifteen miles south of Camden. This begins a series of frequent long stays between 1876 and 1884 at the Stafford farm (they were tenant farmers), which Whitman often refers to as Timber Creek or White Horse. Whitman is attracted to the family atmosphere and to the natural setting, both of which seem to contribute greatly to his recovery of health. *Specimen Days* includes numerous pieces describing the natural joys of the place, especially his delight in bathing nude in the creek (PW, 1:150–152). But it is Harry Stafford who is the main attraction, and Whitman quickly becomes to him the parent/lover figure he seems also to be to Peter Doyle. When he stays with the Staffords he shares Harry's room (CORR, 3:131).

26 JUNE. Whitman writes to Rossetti informing him that the one hundred volumes of *Leaves* and *Two Rivulets*

have been exhausted and that he has ordered a second printing of six hundred volumes of each (CORR, 3:51). Whitman is busy in the first half of this year with orders for the first one hundred volumes, with the majority going to England as part of the subscription raised there to relieve the poet's supposed want. Scholars remain perplexed by Whitman's part in this English/American controversy, but there is no doubt that he saw in it an opportunity (which he grasped) to sell his books (CORR, 6:xi–xxxvi). In discussing the affair with Traubel in 1888, Whitman admits some guilt in not always having put things "into right perspectives" (WWC, 1:344).

4 JULY. The Centennial Exposition opens in Philadelphia. Whitman does not attend, largely for health reasons, but probably also because he is indignant that Bayard Taylor has been invited to write the official opening poem.

10 JULY. "A Death Sonnet for Custer" (later "From Far Dakota's Cañons") appears in the *New York Tribune*. The poem is a memorial to General George Armstrong Custer, killed at Little Bighorn in Montana in June.

12 JULY. Walter Orr Whitman, son of George and Louisa, dies. Proud and fond of his namesake nephew, Whitman finds the infant's death "a bitter cup" (CORR, 3:56).

PROBABLY IN JULY. Jeff Whitman and his daughters, Mannahatta and Jessie, arrive in Camden for a visit (Binns, 265).

10 SEPTEMBER. Anne Gilchrist and three of her grown children, Beatrice, Herbert, and Grace, arrive in Philadelphia (DN, 1:41); her son Percy remains at home. Grace Gilchrist later publishes a reminiscence, "Chats with Walt Whitman," in *Eclectic Magazine* (April 1898) (reprinted in Myerson, *Time*, 151–166).

14 AND 15 SEPTEMBER. Accompanied by John Burroughs, Whitman visits Gilchrist in Philadelphia (DN, 1:42).

16 SEPTEMBER. Whitman takes his niece Hattie to an opera at the Philadelphia Academy, Donizetti's *La Favorita*, with Pasquale Brignoli. He finds the tenor aria "Spirito gentil" "superb" (DN, 1:42).

25 SEPTEMBER. Walt gives Harry Stafford a ring (DN, 1:44).

26 SEPTEMBER. Walt takes back the ring (DN, 1:44). The matter of the ring continues for some months, with Whitman seeming to want Harry to wear it yet repeatedly taking it away, perhaps at Harry's displays of anger or jealousy. Harry suffers bouts of depression and struggles with anger and a bad temper; Whitman tries to help him but often seems to exacerbate Harry's problems.

1–3 OCTOBER. Whitman visits the Staffords (DN, 1:44).

19 OCTOBER. Charles Eldridge visits Whitman (DN, 1:44).

24 OCTOBER. Whitman attends the Centennial Exposition with his nieces and is wheeled about in a chair (DN, 1:47).

25 OCTOBER. Mannahatta and Jessie return to St. Louis (Jeff had returned earlier in the summer); before leaving, Hattie has her photograph taken (CORR, 3:69, n14, n15).

28–31 OCTOBER. Whitman is at the Stafford farm, then visits Gilchrist on the evening of 31 October (DN, 1:47).

1 NOVEMBER. In the front room of George and Louisa's house, Harry and Walt have a serious talk, and Walt gives Harry the ring again (DN, 1:48).

17 NOVEMBER. Whitman begins supplying the Camden Children's Home with his photographs for benefit sales (DN, 1:48).

AROUND 17 NOVEMBER. Harry writes Walt that when he put the ring on his finger he knew only death would cause him to part with it (CORR, 3:7).

25 NOVEMBER. At the farm, Walt has a "Memorable talk" with Harry and "settles the matter," presumably their relationship (DN, 1:49).

13 DECEMBER. Whitman writes to Peter Doyle apologizing for not writing sooner (CORR, 3:67). Unless lost, there have been no letters to Doyle since 15 January of this year. Whitman writes to Doyle again on 20 and 27 December, referring vaguely to a possible visit to Washington.

ON THE SAME DATE. Whitman writes to John H. Johnston accepting an invitation for a week-long visit to his home at 113 East Tenth Street; he informs Johnston that his "adopted" son will accompany him (CORR, 3:67); the "son" is Harry Stafford.

19 DECEMBER. In a note to Johnston, Whitman refers to his "nephew" who will share his room and his bed during their stay (CORR, 3:68).

ON THE SAME DATE. In the evening, Whitman sits in his room in a "very profound meditation," from which he emerges "happy and satisfied . . . (that this may last now without any more perturbation)" (DN, 1:51).

20 DECEMBER. Whitman writes to Johnston, enclosing a check for $35 and asking him to choose a good gold watch intended, he says, as a Christmas present "for a young man" (CORR, 3:70).

1877

6–10 JANUARY. Whitman visits the Staffords (DN, 1:52).

10–16 JANUARY. Whitman is with the Gilchrists in Philadelphia (DN, 1:52).

16 JANUARY. Whitman writes to John Burroughs from the home of Anne Gilchrist (CORR, 3:74). Gilchrist has rented a house at 1929 North Twenty-second Street, where a room is set up for Whitman's use according to his specifications. He often stays for a week at a time or comes by ferry for tea and an evening visit. Between these visits and those in the homes of Harry Stafford and John H. Johnston, Whitman considerably lessens his time with George and Louisa, whose home lacks what he calls "spirit" (CORR, 3:74). Whenever possible he continues a practice of Sunday tea or breakfast with the family of Colonel John R. Johnston, a Camden artist (CORR, 2:256), or with the family of James Matlack Scovel.

18–23 JANUARY. Whitman is with the Staffords (DN, 1:52).

24 JANUARY. Whitman writes to Edward Cattell not to call again at the Stafford home nor to mention this letter. Promising to explain when they meet, he offers assurance that, while there is nothing about "it" that he is ashamed of, he wishes "it" kept "entirely between you and me"; he concludes by professing love for both Harry

Stafford and Cattell and urges Edward to come to see him in Camden (CORR, 3:77). Edward Cattell is a young farmhand and friend of the Staffords' whom Whitman had met in May 1876. He and Whitman seem to be close, for Whitman writes of moonlit meetings by the pond (DN, 1:61). Just as he has a circle of young male literary friends, Whitman also has a circle of young male laborer friends at Timber Creek: Harry and his brother Elmer, their uncle Montgomery, and Edward Cattell. He later introduces Herbert Gilchrist and Edward Carpenter into this circle.

28 JANUARY. Whitman participates in a commemoration of the 140th anniversary of the birth of Thomas Paine held at Lincoln Hall, Philadelphia (his remarks are reprinted in PW, 1:140–142).

JANUARY. "To Walt Whitman," a poem by Joaquin Miller, appears in the *Galaxy*.

7–13 FEBRUARY. Walt is with the Staffords (DN, 1:52).

15–21 FEBRUARY. Walt is with the Gilchrists; Burroughs visits him there (DN, 1:52).

13 MARCH. Whitman writes to John Burroughs from the home of John H. Johnston where he and Harry are staying; he accepts an invitation to visit Burroughs (16–20 March) and asks if he can bring Harry (CORR, 3:79). Burroughs later enjoys having both of them at his home at Esopus-on-Hudson, New York, but complains of difficulty in getting them up to breakfast on time and is vaguely troubled by their wrestling matches (Barrus, 164).

14 APRIL. Walt takes a railroad jaunt through southern New Jersey (NUPM, 3:991).

24–30 APRIL. Whitman visits the Staffords.

29 APRIL. Harry and Whitman quarrel frequently, and on this date some sort of "scene" with Harry takes place at the Stafford home (DN, 1:54).

2 MAY. Edward Carpenter visits Whitman in Camden for the first time and they stroll the streets of Philadelphia. Whitman shows the date as 1 May (DN, 1:54), which may have been the date of the "previous unsuccessful call" Carpenter claims to have made (see Carpenter, 3). Whit-

man is back and forth between Kirkwood and Camden throughout most of May, and Carpenter visits him in both places. Carpenter later accompanies Whitman to Philadelphia to stay with Anne Gilchrist.

EARLY IN MAY. John Burroughs's *Birds and Poets*, with a chapter on Whitman, is published.

MID-MAY. A portrait of Whitman by George W. Waters (for which the poet has sat while visiting with John H. Johnston the previous winter) is delivered to his Camden address (CORR, 3:83).

18 JUNE. Whitman writes to Harry Stafford from the Gilchrist home "not a night passes but I think of you" (CORR, 3:86).

20 JUNE. Still in Philadelphia, Whitman writes to Peter Doyle that he thinks of him often and that he would like to give him "a good buss — often" (CORR, 3:87).

25 JUNE. Walt goes to the Stafford farm.

EARLY JULY. Louisa and George Whitman have a stillborn male child (CORR, 3:90). The teenage James Gibbons Huneker calls on Whitman who, for $2 (to go to "some asylum" in Camden), autographs Huneker's 1867 edition of *Leaves*. He also gives Huneker a copy of the engraving frontispiece from the 1855 edition, along with a photograph of his mother (Huneker, 416). Huneker later becomes an internationally known critic of the arts.

13–20 JULY. Whitman visits the Stafford farm; Herbert Gilchrist comes and paints a picture of the creek where Whitman enjoys bathing (CORR, 3:138).

20 JULY. Whitman tells the Staffords (but not Harry) he is returning to Washington (CORR, 3:6), then quickly changes his mind.

12 AUGUST–10 SEPTEMBER. Whitman visits the Staffords (NUPM, 3:996).

16 AUGUST. Walt and the Staffords visit Pitman Grove, New Jersey, site of a Methodist camp meeting (NUPM, 3:996).

LATE SUMMER. Hattie and Jessie visit in Camden; throughout August and September there is a good deal of visiting around by Whitman's friends and relatives. Dr. Richard

Maurice Bucke visits Whitman for the first time. Bucke, an alienist and mystic, supervises the Asylum for the Insane in London, Ontario, and is already devoted to Whitman's poetry; he becomes one of Whitman's staunchest friends and later one of three literary executors.

24 OR 25 SEPTEMBER. Hattie and Jessie leave New Jersey.

14–17 NOVEMBER. Walt visits the Staffords (NUPM, 3:999).

13 DECEMBER. Whitman writes to Beatrice Gilchrist advising her of the dangers of intense study; he relates the story of a female student at the Philadelphia medical school, where Beatrice has come to study, who died in a "lunatic asylum" from the strain (CORR, 3:104). Beatrice, who commits suicide in 1881, is Walt's favorite of the Gilchrist children; he is also fond of Herbert but does not rate him highly as a painter.

24 DECEMBER. Whitman and Joaquin Miller attend a performance of the latter's play, *The Danites of the Sierras*, at the Walnut Street Theatre, Philadelphia (DN, 1:76).

27 DECEMBER. Whitman takes the Gilchrists to see Miller's play (DN, 1:76).

1878

16–23 FEBRUARY. Whitman is at the Stafford home.

20 FEBRUARY. Walt attends a country auction with George Stafford (NUPM, 3: 1001).

24 FEBRUARY. Whitman writes to John Burroughs agreeing to lecture on Lincoln's death sometime around 15 April (CORR, 3:108). Richard Watson Gilder, assistant editor of *Scribner's Monthly* whom Whitman has met at the John H. Johnston home, instigates the lecture plan with Burroughs's help (CORR, 3:110, n15).

MID-MARCH. Whitman experiences an attack of "rheumatism" in his right shoulder, which causes severe pain and the fear that it may result in further paralysis.

13 APRIL. Whitman visits Dr. S. Weir Mitchell, noted specialist in neurological disorders (DN, 1:95).

18 APRIL. Whitman pays a second visit to Dr. Mitchell, who

diagnoses Whitman's paralysis as the result of a ruptured blood vessel in the brain (DN, 1:96). Mitchell's diagnosis is the most accurate Whitman has received. Characters in two of Mitchell's novels, *When All the Woods Are Green* (1894) and *Dr. North and His Friends* (1900), refer to Whitman, some of whom express reservations about Whitman's poetry or his person. One says of Whitman, "He was the most innocently and entirely vain creature I ever knew. The perfect story of his vanity will, I fancy, never be written. It was past belief" (Mitchell, 274).

LATE APRIL. The Gilchrists close their home in Philadelphia and leave for a visit in Northampton, Massachusetts.

27 MAY. Whitman fills an order for a copy of *Leaves* from poet Sidney Lanier in Baltimore (see Miller, "Correspondence"). The order, placed on 5 May, comes with a letter describing Lanier's discovery of *Leaves* in Bayard Taylor's library and the delight it caused (WWC, 1:208); a later change of heart brings an attack on Whitman in Lanier's *The English Novel* (1883).

MAY. Whitman drops plans for the Lincoln lecture, which has been postponed to this month.

14 JUNE. Whitman attends the funeral of William Cullen Bryant in New York City. At the reception following the service, Whitman meets Bryant's coeditor of the *New York Evening Post*, John Bigelow, and his wife, and accepts an invitation to sail up the Hudson to visit their home in West Point.

17 JUNE. Whitman returns from visiting the Bigelows to stay with John H. Johnston, who is now remarried to Alma (Calder) Johnston and living at 1309 Fifth Avenue, New York (CORR, 3:120–121). (For Alma Johnston's impressions of Whitman, see Myerson, *Time*, 260–273.)

ON THE SAME DATE. Whitman spends the evening at the home of Richard Watson Gilder, where he meets, among others, the great Polish actress Helena Modjeska (NUPM, 3:1012).

22 AND 23 JUNE. Whitman writes to his niece Mannahatta who, with her sister, Jessie, is visiting in Camden, and to Anne Gilchrist providing each an almost identical

account of his adventures in the region of the lower Catskill Mountains with John and Ursula Burroughs. The account appears in the *Tribune* for 4 July as "A Poet's Recreation" (reprinted [abbreviated] in PW, 1:165–172).

25 JUNE. Back in New York City, Whitman goes sailing — spending most of his time in the ship's pilot house (Miller, "Correspondence").

3 JULY. Whitman visits the *Tribune* office and goes "Up, up, up in the elevator some eight or nine stories" (DN, 3:55).

6 JULY. Whitman sits for photographs taken by New York celebrity photographer Napoleon Sarony (CORR, 3:126).

ON THE SAME DATE. Whitman writes to Harry Stafford from the Johnston home that, though he meets many new friends, "I want to see you very much" (CORR, 3:126).

9 AUGUST. Whitman writes to Tennyson reminding him of his letter of September 1876 to which there has been no response (CORR, 3:133).

24 AUGUST. Tennyson replies with apologies: he is overburdened with letters and suffers poor eyesight. Misaddressed, the letter does not reach Whitman until 21 October (CORR, 3:134, 139).

24 OCTOBER. An article, "Gathering the Corn," appears in the *New York Tribune*. It later appears in *Good-bye My Fancy* (1891) (reprinted in PW, 2:669–671).

OCTOBER. "Shakspere-Bacon's Cipher" appears in the *Cosmopolitan*. "The Gospel According to Walt Whitman," an essay by Robert Louis Stevenson, appears in the London *New Quarterly*. In a well-balanced evaluation, the author sees Whitman more as a social critic than poet.

11 DECEMBER. Whitman spends the evening with Dr. Bucke and his wife, Jessie, who are visiting in Philadelphia (CORR, 3:142).

22 DECEMBER. Whitman breakfasts with purser John L. Wilson on the steamboat *Whilldin*, moored in a Philadelphia dock (CORR, 3:144).

28 DECEMBER. Perhaps as a belated Christmas gift, Whitman orders a standing rattan work basket for his sister-in-law Louisa (CORR, 3:143).

1879

22 JANUARY. Harry Stafford visits Walt in Camden with news that his family will move in March to Glendale, New Jersey, where they will operate a corner store (CORR, 3:147).

MID-JANUARY. Walt takes a railroad jaunt to Atlantic City, New Jersey. The journey is the source for "Winter Sunshine."

26 JANUARY. "Winter Sunshine. A Trip from Camden to the Coast" appears in the *Philadelphia Times* (see PW, 1:330–338).

1 FEBRUARY. Whitman attends a reception at the home of Philadelphia publisher George W. Childs (DN, 1:132).

10 FEBRUARY. Walt has a visit from Harry Stafford (DN, 1:134).

14 FEBRUARY. "Uncle Walt" sends a Valentine card to five-year-old Amy Dowe, niece of Louisa Haslam Whitman, who is visiting in Camden (CORR, 3:151, n31); he also sends cards to three male friends (DN, 1:135).

16 FEBRUARY. The bust of Whitman executed by sculptor William Sidney Morse arrives; Whitman pronounces it "wretchedly bad" (DN, 1:135). A later bust by Morse is much to Whitman's liking (see chapter 7).

8 MARCH. "The First Spring Day on Chestnut Street" appears in the *Progress*, a Philadelphia magazine owned by Whitman's friend John W. Forney (see PW, 1:188–190). Whitman had known Forney in Washington as editor of the *Daily Morning Chronicle*.

16 MARCH. Whitman attends an all-male dinner party in Philadelphia; among the guests is architect Frank Furness (CORR, 3:150).

18 MARCH. Whitman receives a letter of praise from a stranger, William H. Riley of Sheffield, England, a friend of John Ruskin's. Riley claims Ruskin shares his admiration of Whitman; Whitman immediately sends a book and photographs to Ruskin (CORR, 3:149).

19 MARCH. Though they are still estranged, Whitman sends copies of *Leaves* and *Two Rivulets* to William O'Connor (DN, 1:138).

MARCH. Plans begin again for Whitman to deliver a Lincoln lecture the following month in New York; Burroughs and Johnston handle the arrangements (CORR, 3:151).

9 APRIL. Whitman leaves for New York, where he will stay with the Johnstons until 14 June; he has agreed to sit again for a portrait while there, this time by G. M. Ottinger (CORR, 3:151, n32).

13 APRIL. On Easter Sunday Walt walks along Fifth Avenue in New York City from Eighty-fifth to Ninetieth Streets and observes Central Park. He finds the stone wall enclosing the park "grim" and thinks, "Perhaps, (though I am not sure,)," the design is a success but that the natural beauty of Prospect Park in Brooklyn has been spoiled by the theories of Frederick Law Olmsted, who codesigned both parks (NUPM, 3:1016–1017).

14 APRIL. Whitman delivers his first Lincoln lecture at Steck Hall, Fourteenth Street, New York. Drawing upon Peter Doyle's account of the events in Ford's Theater (see chapter 4) and adding his own recollections of the president, Whitman fashions a moving address (PW, 1:497–509), which includes a parenthetical reference to the scent of lilacs in bloom at the time of the assassination; the association of scent and event informs the later "When Lilacs Last in the Dooryard Bloom'd." Between this date and April 1890 Whitman gives ten lectures on Lincoln, in many cases following them with readings from *Leaves* or from the works of other poets.

23 APRIL–3 MAY. Whitman visits John and Ursula Burroughs.

28 APRIL. Whitman visits Frederick Louis Ritter, professor of music at Vassar College, Poughkeepsie, New York, who in 1880 composes a setting of "Dirge for Two Veterans" (CORR, 3:153, 174).

APRIL. "Three Young Men's Deaths" appears in *Cope's Tobacco Plant* (see PW, 1:155–158).

10 MAY. "Broadway Revisited" appears in the *New York Tribune* (see PW, 1:16–21, 338–339).

12 MAY. Whitman attends the theater with Anne Gilchrist and daughter Grace (CORR, 3:154). Having returned from Massachusetts, the Gilchrists are staying in New York prior to returning to England.

17 MAY. "Real Summer Openings," a description of Whitman's journey up the Hudson, appears in the *Tribune* (see PW, 1:190–196, 339–341).

24 MAY. "These May Afternoons" appears in the *Tribune* (see PW, 1:196–202, 341–342).

26 MAY. Whitman visits the U.S. *Minnesota* moored in New York and takes dinner with the officers in the Ward Room. He writes Harry Stafford that he enjoyed best the trip by rowboat to and from the ship (CORR, 3:155). (A visit on the previous day is described in PW, 1:201–202).

9 JUNE. The Gilchrists sail for Europe (DN, 1:145). A farewell meeting between Whitman and Anne Gilchrist occurs at the Johnston home, but no record exists of what is said.

16 JUNE. Whitman's postcard to Peter Doyle advising of his return to Camden refers to a meeting between the two prior to his New York stay (CORR, 3:159).

2–9 JULY. Whitman visits the Staffords in their new home in Glendale, New Jersey, but misses the creek where he had bathed and leaves earlier than planned (CORR, 3:162).

31 JULY. Whitman visits the National Teachers Reception at the Exposition Building and sees on exhibit the phonograph and the telephone (DN, 1:150). (A 1951 radio broadcast presented what was said to be an 1889 recording of Whitman reading four lines of his poem "America"; to date there is no verification of this; see Folsom, "The Whitman Recording.")

JULY–AUGUST. Hattie and Jessie are in Camden for what is now an annual visit.

10 SEPTEMBER. Whitman leaves for St. Louis with John W. Forney and newspaper reporters J. M. W. Geist, E. K. Martin, and W. W. Reitzel (Berthold and Price, 175).

Forney is to address the Old Settlers of Kansas Committee at a celebration in Lawrence of the passage of the Kansas-Nebraska Act of 1854, which created the territories. Whitman, formerly a Free-Soiler, has maintained an interest in the progress of Kansas (NUPM, 3:1028– 1053, reprints Whitman's notes from the trip; see also DN, 1:163–166; and Eitner).

12 SEPTEMBER. Whitman arrives in St. Louis. Jeff takes Walt and his party on a tour of the city, including the water works where he is employed. Walt stays overnight with Jeff's family before going on to Lawrence. Always excited by the size of America, Whitman writes to Louisa Whitman that he is a thousand miles from Philadelphia (Berthold and Price, 175; CORR, 3:164). This is Whitman's first trip to the American West, and he is enormously impressed, especially by the Great Plains of Colorado and Kansas, proclaiming them all "that America is for" (CORR, 3:170). He writes to Louisa from the moving car of his train while crossing into Colorado that a mountain sunset, though only of ten minutes' duration, will never be forgotten (CORR, 3:165). In Kansas he meets cowboys and a former soldier from his hospital days at whose home he stays (24 and 25 September). In Denver he and the reporters (Forney has already left for home) stay at the American House hotel. Early in October he has a sudden relapse and is forced by this illness and a lack of funds to remain with Jeff until January 1880 (Allen, *Solitary Singer*, 488).

17 OCTOBER. An unsigned interview with Whitman is published in the *St. Louis Post-Dispatch*. Whitman prepares other such releases while on his western trip (CORR, 3:164, n92) and may have submitted this himself.

5 NOVEMBER. Walt writes to Peter Doyle telling of his two-month journey (CORR, 3:167).

15 NOVEMBER. "A Poet's Western Trip" appears in the *Washington Star*.

7–11 DECEMBER. Whitman experiences "*Very bad spells,*" which cause him to think he may be dying (DN, 1:161).

17 DECEMBER. A new poem, "What Best I See in Thee," ap-

pears in the *Philadelphia Press*. The poem praises General Ulysses S. Grant on the occasion of his return from a world tour.

25 DECEMBER. James T. Fields sends Walt (by way of John Burroughs) an anonymous gift of $100, which allows him to leave for home early in 1880 (Barrus, 189).

1880

4 JANUARY. Whitman leaves St. Louis for the trip home (NUPM, 3:1042). The exact date of his return is uncertain; Whitman gives it as 5 January in his notebook (NUPM, 3:1048), which is not possible.

JANUARY. Dr. Bucke begins gathering information for his proposed biography of Whitman (CORR, 3:172, n11).

25 MARCH. Colonel Robert Ingersoll, attorney and avowed agnostic, introduces himself by letter, professing great admiration (CORR, 3:175, n14).

MARCH. William Sloane Kennedy, soon to be an important member of the circle of Whitman's friends, is mentioned for the first time in Whitman's notebook — as a "college man" (DN, 1:172).

3 APRIL. "A Riddle Song" appears in the first number of the *Tarrytown* (New York) *Sunnyside Press*.

5–8 APRIL. Whitman visits the Staffords.

15 APRIL. Whitman delivers his lecture on the "Death of Abraham Lincoln" at Association Hall, Philadelphia.

17 APRIL. "A Riddle Song" appears in the *Progress*, a Philadelphia magazine.

23 APRIL–4 MAY. Whitman visits the Staffords.

9 MAY. During an evening visit with the Johnston family in New York, Whitman hears a contralto singing in a nearby church (see "A Contralto Voice," PW, 1:235).

22 MAY. "Emerson's Books (the Shadows of Them)" is published in the *Literary World*.

25 MAY. Dr. Bucke arrives in Camden; he and Whitman attend a lecture by Robert Ingersoll, Whitman's first personal contact with the orator (CORR, 3:175, n14; DN,

1:185). Ingersoll quickly becomes part of the Whitman circle.

1 JUNE. Whitman writes a new will naming George and Louisa as executors and leaving the major part of his assets to Edward (NUPM, 3:1068; CORR, 3:180, n33).

3 JUNE. Accompanied by Dr. Bucke, Whitman leaves Philadelphia by train for a trip to Ontario, Canada, to visit with the doctor and his wife.

4 JUNE. Walt sees Niagara Falls for the second time, the first having been on his return from New Orleans in 1848.

22 JUNE. "Summer Days in Canada" appears in the *London* (Ontario) *Advertiser*, the *Camden Daily Post*, and the *Philadelphia Press* (see PW, 1:236–241, 345–346). While in London, Ontario, Whitman stays at the Bucke home on the grounds of the Asylum for the Insane and makes many friends among the attendants, with whom he later corresponds. His visit includes short voyages on Lake St. Clair and Lake Huron and excursions on the St. Lawrence River. Whitman sees Montreal, Quebec, the Thousand Islands, Cape Eternity, and various historical sites, covering in all some three thousand miles. In his diary he describes Canada as "A grand, sane, temperate land, the amplest and most beautiful," fed by rivers and lakes that form "the great central current the glorious mid-artery of the great Free *Pluribus Unum* of America" (DN, 3:645). On the return trip, Dr. Bucke travels with Whitman as far as Niagara Falls, where Whitman is met by Peter Doyle, who accompanies him to New Jersey. (For Bucke's description of the visit, see Myerson, *Time*, 246–248).

JUNE. "Patroling Barnegat" appears in the *American*, a Philadelphia magazine.

25 AUGUST. Whitman sends $20 to Louisa for Eddie's board (DN, 1:198). No matter where he is or what his circumstances, Whitman never fails in this responsibility.

EARLY OCTOBER. Whitman returns to Camden.

9–13 OCTOBER. Walt visits the Staffords. While there he writes in his notebook: "Autumn nights. It is the Indian summer of the year — Is it not also the Indian summer of my life?" (NUPM, 3:1089).

30 OCTOBER. "My Picture-Gallery" appears in the *American*.

6–16 NOVEMBER. Whitman is at the Staffords; Harry is now a telegraph operator at an Atlantic City railroad station. On 12 November Whitman and Susan Stafford drive to see the farm at Timber Creek in Kirkwood, and Whitman revisits the creek (CORR, 3:192, 193).

17 NOVEMBER. This may be the date of Percy Ives's first visit with Whitman (DN, 1:188). Ives is the son of the Detroit artist Lewis T. Ives and grandson of a Long Island friend, Elisa Seaman Leggett. He visits often during his three-year stay in Philadelphia while studying at the Pennsylvania Academy of the Fine Arts and does pencil sketches and an oil portrait of Whitman (see Krieg).

21 NOVEMBER. William Sloane Kennedy visits Whitman for the first time (CORR, 3:214, n54). Kennedy is on the staff of the *Saturday Evening Post* published in Philadelphia (NUPM, 3:1136); Whitman likes him and writes to Burroughs that Kennedy "has *the fever called literature* and I shouldn't wonder if he was in for it, for life" (CORR, 3:218).

25 NOVEMBER. Whitman has Thanksgiving dinner with the family of Damon Kilgore, a distinguished Philadelphia lawyer (CORR, 3:199, n85).

26 NOVEMBER. Whitman writes to Richard Watson Gilder asking advice regarding copyright laws that might allow him to prevent the New York publishing firm of R. Worthington from selling copies of *Leaves of Grass* printed from the 1860 plates (CORR, 3:195). A year earlier Worthington had bought the plates of the 1860 edition and begins selling copies in this year (for details see NUPM, 3:1096–1097; CORR, 3:196–197, n81).

NOVEMBER. "The Dalliance of the Eagles" appears in *Cope's Tobacco Plant*.

IN THE SAME MONTH. *Scribner's Monthly* carries Edmund Clarence Stedman's essay "Walt Whitman," in which he sees Whitman working out a "perfect democracy and the salvation of the world" but refuses to condone the sexual poems. While not a member of the Whitman circle, Stedman is an old acquaintance from Pfaff's; Whitman has met him again in Washington and yet again at the New York home of John H. Johnston. His careful essay is too equivocal for Dr. Bucke, while Burroughs thinks it will "do good." Whitman finds it "quite funny" (CORR, 3:193).

5 DECEMBER. Dr. Bucke is in Philadelphia, and he and Whitman spend an afternoon and evening at the Girard House (CORR, 3:201, n89).

16 DECEMBER. Whitman enjoys what is for him a fairly typical evening, repeatedly crossing by ferry the Delaware River between Camden and Philadelphia (CORR, 3:201).

25 DECEMBER. Christmas dinner is with Mr. and Mrs. Lung, Louisa and George's neighbors on Stevens Street in Camden (DN, 1:217).

IN THIS YEAR. Whitman is elected to the Society of Old Brooklynites and accepts as a "necessary courtesy" (WWC, 1:374).

CHAPTER SEVEN

1881-1887

Life, life an endless march . . .
— "Going Somewhere," 1887

As his health and energy decline, Whitman is more dependent upon others but continues working on "the principal
object" in his life, *Leaves of Grass*. His friends, including
the long-estranged William O'Connor, rally when the 1881
edition is banned in Boston in 1882; reissued by a Philadelphia press the next year, it sells very well, largely because of
the scandal involved. In 1882 Whitman publishes *Specimen
Days & Collect*, a collection of prose writings the nearest
thing to autobiography he will produce and which provides
a rough chronology of some parts of his life. Oscar Wilde
comes to call twice in 1882. Dr. Bucke publishes a biography of Whitman in 1883. In 1884 Harry Stafford marries
(he will become a father two years later), and Walt buys a
house in Camden; by the following year he has hired a
housekeeper and acquired pets. New friends enter his life in
this period, among them Robert Pearsall Smith and his
family and Thomas B. Harned, while some old ones, such as
Thomas Donaldson and Sylvester Baxter, take on new importance. Donaldson raises funds in 1885 sufficient to buy
a horse and buggy, which allow Whitman some of the
mobility lost through his paralysis. In the same year in
England, Anne Gilchrist dies of breast cancer; two years
later Whitman writes the poem "Going Somewhere" as "a
memory-leaf " in her honor. Eighteen eighty-six brings the
sudden death of his niece Mannahatta.

Whitman resumes giving the Lincoln lecture at events
organized by friends as a benefit for him in 1886 and in the
following year. Money also comes from England, where
about eighty admirers have contributed, and in the United
States efforts are made to have a government pension in-
stituted, though Whitman refuses to support the effort.

Another venture on his behalf is the "cottage fund" raised in 1886, by which well-wishers such as Mark Twain and Andrew Carnegie hope to see Whitman settled in a country house of his own for the summer months. Though a substantial sum is raised, Whitman never builds the house. He does begin work in 1886, however, on another book of poetry and prose to be called *November Boughs*. His poetic output declines to short pieces produced for magazines and newspapers, often for the income they provide. Translations of Whitman poems into French appear in summer of 1886 and signal his influence among the French symbolist writers. In 1887 the Whitman image is further perpetuated in photographs by G. C. Cox, in a bust by William Sidney Morse, and in oil by both John W. Alexander and Herbert Gilchrist. By the end of the decade William O'Connor is in very poor health and in 1887 visits Whitman for what proves to be the last time. In the same year Thomas Eakins is believed to have made his first visit to Whitman; late in the year he begins his portrait of the poet. In the summer of 1887 Algernon Swinburne attacks Whitman for vulgarity. Peter Doyle recedes still further from Whitman's attention but visits at least twice in these years.

1881

16 JANUARY. Whitman concludes a letter to George and Susan Stafford by saying he is about to visit a very sick friend, a ferryman, for whom he will provide a bottle of brandy for medicinal milk punch (CORR, 3:207).

27 JANUARY. Writing to Harry Stafford about a Robert Ingersoll book that has brought unfavorable comment from Harry's minister, Whitman tells him that "True religion . . . consists in *what one does* square and kind and generous and honorable all days." (CORR, 3:207). The letter of 16 January to Harry's parents supports this belief.

29 JANUARY. Part one of "How I Get Around at 60, and Take Notes" appears in the *Critic*. Six installments are published between 29 January 1881 and 15 July 1882

(see PW, 2:347–351). The *Critic* is a weekly newspaper started in this year by Jeanette Leonard Gilder, former literary columnist for the *New York Herald* and sister of poet Richard Watson Gilder, who in this year becomes editor of the *Century*. Both Gilders are friends of Whitman's.

JANUARY. Whitman has a visit from Harry Stafford and his young uncle, Montgomery; James B. Marvin of Boston also visits.

7 FEBRUARY. Harry Stafford visits, and Whitman gives him a copy of *Leaves of Grass*, which he begins reading for the first time in their five-year relationship (CORR, 3:211).

12 FEBRUARY. "Death of Carlyle," an essay, appears in the *Critic* (see PW, 1:248–253).

20 FEBRUARY. Whitman writes to Henry Wadsworth Longfellow requesting an autograph for a Canadian friend (CORR, 3:212). The autograph is intended for a friend of Dr. Bucke's; Longfellow complies with "great pleasure" (CORR, 3:212, n49).

22 FEBRUARY. Whitman writes to Susan Stafford describing his day in Philadelphia: a ride on a Market Street coach, a walk on Arch and Chestnut Streets looking at the crowds ("oceans of women, drest to kill") and in store windows, then a visit to Colonel Forney's office where a rattan easy chair is kept for him in a bay window (CORR, 2:213). Whitman has kept close to home for most of January and February because of ill health, including dizziness, indicating hypertension.

28 FEBRUARY. Whitman writes to Harry Stafford reassuring him of his "loving friendship" and of his awareness that, had he not known Harry and his family, he never would have regained his health; memories of their "storms and squalls" have been dismissed, leaving only good memories in which "you, my darling boy, are the central figure" (CORR, 3:215).

FEBRUARY. "The Poetry of the Future," an essay, appears in the *North American Review* (reprinted as "Poetry To-day in America-Shakspere-The Future" in PW, 2:

474–490). William Sloane Kennedy's essay "A Study of Whitman" appears in the *Californian*.

8 MARCH. Whitman attends the funeral of an unidentified friend, perhaps the ferryman whom he visited in January, has a visit from George Parsons Lathrop of Boston, votes in the election, and takes a jaunt to Philadelphia (CORR, 3:217). Lathrop, the journalist son-in-law of Nathaniel Hawthorne, has come to arrange for Whitman's Lincoln lecture to be given in Boston in April (Allen, *Solitary Singer*, 491).

11 MARCH. Whitman leaves for a weekend visit with the Staffords (DN, 1:233).

18–22 MARCH. Whitman visits the Staffords (DN, 1:234).

23 MARCH. Eddie Whitman is sent to live with the family of William V. Montgomery in Glen Mills, Pennsylvania, about forty miles from Camden; Whitman contributes $16 per month for his care (DN, 1:234). Eddie has lived with Walt at the home of George and Louisa Whitman from the time of Whitman's mother's death. The cost of Eddie's board at the Montgomerys was to have been shared by the three remaining brothers, but a letter from Jeff (29 October 1882) acknowledges that he has fallen behind in his payments (Berthold and Price, 178).

2–7 APRIL. Whitman is at the Staffords (DN, 1:235).

9 APRIL. Part two of "How I Get Around at 60, and Take Notes" appears in the *Critic*.

13 APRIL. Whitman goes to Boston (DN, 1:237).

15 APRIL. Whitman gives his Lincoln lecture in the Hawthorne Room of the St. Botolph Club, Boston. While in Boston he stays at the Revere House, is feted at a reception given by Mrs. John T. Sargent, and sees William Dean Howells and James T. Fields, among others. (In PW, 1:264–269, Whitman provides an account of the visit.)

16 APRIL. Whitman returns Longfellow's call, remarking later that Longfellow was the only "eminence" he called on in Boston (PW, 1:266).

17 APRIL. Sculptor Truman Howe Bartlett makes a plaster

cast of Whitman's hand. In 1884 Bartlett will send a cast of the hand to Paris to be bronzed (CORR, 3:354, n7).

ON THE SAME DATE. Whitman visits Memorial Hall at Cambridge, where wall tablets bear the names of Harvard students who died in the Civil War (PW, 1:269).

18 APRIL. At the home of Quincy Shaw, Whitman views a collection of paintings by Jean-François Millet and is greatly affected (PW, 1:267–269). He is also much impressed by the "many *fine-looking gray-hair'd women*" he sees in Boston (PW, 1: 266).

APRIL. "Patroling Barnegat" appears in *Harper's Monthly*.

7 MAY. Part three of "How I Get Around at 60, and Take Notes" appears in the *Critic*.

8 MAY. Whitman writes to James R. Osgood, Boston publisher, giving specifics for a planned new edition of *Leaves of Grass*; he adds a warning that "the old pieces, the *sexuality* ones," are to be retained (CORR, 3:224). Osgood has been suggested to Whitman by Whitman's friend John Boyle O'Reilly, editor of the Boston Catholic newspaper, the *Pilot*. Between this date and the end of June when he receives sample pages, Whitman and Osgood are in close agreement on the new edition; trouble does not occur until critics attack the work on moral grounds.

13–20 MAY. Whitman visits the Stafford home (DN, 1:240).

14 MAY. "Bumble-Bees and Bird Music" appears in the *American* (see PW, 1:122–126).

4 JUNE. "A Summer's Invocation" (later "Thou Orb Aloft Full-Dazzling") appears in the *American*.

11–15 JUNE. Whitman is with the Staffords (DN, 1:244).

6 JULY. Whitman writes to his sister-in-law Louisa in Connecticut where she is visiting and refers to the shooting of President James A. Garfield. Whitman had met Garfield in Washington in 1864. While Louisa is away Whitman spends the warm summer days mostly alone in the house at Camden with just the dog, Tip; he takes his meals with a neighbor, Mrs. Caroline Wroth, at 319 Stevens Street (DN, 1:247; CORR, 3:232, 234).

16 JULY. Part four of "How I Get Around at 60, and Take Notes" appears in the *Critic*.

23 JULY. Whitman meets Dr. Bucke in Jersey City; they proceed to the home of Helen and Arthur Price in Woodside, Long Island (CORR, 3:234, n25).

25 JULY. Whitman leaves Woodside, and he and Dr. Bucke spend four days vacationing, first in Far Rockaway, Long Island (25 July), where he has a "naked ramble" on the beach, then in Long Branch, New Jersey, and finally in his native West Hills and Cold Spring, Long Island (29 July) (CORR, 3:237).

1–6 AUGUST. Whitman visits Edgar M. Smith in New York City (DN, 1:251).

3 AUGUST. Whitman visits the offices of the *Critic* and the *Tribune* in New York (DN, 1:251).

4 AUGUST. "A Week at West Hills" appears in the *New York Tribune* (see PW, 1:5–8, 352–354).

6–19 AUGUST. Whitman is at the summer home of John H. Johnston in the Mott Haven section of New York City (CORR, 3:236; DN, 1:251).

11 AUGUST. Whitman calls on Richard Worthington and tells him "emphatically" that he is not to print further copies of *Leaves* from the 1860 plates he has purchased (DN, 1:252).

15 AUGUST. "City Notes in August" appears in the *New York Tribune* (reprinted [abridged] in PW, 1:273–276, 354–355).

16 AUGUST. Whitman visits Pfaff's at its new Twenty-fourth Street location to breakfast and reminisce with Charles Pfaff (PW, 2:277), takes a "jaunt to Brooklyn" to visit the office of the *Eagle*, and, with John H. Johnston, rides up Broadway and through Central Park (DN, 1:253).

ON THE SAME DATE. Whitman sees John Mulvaney's painting "Custer's Last Rally" (DN, 1:252; see PW, 1:275–276).

19 AUGUST. Whitman arrives in Boston to oversee the printing of the new edition of *Leaves of Grass* (DN, 1:253). He stays at the Hotel Waterson, 8 Bulfinch Place (DN, 1:260, n1334), where the landlady is Mrs. Eva Moffit, and spends

part of every day at the printing office of Rand, Avery & Co. reading proofs (see Myerson, *Time*, 76–89).

EARLY SEPTEMBER. Whitman receives news of the suicide death of Beatrice Gilchrist. The suicide comes about a year and a half after Gilchrist had abandoned her medical career suddenly in the spring of 1880.

10 SEPTEMBER. "Spirit That Form'd This Scene" appears in the *Critic*. The poem harks back to Whitman's western trip in 1879, and the subhead reads "Written in Platte Cañon, Colorado."

17 SEPTEMBER. Whitman goes to stay at the home of Franklin B. Sanborn in Concord, Massachusetts; an evening reception includes Amos Bronson Alcott and his daughter, Louisa May, and the Emersons. Whitman finds Emerson quiet but alert, clear-eyed, with his "well-known expression of sweetness" (PW, 1:279). Emerson is experiencing severe memory loss and aphasia at this point in his life. While in Concord Whitman visits the graves of Hawthorne and Thoreau in Sleepy Hollow cemetery, the battlefield with its monument bearing Emerson's poetic inscription, the Old Manse where Emerson wrote *Nature*, and Walden Pond where, on the site of Thoreau's cabin, he adds his contribution to the commemorative mound of stones left by other visitors (PW, 1:280).

18 SEPTEMBER. Whitman dines with the Emerson family (PW, 1:279–280).

19 SEPTEMBER. Whitman returns to Boston; President Garfield dies.

27 SEPTEMBER. "The Sobbing of the Bells," a poem on the president's death, appears in the *Boston Daily Globe*.

SEPTEMBER. Joaquin Miller is in Boston and visits Whitman daily; Longfellow visits; Whitman meets Oliver Wendell Holmes and Henry James (CORR, 3:246).

11 OCTOBER. Whitman and a Boston journalist, Sylvester Baxter, attend a performance at the Globe Theatre of *Romeo and Juliet* starring the Italian actor Ernesto Rossi (DN, 1:263; Myerson, *Time*, 84).

15 OCTOBER. Whitman hosts an open house at his boarding place for his Boston friends and the printers who have set

his book; by Whitman's count, three hundred people attend (CORR, 3:251).

22 OCTOBER. Whitman leaves Boston for New York City, where he joins Dr. and Jessie Bucke at the Grand Union Hotel (CORR, 3:249).

24 OCTOBER. Whitman goes to stay with the Johnstons in New York.

25 OCTOBER. Whitman takes a carriage drive through the upper part of New York, finding it a kind of "fairy land" of natural beauty (CORR, 3:250).

28 OCTOBER. While in New York, Whitman dines with John Burroughs at "Oriental" and visits the offices of the *Century* and the *Critic* (DN, 1:268).

EARLY NOVEMBER. The sixth edition (1881) of *Leaves of Grass* is published. It is 382 pages. Some copies are bound in gold cloth with a butterfly on the forefinger of a hand stamped in gold on the backstrip. There is a high degree of permanence about this edition: poems are revised for the last time, and titles and the placement of poems are settled. The edition boasts twenty new poems scattered throughout, none major, though "Dalliance of the Eagles" is important. "Pioneers! O Pioneers!" is now part of a new group, "Birds of Passage." The group titled "Sea-Shore Memories" in the previous edition is now "Sea-Drift" and is expanded. The "Drum-Taps" section is also expanded. "There Was a Child Went Forth" appears in a new group, "Autumn Rivulets." Another new group, "From Noon to Starry Night," includes poems that span Whitman's poetic career. Perhaps most important, "Walt Whitman" is now "Song of Myself," with the 1854 portrait of a bohemian Whitman on the facing page. A final new group, "Songs of Parting," ends with "So Long!" While the arrangement appears to be a record of Whitman's life and work, it is a "*poetic record,*" not an autobiography (Allen, *Handbook*, 152).

3 NOVEMBER. Whitman returns to Camden (DN, 1:270).

5 NOVEMBER. An anonymous review of the new edition of *Leaves* appears in the *Critic*. Neither written nor pre-approved by Whitman, the piece (reprinted in Hindus,

182–185) takes a fresh approach, including the claim that his use of foreign words parallels America's absorption of individuals from various nations.

28 NOVEMBER. Whitman writes to Anne Gilchrist for the first time since learning of the death of her daughter (CORR, 3:253–254). The letter is brief and unconsoling.

3 DECEMBER. Part five of "How I Get Around at 60, and Take Notes" appears in the *Critic*.

12 DECEMBER. Whitman attends the funeral of John W. Forney (DN, 1:276). Forney, who traveled with Whitman to Kansas, died on 9 December.

20 DECEMBER. Whitman warmly endorses a request from John Fitzgerald Lee, a student at Trinity College, Dublin, to translate *Leaves* into Russian and provides a preface (CORR, 3:259, 261). Nothing comes of this, perhaps because in the following year a copy of *Leaves of Grass* is removed from the shelves of the National Library, Dublin (CORR, 3:300, n30); in 1888 Whitman mistakenly tells Traubel he has been banned in Russia (WWC, 3:47).

22 DECEMBER. Whitman writes to T. W. H. Rolleston about the German translation of *Leaves* that Rolleston is preparing (CORR, 3:260).

29 DECEMBER. Whitman goes to visit the Staffords, remaining until 9 January 1882 (DN, 2:280).

IN THIS YEAR. In his Johns Hopkins lectures, Sidney Lanier claims that Whitman is not a democrat but "the most incorrigible of aristocrats" and his poetry "a product which would be impossible except in a highly civilized society" (Myerson, *Time*, 72).

1882

11 JANUARY. Whitman enjoys a sight on the Delaware River of what seems to him a perfect combination of nature and technology, a new ferryboat at high tide (see "Only a New Ferry Boat," PW, 1:283).

18 JANUARY. Whitman welcomes Oscar Wilde to his Camden home. Walt is delighted with Wilde and afterward

refers to him as "manly" (Allen, *Solitary Singer*, 502).
Six years later he tells Traubel: "Everybody's been so in
the habit of looking at Wilde cross-eyed, sort of, that they
have charged the defect of their vision up against Wilde
as a weakness in his character" (WWC, 2:289). As to
Wilde's writing, Whitman's final verdict is that though
Wilde writes "exquisitely . . . there seems to be a little
substance lacking" (WWC, 2:192).

24 AND 25 JANUARY. Jeff Whitman visits Walt (DN, 2:282).

25 JANUARY. Whitman writes to Harry Stafford claiming to
understand and like him more than anyone else does
(CORR, 3:264).

31 JANUARY. Whitman writes the despondent Harry advice
on how to avoid "blue spells"; he also tells him Oscar
Wilde has sent a photograph of himself a foot and a half
long (CORR, 3:265). The photograph was taken by the
New York photographer Napoleon Sarony and was in
return for two photographs Whitman had given Wilde,
one of them intended for Swinburne (Ellmann, 168).
Wilde is still in the United States, lecturing in various
cities.

JANUARY. A review in the *Dial* of the 1881 *Leaves* attributes
to Whitman's lack of humor his inability to distinguish
between the erotic and the "bestial" (Hindus, 186−189).

7 FEBRUARY. Whitman returns, with revisions, Dr. Bucke's
manuscript of his biography, claiming it will "justify itself" (CORR, 3:266). The revisions are extensive and will
become even more so; by the time the biography is published, the work is more Whitman's than Bucke's.

16 FEBRUARY−6 MARCH. Whitman is with the Staffords
(DN, 2:284).

1 MARCH. Oliver Stevens, Boston district attorney, writes to
Osgood & Company that *Leaves of Grass* should be with-
drawn from circulation because it falls within the statute
governing "obscene literature." (For the text of the letter, see DN, 2:285, n1488.)

4 MARCH. James Osgood informs Whitman of Stevens's letter and suggests suspension of publication while revisions are made (CORR, 3:267, n16).

7 MARCH. Whitman writes to Osgood indicating he is willing to make some revisions (CORR, 3:267).

13 MARCH. Whitman takes a day trip to Atlantic City and dines with friends, Dr. and Mrs. T. K. Reed (DN, 2:286).

21 MARCH. Whitman writes to Osgood suggesting that Osgood publish the book of prose writings he is preparing, to be called *Specimen Days and Thoughts*, and also Bucke's biography (CORR, 3:269). It seems clear from this suggestion that Whitman does not expect Osgood to withdraw from publication of *Leaves*.

23 MARCH. Having received Osgood's list of suggested deletions, Whitman rejects it outright and agrees only to minor revisions of some of the "Children of Adam" poems (CORR, 3:270). Osgood has suggested dropping "A Woman Waits for Me," "The Dalliance of the Eagles," "To a Common Prostitute," and "Spontaneous Me," as well as about 150 lines from other poems. Whitman agrees only to change some lines in "I Sing the Body Electric," "A Woman Waits for Me," and "Spontaneous Me" (CORR, 3:271, n23).

24 MARCH. Henry Wadsworth Longfellow dies.

24–31 MARCH. Whitman visits the Staffords (DN, 2:287).

8 APRIL. "Death of Longfellow" appears in the *Critic* (see PW, 1:284–286, 355).

10 APRIL. In light of Whitman's refusal to comply with revisions deemed necessary, Osgood & Company declines to continue publication of *Leaves* (CORR, 3:273, n34). A settlement of royalties and plate ownership is effected in May, and for a short time Whitman returns to his former practice of self-publication.

22–27 APRIL. Whitman is with the Staffords (DN, 2:291).

26 APRIL. Ralph Waldo Emerson dies.

AROUND 28 APRIL. William O'Connor learns from Dr. Bucke of the suppression of *Leaves* and begins immediately to protest the action to various government officials in Washington (Barrus, 210–211).

3 MAY. Whitman resumes correspondence with William O'Connor. During their ten-year estrangement, Whitman has sent O'Connor copies of his published work,

but they have not corresponded. The resumption comes about when Bucke (who has found O'Connor eager to be helpful in the matter of a planned biography) suggests that O'Connor be enlisted to protest the Boston banning of *Leaves*. Though there is no reference to the earlier disagreement in their letters, Whitman writes to John Burroughs on 13 August that he and O'Connor have resumed corresponding "on the same terms as of yore" (CORR, 3:301).

6 MAY. "By Emerson's Grave" appears in the *Critic* (see PW, 1:290–291).

7 MAY. Addressing him as "Dear William O'Connor," Whitman writes O'Connor details of the controversy surrounding the 1881 *Leaves* (CORR, 3:276).

10 MAY. Oscar Wilde returns for a second visit.

17 MAY. Whitman informs O'Connor that the Boston banning has been instigated by Massachusetts State Attorney General George Marston and suggests he target him (CORR, 3:279). Later Whitman discovers that Anthony Comstock, the moral crusader, is also involved, and a 27 August letter to the *New York Tribune* from O'Connor castigates Comstock. (See Loving, *Whitman's Champion*, 233–236.)

25 MAY. A letter from O'Connor defending Whitman appears in the *New York Tribune*. Dr. Bucke also writes to the *Springfield* (Mass.) *Republican* (23 May) protesting the banning. O'Connor keeps up the *Tribune* defense by replying to criticisms of his letter and is aided in this by Whitman, who supplies needed information (CORR, 3:285–288).

31 MAY. On his sixty-fourth birthday Whitman writes to a German admirer stating that he weighs 190 pounds, is "clumsy" from his partial paralysis but mentally active, and has accomplished the "principal object" of his life (CORR, 3:288).

3 JUNE. "Edgar Poe's Significance," an essay, appears in the *Critic*.

28 JUNE. Whitman enters into an agreement with Rees

Welsh & Company, Philadelphia, to publish *Leaves* and his prose writings, *Specimen Days & Collect* (DN, 2: 297).

JUNE. "A Memorandum at a Venture" appears in the *North American Review* (reprinted in PW, 2:491–497). In this essay Whitman defends his "Children of Adam" poems as examples of "a new departure" from the two prevailing attitudes in the United States toward sexual matters, repression and pornography.

3–5 JULY. Whitman visits the Staffords (DN, 2:297).

7 JULY. O'Connor writes Whitman that the Postmaster General has ruled in favor of allowing *Leaves* to pass through the mail, O'Connor and Robert Ingersoll having successfully argued the matter to the Postmaster General. This ruling reverses the Massachusetts postmaster's edict (Barrus, 219).

15 JULY. The sixth and final installment of "How I Get Around at 60, and Take Notes" appears in the *Critic*.

MID-JULY. Rees Welsh issues a thousand copies of the previous year's printing of *Leaves of Grass*, which sell out in two days; printing of *Specimen Days & Collect* begins. Because of the publicity resulting from the Boston banning, this edition of *Leaves* quickly sells out its first four printings and goes into a fifth. With the help of O'Connor, who writes (on 28 August) that he will do his best to keep up the controversy, Whitman makes more than $1,000 in royalties (CORR, 6:xxix). In November David McKay buys the booklist and becomes, in effect, the publisher of Whitman's books.

SUMMER. John Burroughs spends the summer in England visiting Anne Gilchrist, William Rossetti, and other friends of Whitman's.

8 SEPTEMBER. *Specimen Days & Collect* is published. *Specimen Days & Collect* contains *Democratic Vistas* (1871), *Memoranda During the War* (1875), *Two Rivulets* (1876), autobiographical material written in 1882, materials taken from Whitman's war notebooks (1862–1865), diary notes (including records of his time at Timber Creek

with the Staffords and of his 1879 western trip), and previously published essays and articles from 1876 to 1881. (For the complete publication history of *Specimen Days* see *PW*, 2:viii; since *Specimen Days* contains many references to specific dates, it should be consulted for additional chronological data.)

10 OCTOBER. Whitman meets Thomas Donaldson, a Philadelphia attorney who becomes a friend, admirer, and later a biographer in *Walt Whitman, the Man* (1896) (DN, 2:298).

17–28 OCTOBER. Whitman is ill of a liver disorder, and a newspaper story puts him at death's door of Bright's disease.

28 OCTOBER. Walt sends Jeff a telegram denying the story after Jeff has twice telegraphed his concern (Berthold and Price, 176).

9 NOVEMBER. Whitman sells his lot at 460 Royden Street, Camden, for $525 (DN, 2:304).

13 NOVEMBER. Whitman dines with John H. Johnston in Philadelphia (DN, 2:305).

18–27 NOVEMBER. Whitman visits the Staffords (DN, 2:306).

NOVEMBER. The first mention of Robert Pearsall Smith appears in Whitman's Daybook (DN, 2:305).

16 DECEMBER. Whitman's essay on "Robert Burns" appears in the *Critic*. It is reprinted in expanded form in *November Boughs*.

23–25 DECEMBER; 30 DECEMBER–2 JANUARY 1883. Whitman visits Robert Pearsall Smith and Hannah Whitall Smith at their home, 4653 Germantown Avenue, Germantown, Pennsylvania. The wealthy Quaker family consists of Robert Pearsall Smith, a Philadelphia glass manufacturer; Hannah Whitall Smith, a leader of the pentecostal movement and a founder of the Woman's Christian Temperance Union; a son; and two daughters, one of whom, Mary Whitall Smith, has sought Whitman out in Camden after hearing of him at Smith College.

1883

30 JANUARY. Whitman writes to Harry Stafford that, with the publication of the two books containing all his (chosen) prose and poetry, he does not know "what to look forward to" (CORR, 3:322). With the "principal object" of his life accomplished, Whitman describes himself to John Burroughs on 2 February as "like a skipper who has come into port at last & discharged cargo" (CORR, 3:325).

JANUARY. Jeff Whitman visits Walt (DN, 2:308).

3 FEBRUARY. "The Bible as Poetry," an essay, appears in the *Critic*.

7 FEBRUARY. Whitman joins Burroughs in Philadelphia (DN, 2:310).

21 FEBRUARY. Whitman leaves for a few days' visit with the Smith family in Germantown. These visits become more numerous and of longer duration, as Whitman seeks a new family environment to replace the Stafford home, now often crowded with grown children and boarders. George and Louisa are preparing to move into a house George is building in Burlington, New Jersey, and Whitman does not plan to go with them (CORR, 3:328).

6 MARCH. Whitman receives his first dividend on two hundred shares of stock in Sierra Grande Mines, New Mexico (DN, 2:311). These shares are a gift from Robert Pearsall Smith but will pay only a few dividends before becoming worthless (DN, 2:308, n1642).

14–16 APRIL. Whitman visits the Staffords (DN, 2:313).

12–15 MAY. Whitman is with the Staffords (DN, 2:314).

23 MAY. Jeannie O'Connor, daughter of William and Ellen O'Connor, dies in Providence, Rhode Island. Whitman was always very fond of Jeannie and usually referred to her as "little Jennie."

20 JUNE. Dr. Bucke's biography of Whitman is published. A comprehensive work, Bucke's *Walt Whitman* includes a biography, sketches of Whitman in old age, a history and analysis of *Leaves*, and a collection of Whitman criticism

from 1855 to 1883. It is highly subjective and laudatory, reflecting Whitman's own image of himself.

3–17 JULY. Whitman visits the Staffords (DN, 2:314).

4–28 AUGUST. Whitman is at the Smith home (DN, 2:315) but returns to Camden every other day, probably to collect his mail (CORR, 3:347).

AUGUST. Elbert Hubbard dates his visit with Whitman (in *A Little Journey to the Home of Whitman*, [1900]) to this month. He is confused, however, for he provides a wonderful word picture of the Mickle Street house and its inhabitants, though Whitman did not move there until 1884. He may have visited Whitman at Stevens Street.

IN THE SAME MONTH. Mannahatta and Jessie visit in Camden until 1 December (DN, 2:317).

16 SEPTEMBER. Whitman meets former Florida senator Simon B. Conover at the Camden home of James Matlack Scovel (DN, 2:318).

23 SEPTEMBER. Whitman dines with Simon B. Conover (DN, 2:319).

26 SEPTEMBER–10 OCTOBER. Whitman visits Ocean Grove, New Jersey, staying at the Sheldon House and enjoying the beach; Burroughs joins him there for a time (CORR, 3:353). Whitman's pleasure at the beach is not limited to daylight; in his diary he describes nights when all alone he has "the whole performance" of the ocean to himself, "beyond all operas or finest vocalism or band." A notebook entry, "Ever that ceaseless, sulking, guttural of the sea as if to me its wrongs and toils in confidence" (DN, 2:319, n1714), later becomes, in "With Husky-Haughty Lips, O Sea!," "Outsurging, muttering from thy soul's abysms, / The tale of cosmic elemental passion, / Thou tellest to a kindred soul."

AROUND 20 OCTOBER. Whitman spends a few days with the Smiths (CORR, 3:354).

30 OCTOBER. Harry Stafford visits Whitman in Camden (DN, 2:322). Not long after this visit Harry goes to London, Ontario, to work in Dr. Bucke's asylum, where he finds the rules oppressive (CORR, 3:357, n20).

17 NOVEMBER. "Our Eminent Visitors (Past, Present, and Future)" appears in the *Critic*.

4 DECEMBER. Whitman dines with Thomas Donaldson (DN, 2:324).

7 DECEMBER. Peter Doyle visits Whitman (DN, 2:325).

9 DECEMBER. Whitman writes to William O'Connor on behalf of Edward Doyle, Pete's brother, who is seeking employment (CORR, 3:358).

15–17 DECEMBER. Whitman visits the Smiths (DN, 2:325).

22–26 DECEMBER. Whitman visits the family of writer Francis H. Williams in Germantown, Pennsylvania (CORR, 3:361).

1884

5 JANUARY. "A Backward Glance on My Own Road" is published in the *Critic*. (Later expanded and retitled "A Backward Glance O'er Travel'd Roads," it is reprinted in PW, 2:711–732.)

30 JANUARY. Whitman attends a performance in Philadelphia of George H. Boker's play *Francesca da Rimini*, starring Marie Wainwright and Lawrence Barrett. Invited backstage by Barrett, he has a brief interview with the American actor but declines an invitation to dine with him (DN, 2:328). Boker, a Philadelphia resident, was among those who in 1885 contributed to the fund to supply Whitman with a horse and buggy.

14 FEBRUARY. In a letter to George and Susan Stafford, Whitman complains of the bad weather but says he must get out and go across the river to Philadelphia or "have the horrors" (CORR, 3:365). Exposure to the weather may be the cause of his illness that begins on 17 February and continues for the next three weeks. On 8 March he needs assistance (probably from Robert Pearsall Smith, who visits him on that date) to call on a consumptive nineteen-year-old friend, Tasker Lay, whose funeral he attends on 12 March. A further pressure is the need to

relocate, as George and Louisa have moved and new tenants are to take possession on 1 April (CORR, 3:367).

28 FEBRUARY. Whitman writes a $16 check to Margaret Goodenough, Mount Laurel, New Jersey, for Eddie's board. Due to ill health, Whitman is not able to mail it until 4 March (White, 91). In his notebook (1 June 1887) Whitman writes that in the last six or seven years he had paid nearly $400 for his brother's board.

FEBRUARY. "An Indian Bureau Reminiscence" is published in *Baldwin's Monthly*, a New York magazine.

20 MARCH. Whitman dines at the home of Thomas Donaldson and meets the English actor Henry Irving and his manager, Bram Stoker. Stoker had written to Whitman in 1872 from his home in Dublin (the letter was not sent until 1876; see chapter 6); he is now traveling with Irving (see Stoker, 92–111).

26 MARCH. Whitman moves to a house at 328 Mickle Street, Camden, which he purchases on 3 April for $1,750 cash (DN, 2:231, 331). The parents of Tasker Lay are tenants in the house, and Whitman takes his meals with them until they move in January 1885.

MARCH. "With Husky-Haughty Lips, O Sea!" is published in *Harper's Monthly*.

22 APRIL. Whitman writes to T. W. H. Rolleston providing an endorsement to be incorporated into Rolleston's preface to the German translation of selections from *Leaves of Grass*. The endorsement includes the statement, "One purpose of my chants is to cordially salute all foreign lands in America's name" (CORR, 3:369). The book is not printed until 1889 and is published in Switzerland.

31 MAY. "A Fabulous Episode" appears in the *Critic*. In it Whitman refutes an allegation that Longfellow had agreed to a conditional acceptance of a dedication to him of the 1855 *Leaves* if some portions were excised (WWC, 2:227).

4 JUNE. Peter Doyle visits Whitman in his new home (DN, 2:335).

18–20 JUNE. Edward Carpenter visits Whitman (DN, 2:337).

20 JUNE. Jeff Whitman and his daughters arrive in Camden for a visit (DN, 2:336).

25 JUNE. Harry Stafford marries Eva Westcott in Camden; Whitman attends the ceremony.

30 JULY. Whitman applies for renewal (for fourteen years) of his copyright to *Leaves*, originally granted in 1856 (CORR, 3:373).

21 AUGUST. Whitman writes to Edwin Booth requesting a photograph of his actor-father, Junius Brutus Booth, about whom he is writing (CORR, 3:376). Whitman greatly admired the acting talent and sonorous voice that made the elder Booth so impressive on the stage (see PW, 2:594–597).

11 SEPTEMBER. Mary Whitall Smith and her future husband, Benjamin F. C. Costelloe, visit Whitman (DN, 2:342).

14 SEPTEMBER. Whitman visits Cape May, New Jersey, and sails on the bay (DN, 2:342).

27 SEPTEMBER. "What Lurks Behind Shakspeare's Historical Plays?" appears in the *Critic*.

10 OCTOBER. "Red Jacket (from Aloft)" appears in the *Philadelphia Press*. The poem commemorates the reburial of an Iroquois warrior, Red Jacket, at Buffalo, New York, on 9 October.

26 OCTOBER. "If I Should Need to Name, O Western World" (later "Election Day, November, 1884") appears in the *Philadelphia Press*.

OCTOBER. At the Smith home, Whitman sits for a portrait by the English painter Edward Clifford (DN, 2:345).

4 NOVEMBER. "The Dead Tenor" appears in the *Critic*. The poem honors Whitman's favorite operatic tenor, Pascuale Brignoli, buried 3 November.

8–10 NOVEMBER. Whitman is with the Smith family (DN, 2:345).

27 NOVEMBER. After declining an invitation from Eva and Harry Stafford, Whitman has Thanksgiving dinner with the Smiths (DN, 2:346).

2 AND 4 DECEMBER. Whitman dines with Dr. Bucke in Philadelphia at the Continental (DN, 2:346). On 4 and

5 December Burroughs joins them, and all three visit the Smiths in Germantown.

14 DECEMBER. Whitman declines an invitation to dine at the Philadelphia home of Talcott Williams (editor of the *Philadelphia Press*) in the company of actors Ellen Terry and Henry Irving (CORR, 3:383).

1885

2 JANUARY. William Sloane Kennedy spends the day with Whitman (Kennedy, 4).

3 JANUARY. Poet and writer Edmund Gosse visits from England, bringing greetings from Whitman's friends there. (For his account of the visit, see Gosse, 95–111.)

6 JANUARY. Whitman has an oyster and champagne dinner with Bartram Bonsall, coeditor of the *Camden Daily Post* (DN, 2:347).

19 JANUARY. Responding to a query from Charles M. Skinner of the *New York Times* about his employment with the *Brooklyn Times*, Whitman refers to himself as having been "an editorial writer" in 1855 or 1856 (CORR, 3:385). This does not necessarily mean he edited the *Times* (see chapter 2).

25 JANUARY. Whitman begins to take meals with Mrs. Mary Davis, 412 West Street, Camden.

JANUARY. "Of That Blithe Throat of Thine" appears in *Harper's Monthly*.

22 FEBRUARY. "Ah, Not This Granite, Dead and Cold," (later "Washington's Monument, February, 1885"), a poem in honor of George Washington, appears in the *Philadelphia Press*.

24 FEBRUARY. Mary Davis becomes Whitman's housekeeper (DN, 2:350, 353). Davis moves in with her many pets — cat (Kitty), dog (Watch, who barked too much for Whitman's liking), parrot, and canary. For some time after Whitman would comment in his letters on "his" canary who sang as he wrote; in 1888 he writes the poem "My Canary Bird." Later, Warren (Warry) Fritzinger,

Davis's foster son, comes to live with them as Whitman's nurse.

28 APRIL. Whitman falls and sprains an ankle, which incapacitates him for some weeks.

16 MAY. "As One by One Withdraw the Lofty Actors" (later "Death of General Grant") appears in *Harper's Weekly*.

4 JUNE. Peter Doyle visits (DN, 2:358). Pete's mother had died on 24 May. He also visited on this same date the year before (DN, 2:357).

20 JUNE. Mary Whitall Smith makes a farewell visit to Whitman before leaving for Europe on 24 June with her entire family. While in England the Smiths visit Anne Gilchrist, Alfred, Lord Tennyson, and other Whitman supporters. Though her brother, Logan, and sister, Alys, return and visit Whitman, the family remains in England, where Mary marries Benjamin Costelloe in 1886; she later will become the wife of art critic Bernard Berenson. Her article "Walt Whitman in Camden" appears in the *Pall Mall Gazette* on 23 December of this year.

BETWEEN 20 AND 23 JULY. Whitman falls again, the result of dizziness (DN, 2:362).

21 JULY. Herbert Gilchrist writes from England about a monetary gift soon to be sent to Whitman by his English friends. In responding on 1 August, Whitman says he will "gratefully accept" (CORR, 3:399). About this time Whitman receives a number of gifts: a watch, silverware, and china from John H. Johnston; a rocking chair from Mary and Blain Donaldson, children of Thomas Donaldson; and sheets and pillowcases from Mary Whitall Smith and her sister, Alys. These gifts were to furnish his home.

16 AUGUST. "Booth and 'The Bowery'" appears in the *New York Tribune* (see PW, 2:591–597).

AUGUST. "Fancies at Navesink," a group of eight poems, appears in the *Nineteenth Century*, a London publication; "The Voice of the Rain" appears in *Outing*, "An Illustrated Monthly Magazine of Recreation."

15 SEPTEMBER. Whitman receives a gift of a horse and small, phaeton-style buggy from some thirty friends,

including Mark Twain, Oliver Wendell Holmes, John Greenleaf Whittier, and Edwin Booth. The surprise gift is the work of Thomas Donaldson (see Donaldson, 172–193).

23 AND 24 SEPTEMBER. In what is no doubt another stroke, Whitman suffers temporary loss of balance and eyesight (DN, 2:369). George and Louisa come on 24 September, William O'Connor soon after, followed by John Burroughs and then Charles Eldridge — each in turn there to attend him.

8 OCTOBER. Whitman visits his brother Eddie in Mount Laurel, New Jersey; he finds him "quite well and hearty" (DN, 2:370).

19 OCTOBER. Accompanied by Dr. William Osler, Whitman visits an opthalmologist, who reassures him concerning his eyesight (DN, 2:370). Osler, later Sir William and the founder of Johns Hopkins Medical University in Baltimore, is a native of Ontario, Canada, and a friend of Dr. Bucke's. At Bucke's request, he had become Whitman's doctor in October 1884; later, Whitman's care is turned over to other physicians (see Leon).

1 NOVEMBER. Thanks to the new conveyance (for which he now has a driver, young William Duckett), Whitman makes his fifth visit to the Staffords since acquiring the gift in mid-September (DN, 2:371). Whitman's visits to the Staffords become too frequent to note individually; often his stay is for only a few hours, and he takes his Sunday dinner with the family almost weekly. His driver is paid through an annual subscription of friends, including George W. Childs and Horace H. Furness (Myerson, *Time*, 283–308).

14 NOVEMBER. Probably intended for use in the new buggy, Louisa Whitman makes her brother-in-law a gift of a wolfskin lap robe (DN, 2:372). In later years Whitman has this over the back of a large chair at all times; it can be seen clearly in the photographs taken by Thomas Eakins.

26 NOVEMBER. Whitman has Thanksgiving dinner at the home of Harry Stafford's sister, Deborah, now Mrs. Joseph Browning (DN, 2:372).

28 NOVEMBER. Whitman visits Atlantic City (DN, 2:374).

30 NOVEMBER. Whitman receives word from Herbert Gilchrist of the death of his mother, Anne Gilchrist, of breast cancer (CORR, 3:408).

NOVEMBER. "Slang in America" appears in the *North American Review*.

IN THE SAME MONTH. Lawrence Barrett, the actor, sends Whitman a check for $10; Thomas Donaldson provides a ferry pass for the horse and buggy (DN, 2:372).

14 DECEMBER. Harry Stafford visits Whitman (CORR, 3:413).

DECEMBER. "Some Diary Notes at Random" appears in *Baldwin's Monthly*.

1886

1 JANUARY. Whitman has dinner with a Camden friend, Dr. George Hendry Shivers (CORR, 4:16).

10 JANUARY. A daughter, Dora, is born to Harry and Eva Stafford (DN, 2:377).

2 FEBRUARY. Whitman delivers his Lincoln lecture at the Pythian Club in Elkton, Maryland (CORR, 4:19).

22 FEBRUARY. Whitman begins sitting for a portrait by John W. Alexander. Walt will not think well of the portrait, finished in 1887, which is now at the Metropolitan Museum of Art, New York.

1 MARCH. Whitman gives his Lincoln lecture at Morgan Hall, Camden (DN, 2:380).

18 MARCH. In a letter to John Burroughs, Whitman refers for the first time to a projected book of prose and poetry written since 1882, to be called *November Boughs* (CORR, 4:22).

15 APRIL. Whitman delivers his Lincoln lecture at the Chestnut Street Opera House, Philadelphia, a group of actors and journalists having arranged the event for his benefit (CORR, 4:24; Donaldson, 103–109).

APRIL. Dr. Bucke spends three days with Whitman before sailing for England (CORR, 4:24).

18 MAY. Whitman delivers his Lincoln lecture in Haddonfield, New Jersey, to benefit a church building fund (CORR, 4:24, n34).

30 MAY. Whitman acknowledges another gift of money from William Rossetti and some eighty friends in England, including Henry James, Robert Louis Stevenson, John Addington Symonds, and Edward Carpenter (CORR, 4:30).

22 JUNE. Whitman writes to the editor of the *Philadelphia Press* on behalf of William Duckett, who is seeking employment. Duckett, Whitman's driver, had moved into the Mickle Street house in May; he leaves in early June (DN, 2:384), only to return the following year. In 1889 Mary Davis will succeed in suing him for $150, eighteen months' back rent (WWC, 4:64–66).

3–6 JULY. Whitman vacations at the Minerva House, Sea Isle City, New Jersey (DN, 2:389).

11 JULY. "How I made a Book — or tried to" appears in the *Philadelphia Press*. It is later incorporated into *November Boughs*.

14 AUGUST. "A Thought on Shakspere" appears in the *Critic*.

3 SEPTEMBER. Jeff's daughter Mannahatta dies in St. Louis of an intestinal disorder at age twenty-six (Berthold and Price, 184, n2).

24 NOVEMBER. Novelist Hamlin Garland writes to introduce himself as an "enthusiastic" reader of Whitman's books (Myerson, *Time*, 316–318).

NOVEMBER. "Robert Burns As Poet and Person" appears in the *North American Review* (see PW, 2:558–568).

1887

1 JANUARY. "A Word about Tennyson" appears in the *Critic* (see PW, 2:568–572).

11 JANUARY. Whitman deposits $393.61, a New Year's gift from his friends in England, in his Philadelphia bank (WWC, 4:512).

12 JANUARY. Whitman writes in his daybook that "in walk-

ing power" he is feeble and that he can only "read &
write rather aimlessly" (DN, 2:405).

15 JANUARY. Tennyson writes his thanks for Whitman's
words of praise for "Locksley Hall" in "A Word about
Tennyson."

17 JANUARY. A bill that would grant a pension of $125 per
month to Walt Whitman is introduced in the House of
Representatives. Offered by Henry B. Lovering of Lynn,
Massachusetts, the bill (Report No. 3856) cites Whitman's Civil War service and is supported by the testi-
mony of William O'Connor, John Swinton, Dr. Bucke,
and Dr. D. W. Bliss, who had been in charge of the Armory Square Hospital (Donaldson, 162–171). On 8 December 1886 Whitman had withheld his consent to this
request, claiming, "I do not deserve it" (CORR, 4:56).
The matter is not pressed, and no final action taken.

22 JANUARY. Whitman recites "The Mystic Trumpeter"
and "A Word Out of the Sea" at the Contemporary Club
in Philadelphia, where Horace Traubel and anthropolo-
gist Daniel G. Brinton, another friend of Whitman's, are
members (WWC, 4:512).

25 JANUARY. "New Orleans in 1848" appears in the *New
Orleans Picayune*, a special edition celebrating the newspaper's fiftieth year. The article recounts Whitman's
experiences while working on the paper (see PW, 2:
604–610).

JANUARY. "Some War Memoranda Jotted Down at the
Time" appears in the *North American Review* (see PW,
2:584–589).

22 FEBRUARY. Whitman addresses the Contemporary Club
in Philadelphia (Traubel, Bucke, and Harned, 130–131).

FEBRUARY. Whitman and Mary Davis are driven to Phila-
delphia to attend a Saturday matinee of the melodrama
Clito, starring the English actor Wilson Barrett and a
Miss Eastlake (WWC, 4:513).

20 MARCH. Moncure Conway visits from England (DN,
2:413).

25 MARCH. Whitman visits Harry Stafford in the hospital
where he is being treated for throat trouble; Stafford

stays with Whitman for about a month after the surgery (DN, 2:413). The first notice by Whitman of this throat ailment is at the time of Stafford's marriage in June 1884. The problem recurs, and surgery is performed twice in April of this year (CORR, 4:80, 82). By January 1888 the condition is "the same as ever" (CORR, 4:139), and Stafford is unwell for some time after. A visitor from England, Charles Rowley, tells of seeing Harry in the Camden house on 6 April, adding, "He is deeply attached to Whitman. . . . It was very touching to see him affectionately kiss Whitman" (Peattie, 249).

5 APRIL. Whitman delivers the Lincoln lecture to the Unitarian Society in Camden (CORR, 4:78).

10 APRIL. Whitman visits Mr. and Mrs. Talcott Williams in Philadelphia (CORR, 4:81).

14 APRIL. Whitman delivers his Lincoln lecture in Madison-Square Theatre, New York, before a large audience that includes Andrew Carnegie (who pays $350 for his box), James Russell Lowell, and Augustus Saint-Gaudens. Also present are the politically exiled Cuban journalist José Martí, whose account in *La Nación* (Buenos Aires) spreads Whitman's fame in Latin America, and Stuart Merrill, the native Long Islander who has become a major figure in the French symbolist movement and who presents Whitman with a copy of Jules Laforgue's translations of some of Whitman's poems into French (Erkkila, 78). Whitman is dressed "in a dark sack coat, with dark-gray waistcoat and trousers, low shoes, and gray woollen socks" (Kennedy, 26). After the lecture he is presented with a bouquet of lilacs and then reads "O Captain! My Captain!" The following year Whitman claimed to be "almost sorry I ever wrote the poem" ("O Captain!") because it was so often referred to as his "best" (WWC, 2:304). William Duckett accompanies Whitman to New York, and the two stay at the Westminster Hotel, where a reception is held.

15 APRIL. Whitman is photographed by G. C. Cox at his studio at Twelfth Street and Broadway (CORR, 4:82, n50). The photographs (Whitman dubs his favorite "The

Laughing Philosopher") are to be approved in proofs, autographed, and sold, with Whitman receiving a royalty. No proofs arrive, however, and when the photographs are advertised in the newspaper on 1 September, Whitman is ready to take legal action. He is mollified when Cox sends the photographs on 15 September for autographing; royalties are subsequently paid (WWC, 5:306).

16 APRIL. "Five Thousand Poems" appears in the *Critic*.

28 APRIL. Whitman and William Duckett drive four miles to "Billy" Thompson's on the Delaware River at Gloucester, New Jersey, where, with Thomas Harned and James Matlack Scovel, they enjoy a dinner of baked shad and champagne (CORR, 4:89). Thompson is a restauranteur who annually opens the season with a dinner of shad and champagne in honor of Whitman (Kennedy, 15).

25 MAY. Whitman writes to thank Sylvester Baxter for his "kind project for me" (the raising of funds from Whitman supporters toward the purchase of a country house) and indicates his willingness to accept a summer home in the country, a "4-or-5-room house," the choice of place and design to be his (CORR, 4:93). William Sloane Kennedy takes over the project, and a total of $788 is raised; Whitman accepts the money but never builds the house (Kennedy, 10−11).

29 MAY. Whitman receives a letter from Dr. John Johnston and J. W. Wallace, both of Bolton, England, who are admirers of his work; it is the first in a series of communications between them and Whitman that will continue to his death. The two men are leaders of a group who call themselves the "Bolton College," middle-class socialists who find Whitman's poetry inspiring to their cause. (See Blodgett, 212−215; and "Whitman's Disciples.")

SPRING. Whitman has a surprise visit from John Newton Johnson, an Alabama cotton farmer and an admirer of many years. Johnson has come on a mission: to chastize Whitman for "toning down" *Leaves of Grass* in its later editions. Finding that the poet does not grant him lengthy audiences (Whitman likes him but finds his enthusiasm tiring), Johnson remains in the Camden vicinity for thirty-nine days, seeing Whitman often but briefly (Kennedy, 19–21).

1 JUNE. Whitman writes in his notebook, "To day I begin my 69th Year — almost altogether disabled in walking power & bodily movement" (DN, 2:425).

3 JUNE. Herbert Gilchrist arrives from England for the first time since the death of his mother (DN, 2:426).

14 JUNE. Whitman writes to Mark Twain, thanking him for his generosity (CORR, 4:101). Twain is among those who have contributed to the horse and buggy purchase and to the "Cottage Fund," concerning which he is quoted in the *Boston Herald* on 24 May as saying, "What we want to do is to make the splendid old soul comfortable" (Barrus, 268).

JUNE. "The Dying Veteran" appears in *McClure's Magazine*.

AUGUST. This month's issue of the London *Fortnightly Review* carries an essay by Algernon Charles Swinburne in which he claims not to recant his original laudatory view of Whitman but finds the poet's thinking questionable, his form lacking, his Eve "a drunken apple woman," and his Venus "a Hottentot wench" (Miller, *Century*, 88). Whitman was not disturbed by this defection though some of his admirers were; John Addington Symonds publishes a refutation of Swinburne in the September *Fortnightly Review* (Blodgett, 117–121).

SUMMER. Herbert Gilchrist and William Sidney Morse both execute likenesses of Whitman, Gilchrist an oil painting and Morse a bust. While Whitman is unhappy with the painting ("he's given me Romeo curls"), he likes the bust well enough to pay for ten castings, some of which he sends to friends in other cities for presentation to art galleries (CORR, 4:120, 121, 131, 132).

20–21 SEPTEMBER. Herbert Gilchrist leaves for England (DN, 2:438).

SEPTEMBER. Philadelphia is "all alive" with the celebration of the centennial of the United States Constitution; Whitman is invited to write and deliver a poem for the occasion but declines because of his health (CORR, 4:122).

18 OCTOBER. William O'Connor visits Whitman on his way back to Washington from Maine (CORR, 4:126). It is the last time they see each other. O'Connor's health is rapidly deteriorating; he has gone to California in hope of recovery and to Maine for treatment from a Dr. Kinnear, but neither trip has helped (CORR, 4:114, n11).

OCTOBER. "Shakspere-Bacon's Cipher" appears in the *Cosmopolitan.*

12 NOVEMBER. Moncure Conway visits Whitman (DN, 2:441).

15 NOVEMBER. Tennyson writes Whitman that though "the mother country" may feel "the daughter" owes much to her, the mother has "much to learn" from the daughter (CORR, 4:131).

26 NOVEMBER. "Yonnondio" appears in the *Critic.*

NOVEMBER. Five poems — "November Boughs," "You Lingering Sparse Leaves of Me," "Not Meagre, Latent Boughs Alone," "'Going Somewhere,'" and "After the Supper and Talk" — appear in *Lippincott's Monthly Magazine.* Whitman has Thanksgiving dinner (turkey and champagne) at the home of Thomas Harned.

15 DECEMBER. "As the Greek's Signal Flame," Whitman's poetic tribute to John Greenleaf Whittier on his eightieth birthday, appears in the *New York Herald.*

25 DECEMBER. Whitman enjoys Christmas with the Harneds (another turkey and champagne dinner) and with Ernest Rhys, who is visiting from England (CORR, 4:137). Rhys is a literary agent who has facilitated the English publication of *Leaves, Specimen Days,* and *Democratic Vistas.* In 1886 he edits *Leaves of Grass: The Poems of Walt Whitman,* a volume of expurgated selections. His visit to the Harneds is recounted in *Everyman Remembers* (reprinted in Myerson, *Time,* 327–332).

DECEMBER. "Twilight" appears in the *Century.* Thomas Eakins begins his portrait of Whitman (DN, 2:444). Whitman's evaluation of this portrait is arrived at slowly; initially unimpressed, he comes to see it as "strong" and "profounder" than others done of him (WWC, 1:39).

CHAPTER EIGHT

1888-1892

An old, dismasted, gray and batter'd ship . . .
— "The Dismantled Ship," 1888

Trials of old age and illness fill the final years of Whitman's life, but there is activity still. Thomas Eakins finishes his portrait in 1888 before the poet's devastating stroke in June. The stroke brings major changes in Whitman's life: the horse and buggy are sold — to be superseded in the next year by a wheelchair — a nurse is required, and visitors often must be turned away. One visitor comes daily, however, young Horace Traubel, who in 1888 begins a record of his visits with the poet. (Traubel's record forms a chronology in itself and supplements the present one from 28 March 1888 to 3 April 1892.) With what Whitman terms "invaluable" help from Traubel, both *November Boughs* and the nine hundred-page *Complete Poetry and Prose of Walt Whitman, 1855–1888* are published in 1888.

William O'Connor dies in May 1889, leaving a great void in Whitman's life. Friends hold a grand seventieth birthday celebration in Philadelphia. In October Whitman is much taken with the light cast into his room by the newly installed electric street lamp. In December he chooses a burial plot in the nearby Harleigh Cemetery.

A birthday dinner in May 1890 features a speech by Robert Ingersoll, with whom Whitman agrees in almost all matters save his agnosticism. Later in the year Ingersoll gives a benefit lecture in Philadelphia to raise funds for Whitman. In July Dr. John Johnston arrives from Bolton, England. In August Whitman finally responds to the repeated queries of John Addington Symonds regarding the meaning of the "Calamus" poems; in doing so he concocts a bit of personal history, his six illegitimate children. Sensing the diminution of his creative genius, Whitman begins to work in September 1890 on a volume to be called *Good-Bye My Fancy*; it is published the following May. As the year winds toward its close it brings another terrible blow, the death of Jeff Whitman. It is left to Walt to notify his sisters, Hannah and Mary, and Eddie, who is now in an insane asylum in New Jersey.

The last full year of Whitman's life finds him drawing closer to his sisters, especially his favorite, Hannah, to whom he now writes often. In May Horace Traubel marries Anne Montgomerie, and the ceremony is performed in the ailing poet's room. Even the birthday celebration is held in the Mickle Street house this year, and *Good-Bye My Fancy* is published in time for its author's birthday. July brings Dr. Bucke's two-month stay in England, and he returns with J. W. Wallace, the Bolton stalwart who becomes, even at this late date, one of Whitman's closest friends. An old nemesis, James Russell Lowell, dies, and Whitman finds it just possible to write a few words in his honor. Sick and nearly worn out, he completes the final version of *Leaves of Grass* in December and makes another will. The winter of 1891–1892 sees the last of the "Good Gray Poet," who dies, surrounded by just a few of those who love him, on 26 March.

1888

27 JANUARY. "To Those Who've Failed" appears in the *New York Herald*.

29 JANUARY. "Halcyon Days" appears in the *New York Herald*.

31 JANUARY. Dr. Bucke visits Whitman on his way to Florida.

JANUARY. Despite poor health (DN, 2:447), Whitman enters into an agreement with the *New York Herald* to provide brief poems for which they will compensate him. Though he often complains of neglect or vilification by newspapers, Whitman not only uses them to publicize himself and his work but finds a market for his writings in many of them. Over the years he publishes frequently in New York's *Daily Graphic*, *Tribune*, and *Herald*, as well as in Philadelphia and Camden papers.

3 FEBRUARY. "After the Dazzle of Day" appears in the *New York Herald*.

11 FEBRUARY. "America" appears in the *New York Herald*.

12 FEBRUARY. "Abraham Lincoln, Born Feb. 12, 1809" appears in the *New York Herald*.

15 FEBRUARY. "True Conquerors" appears in the *New York Herald*.

21 FEBRUARY. "Soon Shall the Winter's Foil Be Here" appears in the *New York Herald*.

23 FEBRUARY. "The Dismantled Ship" appears in the *New York Herald*.

27 FEBRUARY. "Mannahatta" appears in the *New York Herald*.

29 FEBRUARY. "Paumanok" appears in the *New York Herald*.

1 MARCH. "From Montauk Point" appears in the *New York Herald*.

2 MARCH. "My Canary Bird" appears in the *New York Herald*.

9 MARCH. "A Prairie Sunset" appears in the *New York Herald*.

10 MARCH. "The Dead Emperor" appears in the *New York Herald*. It is written for Wilhelm I of Germany, who died on 9 March.

12 MARCH. "The First Dandelion" appears on page one of the *New York Herald*. A three-day blizzard begins in New York, and on 15 March Whitman writes to Bucke of a "terrible" storm of hail and snow for three days' running (CORR, 4:156).

16 MARCH. "The Wallabout Martyrs" appears in the *New York Herald*.

18 MARCH. "The Bravest Soldiers" appears in the *New York Herald*.

19 MARCH. "Orange Buds by Mail from Florida" appears in the *New York Herald*.

28 MARCH. Horace Traubel begins his record of talks with Whitman. This record, later published as *With Walt Whitman in Camden*, is nine volumes. In May of this year Whitman writes three letters to businessmen (including publisher David McKay) introducing Traubel as his agent and in June notes in his Daybook, "Horace Traubel is invaluable to me" (DN, 2:464).

15 APRIL. "Life" appears in the *New York Herald*.

23 APRIL. "To-day and Thee" appears in the *New York Herald*.

24 APRIL. Whitman enjoys a shad and champagne dinner at "Billy" Thompson's (WWC, 1:80–81).

1 MAY. The French critic Gabriel Sarrazin publishes "Poètes modernes de l'Amérique, Walt Whitman" in *La Nouvelle Revue*, in which he hails Whitman as the poet of a form "instinctively audacious, novel, overstepping all literary conventions" (Miller, *Century*, 90). The essay is translated in the United States by Harrison S. Morris, who later claims that Whitman, who knew no French, insisted on editing the translation (Morris, 98–99).

2 MAY. "Queries to My Seventieth Year" appears in the *New York Herald*.

8 MAY. "The United States to Old World Critics" appears in the *New York Herald*.

10 MAY. "Out of May's Shows Selected" appears in the *New York Herald*.

14 MAY. "As I Sit Writing Here" appears in the *New York Herald*.

21 MAY. "A Carol Closing Sixty-nine" appears in the *New York Herald*.

23 MAY. "Life and Death" appears in the *New York Herald*.

27 MAY. "The Calming Thought of All" appears in the *New York Herald*.

29 MAY. Jeff Whitman visits Walt (DN, 2:461).

LATE MAY. The Harneds have a birthday dinner for Walt (WWC, 1:238).

3–4 JUNE. Whitman suffers a stroke during the night of 3 June, followed by perhaps two more the next day.

These episodes almost kill him. Dr. Bucke, in Pennsylvania at the time, sees to his care, after which Dr. Osler takes over. Nurses are kept in attendance from this time to his death. By mid-June Whitman is at work again on *November Boughs*, though with diminished strength. (For details of his illness, see WWC, 1:259 ff.)

10 JUNE. The first of Whitman's male nurses is employed, Nathan M. Baker. Traubel has started a fund among Whitman's friends to provide nursing care.

15 JUNE. Peter Doyle visits Whitman (CORR, 4:174).

27 JUNE. Whitman discusses his recent poem "The Dismantled Ship" with Traubel and says, "that's me — that's my old hulk — laid up at last" (WWC, 1:390).

29 JUNE. Whitman writes a new will naming Dr. Bucke, Horace Traubel, and Thomas Harned as his literary executors; Edward Whitman and his sisters are his principal heirs; Harry Stafford is left a gold watch, Peter Doyle a silver one (WWC, 1:310–312).

14 JULY. Nathan Baker leaves, and Dr. Bucke sends W. A. Musgrove to replace him. Whitman, or perhaps Traubel, does not care for Musgrove, so Bucke later makes arrangements for Edward Wilkins, an employee at the Ontario asylum, to replace him.

31 JULY. Eddie Whitman is brought to visit Walt; Eddie is incapable of intelligent communication, and the brothers talk in monosyllables (WWC, 1:66).

JULY. "Twenty Years" appears in the London *Pall Mall Gazette* and in New York's *Magazine of Art*.

1 AUGUST. Louisa and Jessie Whitman (who is visiting from St. Louis) place Eddie in the annex to the insane asylum in Blackwoodtown, New Jersey (CORR, 4:202); Walt pays his board thereafter, $45.50 every three months (CORR, 4:282), and Eddie "has a good little bedroom to himself" (DN, 2:465).

12 AUGUST. "Over and Through the Burial Chant" (later "Interpolation Sounds") appears in the *New York Herald*. It is Whitman's tribute to General Philip Sheridan, buried in Virginia on this date.

LATE SUMMER—EARLY FALL. *November Boughs* is published. A large book, 140 pages, it is published in Philadelphia by David McKay. It contains twenty essays (some are included in PW) and sixty-four "new" poems (many first appeared in newspapers or magazines) grouped in two clusters, "Sands at Seventy" and "Fancies at Navesink." The preface, "A Backward Glance O'er Travel'd Roads," is the most important feature of *November Boughs*. Here Whitman resigns himself to a hope for future recognition — having failed to gain it in his lifetime — and to the satisfaction of having had his "say" and putting it "on record" himself.

7 SEPTEMBER. No longer able to go about as before, Whitman sells his horse and buggy to the Rev. J. Leonard Corning for $130 (DN, 2:470). Whitman will remain confined to his room until May 1889.

18 SEPTEMBER. Harry Stafford visits Whitman (CORR, 4:212).

26 SEPTEMBER. Hamlin Garland visits Whitman (CORR, 4:218, n64). (The visit is described in Myerson, *Time*, 315—326.)

SEPTEMBER. "Old Age's Lambent Peaks" appears in the *Century*.

OCTOBER. "Army and Hospital Cases" appears in the *Century* (see PW, 2:614—626).

5 NOVEMBER. Edward Wilkins becomes Whitman's nurse (DN, 2:476). Whitman, pleased with Wilkins's services, is willing to put up with his violin practice.

15 NOVEMBER. Hamlin Garland reviews *November Boughs* in the *Boston Evening Transcript*, commenting, "It is no longer in order to assault him, even if we do not agree with him" (Price, *Reviews*, 311—314).

FALL. *Complete Poems and Prose of Walt Whitman, 1855—1888* is published. This nine hundred—page volume includes all the published poetry, *Specimen Days & Collect*, and *November Boughs*. Its publication, a Herculean effort for the aged and ill poet, could not have been possible without the help of Horace Traubel.

1889

5 JANUARY. "To the Year 1889" (later "To the Pending Year") appears in the *Critic*.

25 JANUARY. Oscar Wilde writes "The Gospel According to Walt Whitman," a review of *November Boughs*, in the London *Pall Mall Gazette*; he finds Whitman, near the end of his life, "the herald to a new era" and "the precursor of a fresh type" (Price, *Reviews*, 318–321).

JANUARY. A German translation of selections from *Leaves* is published in Zurich, Switzerland (CORR, 4:287).

20 FEBRUARY. Jeff Whitman visits Walt, who finds that as they grow older they "look curiously alike" (CORR, 4:293).

26 FEBRUARY. Dr. Bucke arrives from Canada for a visit.

FEBRUARY. In *Harper's New Monthly Magazine*, William Dean Howells reviews *November Boughs* and claims, "It is time . . . to own that [Whitman's] literary intention was as generous as his spirit was bold" (Price, *Reviews*, 322–323).

2 MARCH. Dr. Bucke and Horace Traubel visit the ailing William O'Connor in Washington (WWC, 4:252–263).

8 MARCH. A Delaware River ferryman visits Walt, bringing news of scenes and people Whitman has been incapable of visiting for a year (CORR, 4:300).

1 MAY. Whitman's first nurse, Nathan Baker, graduates from medical school, and Dr. Osler gives the address; P. T. Barnum's circus arrives in Camden for a performance (CORR, 4:328). Whitman is not well enough to attend either of these events.

9 MAY. William D. O'Connor dies in Washington.

11 MAY. Whitman takes delivery of a wheelchair (paid for by Camden friends) and, with Wilkins pushing, has his first outing since the June 1888 strokes. Harry Stafford visits (CORR, 4:336–337). For a time Whitman tries to spend part of every day (evenings in the summer months) outdoors in his wheelchair, though he complains of its jostling.

26 MAY. Walt has a visit from "three Hindus" in native costume who bring him gifts of a silk handkerchief from India and a bamboo cane (DN, 2:493).

31 MAY. A great banquet celebration of Whitman's seventieth birthday is held in Morgan Hall, Philadelphia. Unable to attend the banquet, Whitman is carried in afterward and sits on the stage in his wheelchair while speeches in his honor continue for hours. The celebrants have no knowledge of the disastrous flood not far away at Johnstown, Pennsylvania.

2 JUNE. Whitman proposes publication of a pamphlet, *Camden's Compliment to Walt Whitman*, to include the birthday speeches (CORR, 4:343).

7 JUNE. "A Voice from Death" on the Johnstown flood, written at the request of the *New York World*'s editor, appears in the *World*.

7 AUGUST. Whitman sits for the Philadelphia photographer Frederick Gutekunst, who supplies a carriage to transport Whitman to the studio (CORR, 4:364).

17 AUGUST. Whitman has a visit from Carl Sadakichi Hartmann (CORR, 4:368). This is the first recorded visit from the author (a second is on 10 July 1890 [CORR, 5:61]), though in April of this year Whitman had told Traubel he had met him "more than once" (WWC, 5:35). Hartmann, of German-Japanese parentage (Whitman always referred to him as "the Japanee"), writes newspaper articles, one of which, "Walt Whitman. Notes of a Conversation with the Good Gray Poet by a German Poet and Traveller" (*New York Herald*, 14 April 1889; reprinted in Myerson, *Time*, 57–61), includes disparaging comments on other writers attributed to Whitman, which the poet denies (CORR, 4:331). In Boston Hartmann launches, without Whitman's consent, a Walt Whitman Society; when he begins to collect money for his society, Whitman brings pressure to bear to end it (WWC, 2:281; 5:85, 88–89). Whitman continues to see Hartmann, however, evidently because he finds his cultured views impressive (WWC, 2:281).

24 AUGUST. After paying two tax bills amounting to over

$33, Whitman compares the "banditti" of Italy and Greece to this country's "regular legal" and "remorseless" tax collectors (DN, 2:529).

13 SEPTEMBER. The English author and world traveler Sir Edwin Arnold visits Whitman (WWC, 5:506, 509–510). Arnold describes the visit in *Seas and Lands* (1891).

28 SEPTEMBER. "Bravo, Paris Exposition!" appears in *Harper's Weekly*.

10–19 OCTOBER. Whitman has carpentry and masonry repairs done to his house (CORR, 4:381).

21 OCTOBER. Ed Wilkins leaves Whitman's employ to return to Canada and study veterinary medicine. Another nurse has been engaged but fails to appear; Warren (Warry) Fritzinger (Mary Davis's foster son who has been a sailor) takes over, and Whitman is very pleased with his "sailor boy" (CORR, 4:386, 393).

26 OCTOBER. Walt has an old, dead tree removed from in front of his house and wonders, "how long before I go too?" (DN, 2:538).

LATE OCTOBER. *Camden's Compliment to Walt Whitman* is published. Walt's sister Hannah (in Vermont) is very ill (DN, 2:539).

OCTOBER. An electric street light is installed at the corner of Mickle Street and shines into Whitman's room "like moonlight"; he sits in the dark to enjoy it (CORR, 4:384).

13 NOVEMBER. Ellen O'Connor visits Walt, and they talk of "dear William" (DN, 2:540). William O'Connor has left behind a manuscript of a short story, "The Brazen Android," which is later published in *Three Tales* (1892), along with "The Ghost" and "The Carpenter" (this last a story whose central character is based on Whitman); Whitman writes a preface (reprinted in PW, 2:689–691) for the book.

NOVEMBER. "My 71st Year" appears in the *Century*.

5 DECEMBER. Whitman's friend Charles Eldridge is married to Emily Louisa Brown in San Francisco.

24 DECEMBER. Whitman visits the Harleigh Cemetery outside Camden to choose a burial plot; he chooses a lot 20

by 30 feet on a wooded hill and plans a vault within a "plain massive stone temple" (CORR, 4:408).

25 DECEMBER. "A North Star to a South," a poem welcoming the Brazilian republic (later "A Christmas Greeting"), appears in *McClure's Magazine*.

1890

30 JANUARY. A son, George Wescott Stafford, is born to Eva and Harry Stafford (CORR, 5:27, n24).

2 FEBRUARY. "A Death-Bouquet," a prose meditation on death, appears in the *New York Sun*.

FEBRUARY. "Old Age's Ship and Crafty Death's" appears in the *Century*.

MARCH. Harry Stafford is very ill. As a result of this illness, Stafford gives up his railroad job and turns to farming (CORR, 5:32), after which his health improves.

15 APRIL. Whitman gives his Lincoln address to the Contemporary Club at the Philadelphia Art Gallery. He sends an account of the event to the *Boston Evening Transcript*, where it is printed on 19 April.

21 APRIL. The editor of *Lippincott's Monthly Magazine*, Joseph M. Stoddard, invites Whitman to write for the magazine (DN, 2:551).

APRIL. An autobiographical sketch, "Walt Whitman's Life," appears in *Munyon's Illustrated World*. Dodd, Mead & Company, a New York publisher, offers Whitman $500 to produce a sixty thousand–word book on Abraham Lincoln (CORR, 5:39); he considers it but does not accept.

3 MAY. Whitman receives word from William Sloane Kennedy of the death of Charles Pfaff (CORR, 5:44, n54).

14 MAY. Whitman has his longest outing in two years when he goes by carriage to visit his burial plot and for a ride on the Haddonfield, New Jersey, pike (CORR, 4:47).

22 MAY. "For Queen Victoria's Birthday" appears in the *Philadelphia Public Ledger* but is not included in the 1892

Leaves. The previous year Whitman and six others toasted the queen on her birthday, 24 May (DN, 2:492).

31 MAY. Whitman's friends give him a birthday dinner at Reisser's Restaurant in Philadelphia, with Robert Ingersoll as the principal speaker.

MAY. "A Twilight Song" appears in the *Century*, but that magazine's rejection of "On, On the Same, Ye Jocund Twain!" seems like "a sort of douche of very cold water right in the face," which Whitman finds hard to get over (CORR, 5:52). Herbert Gilchrist rents a farmhouse in Centreport, Long Island.

JUNE. Warry Fritzinger takes lessons in massage technique from the head masseur in Dr. S. Weir Mitchell's orthopedic hospital, Philadelphia (CORR, 5:52). Whitman has found Warry's "pummeling," as he calls it, helpful, and it is decided that Warry should learn the proper technique. Warry also takes violin lessons and does carpentry.

MID-JULY. Dr. John Johnston arrives from Bolton, England, to visit Whitman and people and places connected with the poet's life in Huntington and Brooklyn (see Johnston and Wallace).

3 AUGUST. "Old Brooklyn Days" appears in the *New York Morning Journal* (see PW, 2:773–774).

16 AUGUST. "An Old Man's Rejoinder," an article responding to John Addington Symonds's comments on "Democratic Art, with Special Reference to Walt Whitman" in *Essays Speculative and Suggestive* (1890), appears in the *Critic*; Whitman writes that "*Art is one*, is not partial, but includes all times and forms and sorts — is not exclusively aristocratic or democratic." The response appears in *Good-Bye My Fancy* (see PW, 2:655–658).

19 AUGUST. Whitman answers yet another of the persistent queries of Symonds about the meaning of the "Calamus" poems by claiming these questions "quite daze me" and by disavowing the implications Symonds finds there. Concluding on an expansive note, he claims though never married to "have had six children — two are dead" (CORR, 5:73).

SEPTEMBER. Whitman begins work on an annex to *Leaves of Grass* to be called *Good-Bye My Fancy*, which is to contain poems written since the 1888 printing.

1 OCTOBER. Ground is broken for Whitman's tomb and vault, to be made of stone quarried at Quincy, Massachusetts (CORR, 5:98).

21 OCTOBER. Robert Ingersoll delivers a lecture on Whitman as a benefit for the poet at Horticultural Hall, Philadelphia. According to Whitman, 1,600 to 2,000 people, "one third women," attend, with proceeds to him of $869.45 (DN, 2:573).

LATE OCTOBER. Horace Traubel accompanies Dr. Bucke on the return to Canada and stays the remainder of the month.

OCTOBER. "The Human Voice" is published in *Munyon's Illustrated World*; it appears in *Good-Bye My Fancy* as "The Perfect Voice" (PW, 2:673−674).

18 NOVEMBER. Whitman has a visit from Charles Hamilton Aide, a poet and British army officer (CORR, 6:53).

25 NOVEMBER. Thomas Jefferson (Jeff) Whitman dies of pneumonia in St. Louis, while his daughter, Jessie, is visiting in Camden (DN, 2:578). Walt's obituary of his brother appears in the *Engineering Record* 13 December and is reprinted in *Good-Bye My Fancy* (see PW, 2:692−693); Horace Traubel writes an obituary for the *Camden Post* on 20 January 1891 (reprinted in Berthold and Price, 192−193).

28 NOVEMBER. Whitman writes to his brother Edward in the asylum with news of Jeff's death (CORR, 5:123). It is the only extant letter from Walt to Eddie.

NOVEMBER. "Old Poets — and Other Things," an essay, appears in the *North American Review*. Whitman has a new pair of glasses made but prefers his old ones (CORR, 5:117).

DECEMBER. "To the Sun-Set Breeze" appears in *Lippincott's Monthly Magazine*. Whitman gives Mary Davis a plain gold ring as a Christmas gift and writes Bucke that he has always felt "to have her mind [care] for me as long as I live" (CORR, 5:133).

31 DECEMBER—1 JANUARY 1891. Whitman writes encourag-
ingly to his bereaved niece Jessie of the new year beginning with "a dark stormy morning here — but of course
it will clear & brighten up" (CORR, 5:142).

IN THIS YEAR. Whitman's name and face appear in a cigar
advertisement. Horace Traubel begins publication of a
monthly paper, the *Conservator* (1890–1908), much of
which is devoted to Whitman and his themes.

1891

8—10 JANUARY. Whitman writes to his sister Hannah
Heyde. Beginning with a Christmas 1890 greeting, Whitman more often writes directly to Hannah in 1891 than to
her husband, Charles, as had been his habit. He sends her
word of their niece in St. Louis and of their sister Mary, in
Greenport, Long Island. Every letter encloses a gift of
money. His last letter to her is written nine days before his
death.

10 JANUARY. "The Pallid Wreath" appears in the *Critic*.

JANUARY. The sixty-first exhibition at the Pennsylvania
Academy of Fine Arts includes Thomas Eakins's portrait
of Whitman.

3 FEBRUARY. Harry Stafford visits. Feeling well again,
Harry is now eager to give up farming and return to
work with the railroad; but when the lease on the farm
is up and he cannot find work, he and his family move
into his parents' home (CORR, 5:183).

FEBRUARY. Whitman is invited to participate in a sympo-
sium on the "Coming Man" to be published in the *New
York Herald*, and sends his thoughts on the subject
(which are not published in the paper) in a letter dated
3 March.

5 MARCH. The United States Congress passes a bill on international copyright, and Whitman exults, "It is a question of honesty — of morals — of a literature, in fact"
(WWC, 8:54).

12 MARCH. "Ship Ahoy!" appears in the Boston *Youth's Companion*.

19 MARCH. "Old Chants" appears in a magazine called *Truth*.

MARCH. *Lippincott's Monthly Magazine* contains a section devoted to Whitman, including a portrait, a set of four poems — "Sail Out for Good, Eidolon Yacht!," "Sounds of the Winter," "The Unexpress'd," and "After the Argument" — collectively titled "Old Age Echoes," and prose pieces by Whitman and Traubel. The *North American Review* publishes Whitman's essay on "American National Literature" (see PW, 2:663–668), and *Munson's Magazine* publishes "The Commonplace."

2 APRIL. "Old Actors, Singers, Shows, & in New York" appears in *Truth* (see PW, 2:693–699).

3 APRIL. William O'Donovan, a New York sculptor and friend of Thomas Eakins's, visits and proposes a bust of Whitman (WWC, 8:123). O'Donovan makes several visits and on 1 May has photographs of Whitman taken by Samuel Murray, Eakins's pupil; at the poet's death, Eakins, O'Donovan, and Murray fashion a death mask and a cast of his hand (WWC, 9:176, 602, 605).

15 APRIL. Whitman goes out in his wheelchair, his first time out in four months, and finds the experience too "confusing" and the sun "too bright." Whitman is finding many things too taxing, including visitors, whose talk makes him "headachy and deaf." Aside from paralysis, his principal health problems are intestinal blockage and an enlarged prostate.

APRIL. Whitman learns from the artist John W. Alexander that his portrait has been purchased and placed in the Metropolitan Museum of Art, New York (CORR, 4:193). Herbert Gilchrist buys the farmhouse he has been renting on Long Island.

28 MAY. Horace Traubel marries Anne Montgomerie in Whitman's room at Mickle Street. Whitman writes out a certificate documenting the event (WWC, 8:242; Loving and Birney, 104–105). The Traubels travel to Canada

(stopping at Niagara Falls) with Dr. Bucke for their honeymoon and return to Camden 14 June.

30 MAY. Whitman visits the tomb he is having built in Harleigh Cemetery and gives instructions that his body is to be placed between those of his parents (WWC, 8: 245). He agrees to pay $1,500 for the tomb; a contract for $4,678 is later found to be a fraud. To end the matter, Thomas Harned agrees to pay an additional $1,000 (WWC, 8:290; 9:490–491).

31 MAY. A birthday celebration with about forty people is held at Mickle Street; Tennyson sends greetings, as do many, and a gift of 40 pounds comes from Edward Carpenter and others in England. (A transcript of the celebration proceedings appears in WWC, 8:591–606).

MAY. *Good-Bye My Fancy* is published. This sixty-six-page volume of prose and poetry (in the 1892 edition, the second annex to *Leaves of Grass*) is published by David McKay. It ends with the title poem, in which Whitman bids "Good-bye" to his creative imagination.

5 JUNE. Whitman writes Dr. Bucke that he has received eight letters in the mail, seven of which request an autograph (CORR, 5:207). These requests become more numerous as he grows older, but Whitman does not oblige; when the requests include postage he confiscates it.

8 JULY. Dr. Bucke sails from New York on the *Britannic* for a two-month visit in England; Whitman writes him a letter of introduction to Tennyson. Whitman's beloved canary having died, he sends the stuffed bird with Bucke (Warry delivers it to the boat) for his friends in Bolton. It remains as part of the Whitman Collection in the Bolton Library.

JULY. Bucke writes of a "coolness" on the part of Robert and Hannah Smith and Mary Smith Costelloe, which would account for the break in communication that has baffled Whitman (CORR, 5:225, n51). The exact cause of the coolness is never established, but Walt describes Hannah Smith to Traubel as "very evangelical: she takes her doctrine, if she don't take her whiskey, very straight" (WWC,

1:172). Bucke avers that the show of affection from the "Bolton College" friends is deep and genuine.

10 AUGUST. Bucke writes Whitman a long letter describing his visit to Tennyson and the very cordial reception accorded him "for your sake." He says of Tennyson that he "does not make as strong an impression of *great personality* as I expected" (Lozynsky, 247).

12 AUGUST. James Russell Lowell dies. The following day Whitman sends a brief word of tribute to the *Boston Herald*, but his feelings toward Lowell have remained bitter from the time of the latter's denunciation of the 1855 *Leaves*.

4 SEPTEMBER. Dr. Bucke returns. Ellen O'Connor is visiting Whitman from Washington.

8 SEPTEMBER. J. W. Wallace of Bolton arrives on the *British Prince*. Wallace goes to Canada with Bucke. He later visits Whitman's birthplace in West Hills and Andrew Rome in Brooklyn. James and Andrew Rome owned the printing shop in Brooklyn where the 1855 *Leaves of Grass* was printed. In October he visits Timber Creek. (See Johnston and Wallace.)

12 SEPTEMBER. Moncure Conway visits from England to gather information on Thomas Paine for the biography he is writing (CORR, 5:241). Whitman's father was a great admirer of Paine, as was Whitman. In 1877 Whitman gave a lecture in Philadelphia on Paine (PW, 1:140). In 1888 he urged Traubel to write a biography of Paine (WWC, 3:139).

15 SEPTEMBER. In a letter to Dr. John Johnston in Bolton, Whitman makes his first reference to a "really *complete ed'n L of G.*" on which he has begun work (CORR, 5:243). This proves to be the final version, though not actually a new edition, published in 1892.

16 SEPTEMBER. Whitman has an eye examination and will receive new glasses (WWC, 8:514). He complains of being nearly blind, but Traubel often notes his ability to see well at a distance; obviously Whitman had become farsighted.

17 SEPTEMBER. Whitman presses Traubel for details of

telephone use, which the poet has never experienced (WWC, 8:518).

15 OCTOBER. J. W. Wallace, Andrew Rome, and Horace Traubel visit Whitman.

16 OCTOBER. Whitman learns from Wallace that Peter Doyle is living in Baltimore; he speaks of "The noble Pete!," commenting that he hears but little from him (WWC, 9:34).

30 OCTOBER. Essayist Agnes Repplier visits Whitman (CORR, 5:259). Whitman respects Repplier's brilliance and wit but believes her to be one of "the polishers of language . . . above all, erudite — oh! too damned erudite!" (WWC, 4:206).

OCTOBER. William O'Connor's *Three Tales* is published by Houghton Mifflin of Boston (see entry for 13 November 1889). J. E. Reinhalter & Company, Philadelphia, report completion of the Whitman tomb.

2 NOVEMBER. Visitors to Mickle Street this day are Sir Edwin Arnold, journalist John Russell Young, and Major James Pond (CORR, 5:260).

4 NOVEMBER. J. W. Wallace sails for England on the *City of Berlin*.

NOVEMBER. Harry Stafford visits Whitman and finds him restrained; after he leaves, Whitman chides Mary Davis for allowing "everybody" access to his room (WWC, 9: 162, 163).

2 DECEMBER. Whitman's ailing left leg gives way and he falls (WWC, 9:197).

7 DECEMBER. Harry Stafford visits again, this time with his wife and children (WWC, 9:211).

12 DECEMBER. Writing to Dr. Bucke about his poor health, Whitman quotes his father: "Keep good heart — *the worst is to come*" (CORR, 5:272).

17 DECEMBER. Whitman is seriously ill with severe lung congestion and is not expected to recover. Bucke comes as quickly as possible, followed by Jessie Whitman and John Burroughs; in attendance are Dr. Daniel Longaker and Dr. Alexander McAlister.

24 DECEMBER. Whitman makes his final will, again (as in

1888) naming Bucke, Harned, and Traubel as literary executors and leaving almost all of his assets for Eddie's support; Mary Davis and his sisters each receive $1,000; Harry Stafford is left a gold watch; Peter Doyle, a silver watch; Susan Stafford, $250 (WWC, 9:292).

25 DECEMBER. A son is born to Harry Fritzinger (Warren's brother) and named Walt Whitman Fritzinger (WWC, 9:287). In addition to this boy and to George and Louisa's deceased son, there are at least four other children named for Whitman: the son (born 1858) of an old friend, Herman Storms of Passaic, New Jersey (CORR, 5: 215, n31); the son (born 1874) of a former Broadway stage conductor Whitman met in Brooklyn in 1870, John M. Rogers, later of New Britain, Connecticut (Shively, *Lovers*, 129); the son (born 1875) of William H. Millis Jr. of Dover, Delaware; and, probably, the son (born 1868) of Benton H. Wilson of Syracuse, New York. The last two were soldiers in the Armory Square Hospital (Shively, *Drum Beats*, 160, 222).

28 DECEMBER. A hired nurse, Elizabeth L. Keller, begins taking care of Whitman.

1892

1 JANUARY. In a codicil to his final will, Whitman leaves Mary Whitman Van Nostrand $200, Walt Whitman Fritzinger $200, Susan Stafford $200, the gold watch to Horace Traubel, and the silver one to Harry Stafford; nothing is left to Doyle (WWC, 9:292).

27 JANUARY. Whitman sends Dr. Bucke the advertisement for the latest publication of *Leaves* which, he tells him, "supersedes them all by far" (CORR, 5:275). It reads, in part:

> Walt Whitman wishes respectfully to notify the public that the book LEAVES OF GRASS, which he has been working on at great intervals, and partially

issued for the past thirty-five or forty years, is now completed. (CORR, 5: 275, n2)

The 1892 *Leaves of Grass* (often called "the deathbed edition") is completed in December 1891 but published in 1892. It is not a new edition since its two volumes reprint the 1881 edition using the Osgood plates and add two annexes, the poems of *November Boughs* constituting the first and the poems of *Good-Bye My Fancy* the second. In an "Executor's Diary Note, 1891," included in the book, Whitman authorizes the work as the final and complete *Leaves of Grass*.

8 FEBRUARY. Whitman writes to his sister Hannah that he is "probably growing weaker" (CORR, 5:276).

22 FEBRUARY. Walt sits in his big chair for the last time while a new bed, purchased with a fund raised by the *New York Evening Telegram*, is set up in his room (Keller, 165).

FEBRUARY. His letters to Hannah, two in February and two in March, are but one or two lines each. George and Louisa Whitman come to visit often, but Jessie has returned to St. Louis. Traubel keeps Whitman's friends informed of his condition, and Whitman receives messages daily from people in the United States and Europe, especially from his friends in Bolton. Whitman continues his great interest in Edmund Clarence Stedman's selections from *Leaves*; published after his death as *Selected Poems*, it is a sanitized version.

8 MARCH. Elizabeth Keller leaves the Mickle Street house to take another position (Keller, 173).

16 MARCH. Whitman gives Traubel a poem titled "A Thought of Columbus," which seems to date to about November 1891 (see LGC, 581–582). The poem appears in *Once a Week* on 9 July 1892 and is included in the 1897 *Leaves of Grass*, published by Small, Maynard & Co., Boston, which includes fragments of some unpublished works.

24 MARCH. Whitman receives news of Ellen O'Connor's marriage to Albert L. Calder of Providence, Rhode Island (WWC, 9:585).

25 MARCH. In a final effort to ease Whitman's discomfort, a water mattress is installed in his bed.

26 MARCH. At about 6:30 P.M. Whitman dies. Present are Dr. McAlister, Mary Davis, Warry Fritzinger, Horace Traubel, and Thomas Harned. Whitman's last words are to Warry, asking to be turned in the bed: "Warry, shift" (Traubel, Bucke, and Harned, 435).

27 MARCH. Thomas Eakins, Samuel Murray, and William O'Donovan take Whitman's death mask and a cast of one hand; close friends begin to gather.

THAT EVENING. An autopsy is performed in the Mickle Street house by Drs. Cattell, Dercum, Longaker, and McAlister, with Horace Traubel present. Findings include a collapsed left lung and sharply diminished capacity in the right, a stone-filled gallbladder, an invasive abcess on the left side, and tubercles on major organs (Traubel, Bucke, and Harned, 409). The brain is removed and sent to the American Anthropometric Society in Philadelphia, which will later turn it over to the Wistar Institute of Anatomy and Biology for examination of signs of genius; at the institute the brain will be accidentally destroyed (Leon, 105). George Whitman opposes the autopsy but is overruled by Whitman's prior instructions to Dr. Longaker (WWC, 9:604).

28 MARCH. Louisa Whitman asks a Philadelphia minister to officiate at the burial; he is disinvited by Traubel who, with Dr. Bucke and others, has other plans, including a eulogy to be given by Robert Ingersoll (WWC, 9:609). John Burroughs raises an objection to speeches and especially to Ingersoll (WWC, 9:618).

29 MARCH. In the morning on the day of the funeral Warry Fritzinger and Traubel gather Whitman's papers, manuscripts, and letters into barrels for removal to Traubel's home and later division among literary executors (WWC, 9:613). Friends and supporters arrive, and about 11 A.M. general viewing begins; the line of visitors extends three blocks. At the noon lunch hour workers at all manner of trades, shopkeepers, and schoolchildren crowd in; at about 2 P.M., when the funeral procession is to begin, the line has to be cut off (WWC, 9:616; for a list of friends present at the house or cemetery, see WWC, 9:623). Peter

Doyle attends the funeral, arriving and leaving alone. Traubel sees him on the road leaving Harleigh Cemetery and later describes him as expressing by his demeanor "the powers by which he must have attracted Walt" (WWC, 9:620).

WORKS CITED

Allen, Gay Wilson. *New Walt Whitman Handbook*. New York: New York University Press, 1986.

———. *The Solitary Singer*. New York: New York University Press, 1955.

Asselineau, Roger. *The Evolution of Walt Whitman*. Vol. 1. Cambridge: Harvard University Press, 1962.

Bandy, W. T. "An Unknown 'Washington Letter' by Walt Whitman." *Walt Whitman Quarterly Review* 2 (Winter 1984): 23–27.

Barrus, Clara. *Whitman and Burroughs, Comrades*. Boston: Houghton, Mifflin, 1931.

Berthold, Dennis, and Kenneth Price, eds. *Dear Brother Walt: The Letters of Thomas Jefferson Whitman*. Kent, Ohio: Kent State University Press, 1984.

Binns, Henry B. *A Life of Walt Whitman*. New York: Haskell House, 1969.

Blodgett, Harold W. *Walt Whitman in England*. New York: Russell & Russell, 1973.

Blodgett, Harold W., and Sculley Bradley, eds. *Leaves of Grass, Comprehensive Reader's Edition*. New York: W. W. Norton, 1965.

Brasher, Thomas L. *Whitman as Editor of the Brooklyn Daily Eagle*. Detroit: Wayne State University Press, 1970.

Bucke, Richard M. *Calamus: A Series of Letters Written during the Years 1868–1880 by Walt Whitman to a Young Friend (Peter Doyle)*. Boston: Small, Maynard, 1897.

———. *Walt Whitman*. Philadelphia: David McKay, 1883.

Burroughs, John. *Notes on Walt Whitman, as Poet and Person*. New York, 1867. Reprint, New York: Haskell House, 1971.

———. "Walt Whitman and His 'Drum-Taps.'" *Galaxy* 2 (December 1866): 606–615.

———. *Walt Whitman, a Study*. Boston, 1896. Reprint, New York: AMS Press, 1969.

Cargill, Oscar. *Toward a Pluralistic Criticism*. Carbondale: Southern Illinois University Press, 1965.

Carpenter, Edward. *Days with Walt Whitman*. New York: Macmillan, 1906.

Ceniza, Sherry. "'Being a Woman . . . I Wish to Give My Own View': Some Nineteenth-Century Women's Responses to the 1860 *Leaves of Grass*." In Ezra Greenspan, ed., *The Cambridge Companion to Walt Whitman*. Cambridge: Cambridge University Press, 1995.

Chistova, I. "Turgenev and Whitman." *Walt Whitman Quarterly Review* 13 (Summer/Fall 1995): 68–72.

Consolo, Dominick P., ed. *Walt Whitman, Out of the Cradle Endlessly Rocking*. Merrill Literary Casebook Series. Columbus, Ohio: Charles E. Merrill, 1971.

Donaldson, Thomas. *Walt Whitman, the Man*. London: Gay and Bird, 1897.

Eitner, Walter. *Walt Whitman's Western Jaunt*. Lawrence: Regents Press of Kansas, 1981.

Ellman, Richard. *Oscar Wilde*. New York: Knopf, 1988.

Erkkila, Betsy. *Walt Whitman among the French*. Princeton, N.J.: Princeton University Press, 1980.

Folsom, Ed. *Walt Whitman's Native Representations*. Cambridge: Cambridge University Press, 1994.

———. "The Whitman Recording." *Walt Whitman Quarterly Review* 9 (Spring 1992): 214–216.

Furness, Clifton Joseph. *Walt Whitman's Workshop: A Collection of Unpublished Manuscripts*. New York: Russell & Russell, 1964.

Gilchrist, Anne. "A Woman's Estimate of Walt Whitman." *The Radical* (Boston) 7 (May 1870): 345–359.

Glicksberg, Charles I. *Walt Whitman and the Civil War*. Philadelphia: University of Pennsylvania Press, 1933.

Gohdes, Clarence, and Rollo G. Silver, eds. *Faint Clews & Indirections: Manuscripts of Walt Whitman and His Family*. Durham, N.C.: Duke University Press, 1949.

Golden, Arthur, ed. *Walt Whitman's Blue Book: The 1860–61* Leaves of Grass *Containing His Manuscript and Revisions*. 2 vols. New York: New York Public Library, 1968.

Harned, Thomas, ed. *The Letters of Anne Gilchrist and Walt Whitman*. New York: Doubleday, Doran, 1918.

Hindus, Milton. *Walt Whitman: The Critical Heritage*. New York: Barnes and Noble, 1971.

Holloway, Emory. "Walt Whitman's Visit to the Shakers." *Colophon* (Spring 1933).

————. "Whitman as His Own Press Agent." *American Mercury* 17 (December 1929): 483–485.

————. "Whitman on the War's Finale." *Colophon*, Part 1 (February 1930).

————, ed. *The Uncollected Poetry and Prose of Walt Whitman.* Vol. 2. New York: Doubleday and Co., 1921. Reprint, Gloucester, Mass.: Peter Smith, 1972.

Holloway, Emory, and Ralph Adimari, eds. *New York Dissected.* New York: Rufus Rockwell Wilson, 1936.

Holloway, Emory, and Vernolian Schwarz, eds. *I Sit and Look Out, Editorials from the* Brooklyn Daily Times *by Walt Whitman.* New York: Columbia University Press, 1932. Reprint, New York: AMS Press, 1966.

Hudson, Frederic. *Journalism in the United States, from 1690 to 1872.* New York: Harper & Row, 1969.

Huneker, James G. *Essays by James Huneker.* New York: Charles Scribner's Sons, 1929.

Johnston, John, and J. W. Wallace. *Visits to Walt Whitman in 1890–1891 by Two Lancashire Friends.* London: G. Allen and Unwin, 1917. Reprint, New York: Haskell House, 1970.

Kaplan, Justin. *Walt Whitman: A Life.* New York: Simon and Schuster, 1980.

Keller, Elizabeth L. *Walt Whitman in Mickle Street.* New York: Mitchell Kennerley, 1921.

Kennedy, William S. *Reminiscences of Walt Whitman.* Philadelphia: n.p., 1896.

Killingsworth, M. Jimmie. *Whitman's Poetry of the Body.* Chapel Hill: University of North Carolina Press, 1989.

Krieg, Joann P. "Walt Whitman's Long Island Friend: Elisa Seaman Leggett." *Long Island Historical Journal* (Spring 1997): 223–233.

Leaves of Grass Imprints, American and European Criticisms on "Leaves of Grass." Boston: n.p., 1860.

Leon, Philip. *Walt Whitman and Sir William Osler: A Poet and His Physician.* Toronto, Ontario: ECW Press, 1995.

Loving, Jerome. "'Broadway, the Magnificent!', a Newly Discovered Whitman Essay." *Walt Whitman Quarterly Review* 12 (Spring 1995): 209–216.

————. *Civil War Letters of George Washington Whitman.* Durham, N.C.: Duke University Press, 1975.

————. *Emerson, Whitman, and the American Mind.* Chapel Hill: University of North Carolina Press, 1982.

————. "A Newly Discovered Whitman Poem." *Walt Whitman Quarterly Review* 11 (Winter 1994): 117–122.

————. *Walt Whitman's Champion, William Douglas O'Connor.* College Station: Texas A&M University Press, 1978.

Loving, Jerome, and Alice Lotvin Birney. "'A Young Woman Meets Walt Whitman': Anne Montgomerie Traubel's First Impression of the Poet." *Walt Whitman Quarterly Review* 12 (Fall 1994): 104–105.

Lozynsky, Artem, ed. *The Letters of Dr. Richard Maurice Bucke to Walt Whitman.* Detroit: Wayne State University Press, 1977.

Miller, Edwin Haviland, ed. *A Century of Whitman Criticism.* Bloomington: Indiana University Press, 1969.

————. "The Correspondence of Walt Whitman: A Second Supplement with a Revised Calendar of Letters Written to Whitman." *Walt Whitman Quarterly Review* 8 (Winter/ Spring 1991).

Mitchell, Silas Weir. *When All the Woods Are Green.* New York: Century, 1910.

Molinoff, Katherine. *Some Notes on Whitman's Family.* Brooklyn, N.Y.: Katherine Molinoff, 1941.

————. *An Unpublished Whitman Manuscript: The Record Book of the Smithtown Debating Society, 1837–1838.* New York: Comet Press, 1941.

Morris, Harrison S. *Walt Whitman.* Cambridge: Harvard University Press, 1929.

Murray, Martin G. "'Pete the Great': A Biography of Peter Doyle." *Walt Whitman Quarterly Review* 12 (Summer 1994): 1–51.

Myerson, Joel. *Whitman in His Own Time: A Biographical Chronicle of His Life, Drawn from Recollections, Memoirs, and Interviews by Friends and Associates.* Columbia, S.C.: Omnigraphics, 1991.

————, ed. *The Walt Whitman Archive: A Facsimile of the Poet's Manuscripts.* New York: Garland, 1993.

Peattie, Roger. "Four Letters about Whitman in the Angeli-Dennis Papers." *Walt Whitman Quarterly Review* 12 (Spring 1995): 246–252.

Perry, Bliss. *Walt Whitman, His Life and Work*. Boston: Houghton, Mifflin, 1906.

Price, Kenneth M., ed. *Walt Whitman: The Contemporary Reviews*. New York: Cambridge University Press. 1996.

Reynolds, David S. *Walt Whitman's America*. New York: Knopf, 1995.

Rhys, Ernest. *Everyman Remembers*. New York: Cosmopolitan, 1931.

Rodgers, Cleveland, and John Black, eds. *The Gathering of the Forces*. New York: Putnam's Sons, 1920.

Rossetti Papers, 1868–1870: A Compilation by William Michael Rossetti. London: Sands, 1903.

Rubin, Joseph Jay. *The Historic Whitman*. University Park: Pennsylvania State University Press, 1973.

Rubin, Joseph Jay, and Charles H. Brown. *Walt Whitman of the New York Aurora, Editor at Twenty-Two*. Westport, Conn.: Greenwood Press, 1950.

Rusk, Ralph L. *The Life of Ralph Waldo Emerson*. New York: Charles Scribner's Sons, 1949.

Schmidgall, Gary. *Walt Whitman: A Gay Life*. New York, Dutton, 1997.

Shepard, Odell, ed. *Journals of Bronson Alcott, 1799–1888*. Port Washington, N.Y.: Kennikat Press, 1966.

Shively, Charley. *Calamus Lovers: Walt Whitman's Working Class Camerados*. San Francisco: Sunshine Press, 1987.

—————, ed. *Drum Beats: Walt Whitman's Civil War Boy Lovers*. San Francisco: Sunshine Press, 1989.

Sill, Geoffrey. "Whitman on 'The Black Question': A New Manuscript." *Walt Whitman Quarterly Review* 8 (Fall 1990): 69–75.

Stoker, Bram. *Personal Reminiscences of Henry Irving*. Vol. 2. New York: Macmillan, 1906.

Thoreau, Henry David. *Letters to Various Persons*. Boston: n.p., 1865.

Traubel, Horace, Richard M. Bucke, and Thomas Harned, eds. *In Re Walt Whitman*. Philadelphia: David McKay, 1893.

Trowbridge, John Townsend. *My Own Story*. Boston: Houghton, Mifflin, 1903.

Waldron, Randall H., ed. *Mattie: The Letters of Martha Mitchell Whitman*. New York: New York University Press, 1977.

Warren, James Perrin. "Whitman as Ghostwriter: The Case of *Rambles Among Words*." *Walt Whitman Quarterly Review* 2 (Fall 1984): 22–30.

Warren, Joyce W. *Fanny Fern: An Independent Woman*. New Brunswick, N.J.: Rutgers University Press, 1992.

White, William. "An Unknown Check for Ed Whitman's Board." *Walt Whitman Review* 22 (June 1976): 91.

"Whitman's Disciples." *Walt Whitman Quarterly Review* 14 (Fall 1996/Winter 1997; special double issue).

INDEX

A title index to Walt Whitman's works appears at the end of this index; original titles are listed first, with later changes in parentheses.

Abbott, Dr. Henry, 25
Academy (London), 103, 106
Adams, Charles Francis, 21
Agassiz, Alexander, 82
Aide, Charles Hamilton, 169
Alcott, Amos Bronson, 26, 34, 35, 83, 135
Alcott, Louisa May, 55, 135
Alexander, John W., 130, 151, 171
American, 126, 127, 133
American Anthropometric Society, 178
American Phrenological Journal, 28, 31
American Review, 2
Aristidean, 15, 16
Armory Square Hospital, 51, 52, 53, 54, 57, 62, 153, 175
"Armory Square Hospital Gazette," 68
Arnold, Sir Edwin, 166, 174
Ashton, J. Hubley, 70, 99
Ashton, Mrs. J., 97, 99
Astor, John Jacob, 6
Asylum for the Insane (London, Ontario), 118, 126, 162
Athenaeum, 109
Atlantic Monthly, 44, 47, 73, 86
Augsburg Allgemeine Zeitung, 83

Baker, Nathan M., 162, 164
"Banner at Day-Break," 45
Barbiere di Siviglia, Il, 18
Barnum, P. T., 164
Barrett, Lawrence, 145, 151
Barrett, Wilson, 153
Bartlett, Truman Howe, 132, 133
Baxter, Sylvester, 129, 135, 155
Bayne, Peter, 106, 108
Beecher, Henry Ward, 21
Bellini, Vincenzo, 22
Benedict, Mrs. Newton, 65
Benjamin, Park, 10, 11, 13
Berenson, Bernard, 149
Biachi, Hannibal, 57
Bigelow, John, 119
Blake, Harrison, 35
Blake, William, xix, 81, 83, 87
Bliss, Dr. D. W., 153
Bloomer, Amelia, 35
Boker, George H., 145
Bolton, England, xix, xx, 155, 158, 168, 172, 173, 176
Bonsall, Bartram, 148
Bonsall, Henry L., 104, 105
Booth, Edwin, 147, 150
Booth, Junius Brutus, 147
Boston, 24, 40, 42, 43, 44, 54, 62, 71, 73, 86, 104, 106, 129,

Boston (continued)
131, 132, 133, 134, 135, 136,
140
Boston Courier, 42
Boston Daily Globe, 135
Boston Evening Transcript,
163, 167
Boston Herald, 156, 173
Brenton, James J., 8
Bride of Lammermoor, The, 22
Brignoli, Pasquale, 76, 91, 147
Brinton, Daniel G., 153
Broadway Hospital, 47
Broadway Journal, 16
Broadway Magazine (London), 85
Brooklyn, xvii, 1, 3, 4, 5, 6,
15, 17, 18, 20, 21, 22, 23, 24,
29, 30, 31, 32, 34, 35, 41,
47, 48, 49, 51, 52, 58, 61,
62, 64, 67, 68, 70, 72, 78,
81, 82, 84, 86, 87, 89, 90,
92, 95, 96, 122, 168
Brooklyn Academy of Music,
89
Brooklyn Advertiser, 19
Brooklyn Art Union, 23
Brooklyn City News, 45
Brooklyn Daily Eagle, 2, 16,
17, 18, 19, 20, 50, 51, 64, 84
Brooklyn Daily Standard, 47
Brooklyn Daily Times, 26, 30,
36, 37, 148
Brooklyn Daily Union, 55
Brooklyn Evening Star, 24
Brooklyn Weekly Freeman, 21
Brother Jonathan, 11, 14
Brown, Lewis K., 54, 57, 61
Browning, Deborah Stafford,
150

Bryant, William Cullen, 9, 11,
17, 23, 107, 119
Buchanan, Robert, 94, 110, 112
Bucke, Jessie, 108, 120, 136
Bucke, Dr. Richard Maurice,
xviii, 89, 107, 108, 118, 120,
125, 126, 128, 129, 134, 136,
138, 139, 140, 143, 147, 150,
151, 153, 159, 160, 162, 164,
169, 172, 173, 174, 175; *Walt
Whitman*, 143
"Burial of Sir John Moore at
Corunna, The," 12
Burns, Anthony, 24
Burnside, Ambrose, 62
Burroughs, John, xix, 34, 56,
61, 62, 66, 83, 91, 97, 99,
101, 102, 103, 104, 108, 111,
113, 115, 116, 118, 120, 122,
125, 127, 136, 140, 141, 142,
144, 148, 150, 151, 174, 178;
Birds and Poets, 104, 117
(publ'd.); "The Birds of the
Poet," 100; *Notes on Walt
Whitman, as Poet and Person*, xix, 34, 77 (publ'd.),
83; *Walt Whitman, a Study*,
xix, 77; "Walt Whitman
and His 'Drum-Taps,'" 73
Burroughs, Ursula, 97, 120,
122

Calder, Albert L., 176
Californian, 132
Camden, N.J., xviii, 82, 86,
91, 96, 98, 99, 100, 101, 102,
103, 107, 108, 112, 113, 116,
117, 119, 121, 123, 126, 129,
132, 133, 136, 137, 142, 144,
146, 149, 154, 155, 164, 172

Camden Children's Home, 114

Camden Daily Post, 126, 148, 169

Camden New Republic, 102, 104, 105, 108, 111

Camden's Compliment to Walt Whitman, 165

Campbell Hospital, 50, 51

Carlyle, Thomas, 78

Carnegie, Andrew, 130, 154

Carpenter, Edward, 103, 107, 116, 146, 152, 172

"Carpenter, The," 82

Cattell, Dr., 178

Cattell, Edward, 115, 116

Centennial Exposition, 113, 114

Central Park (New York), 122, 134

Century, 131, 136, 157, 163, 166, 167, 168

Channing, Dr. William, 85

Chapin, William, 73

Chase, Salmon P., 49, 58

"Chats with Walt Whitman," 113

Childs, George W., 112, 121

Chronicle (London), 77

Church, Francis P., 73, 78

Church, William C., 73

Cincinnati Daily Commercial, 38, 41

Clapp, Henry, 38, 41

Clare, Ada. *See* McElheney, Jane

Clark, Edward, 5

Clark, James B., 5

Clay, Henry, 43

Clements, Samuel E., 5

Clifford, Edward, 147

Cold Spring, Long Island, 134

Columbian Magazine, 14, 15

Colyer, Hannah, 24

Colyer, Richard, 24

Commonwealth, 72

Compromise of 1850, 22

Comstock, Anthony, 140

Concord, Mass., 29, 135

Conover, Simon B., 144

Conservator, 170

Contemporary Review (London), 94, 106

Conway, Moncure, 26, 30, 73, 77, 78, 79, 82, 106, 110, 111, 153, 157, 173

Cope's Tobacco Plant, 122, 127

Corning, Rev. J. Leonard, 163

Cosmopolitan Magazine, 120, 157

Costelloe, Benjamin F. C., 147, 149

Cottage Fund, 130, 156

Cox, G. C., 130, 154, 155

Critic, 130, 131, 132, 133, 134, 135, 136, 137, 139, 140, 141, 142, 145, 146, 147, 152, 155, 157, 164, 168, 170

Crystal Palace Exhibition, 25

Curtis, Mrs. C. P., 54

Custer, George Armstrong, 113

Custer's Last Rally, 134

Daily Morning Chronicle, 121

Dana, Charles A., 30

Danites of the Sierras, The, 118

Dark Blue (London), 91

Dartmouth College, 81, 96

Davis, Jefferson, 68

Davis, Mary, 148, 153, 166, 169, 174, 175, 177

Davis, Thomas, 85

"Democratic Art, with Special Reference to Walt Whitman," 168

Democratic Party, 11, 14, 18, 21, 85

Democratic Review. See United States Magazine and Democratic Review

Demokratiske Fremblik, 101

Dercum, Dr., 178

Dial, 138

Dickens, Catherine, 13

Dickens, Charles, 13, 85

Dix Hills, Long Island, 9, 15

Donaldson, Blain, 149

Donaldson, Mary, 149

Donaldson, Thomas, 129, 142, 145, 146, 150, 151

Donizetti, Gaetano, 46, 57, 89, 113

Dowden, Edward, 92, 93, 109

Dowe, Amy, 121

Doyle, Edward, 145

Doyle, Francis M., 91, 92, 94

Doyle, Peter, xix, 61, 66, 67, 81, 84, 85, 87, 88, 89, 90, 91, 92, 94, 95, 97, 98, 99, 100, 101, 102, 104, 105, 107, 108, 112, 114, 117, 122, 124, 126, 130, 145, 146, 149, 162, 174, 175, 179

Dr. North and His Friends, 119

Dracula, 109

Drinkard, Dr. William B., 97, 98

Duckett, William, 150, 152, 154, 155

Dyer, Oliver, 36

Eakins, Thomas, 130, 150, 158, 170, 171, 178

Eastlake, Miss, 153

Eckler, Peter, 67

Eclectic Magazine, 113

Egyptian Museum, 25

Einstein, Edwin, 105, 106

Eldridge, Charles, 42, 48, 57, 97, 99, 100, 101, 106, 114, 150, 166

Ellis, F. S., 93

Emerson, Ralph Waldo, 12, 26, 29, 31, 33, 40, 42, 43, 49, 50, 51, 54, 58, 77, 85, 95, 103, 104, 135, 139

Engineering Record, 169

English Novel, The, 119

Ernani, 75

Essays Speculative and Suggestive, 168

Etienne, Louis, 47

Evans, Frederick W., 24

Everyman Remembers, 157

Eyre, Ellen, 48

Farragut, David G., 90

Fern, Fanny. *See* Parton, Sara

Fields, James T., 86, 125, 132

Fight of a Book for the World, The, xix

"Fleshly School of Poetry, The," 94

For Ide og Virkelighed, 91

Forney, John W., 121, 123, 124, 137

Fortnightly Review (London), 73, 77, 79, 86, 156

Foster, Charles H., 62

Fowler, Lorenzo, 20, 28

Fowler, Orson, 21, 28

Fowler & Wells, 27, 28, 30, 32, 37

Francesca da Rimini, 145

Fredricksburg, Va., xviii, 40

Free-Soil, 18, 21, 35, 69, 124

Freiligrath, Ferdinand, 83

Fritzinger, Harry, 175

Fritzinger, Walt Whitman, 175

Fritzinger, Warren (Warry), 148, 166, 168, 172, 175, 177, 178

Fugitive Slave Law, 22

Fulton (steamship), 4

Furness, Frank, 121

Furness, Horace H., 150

Galaxy, 73, 78, 80, 85, 88, 92, 98, 104, 116

Gardner, Alexander, 55, 87

Garfield, James A., 62, 133, 135

Garland, Hamlin, 152, 163

Geist, J. M. W., 123

Gentleman's Magazine (London), 106

Gilchrist, Alexander, xix, 81

Gilchrist, Anne B., xix, 81, 87, 88, 93, 94, 95, 104, 105, 107, 110, 113, 114, 115, 116, 117, 119, 123, 129, 137, 141, 149, 151

Gilchrist, Beatrice, 113, 118, 135

Gilchrist, Grace, 113, 123

Gilchrist, Herbert, 113, 116, 117, 118, 130, 149, 151, 156, 168, 171

Gilchrist, Percy, 113.

Gilder, Jeanette Leonard, 131

Gilder, Richard Watson, 118, 119, 127, 131

Goodenough, Margaret, 146

Good Gray Poet, The, xix, 61, 71 (publ'd.), 77, 83

"Gospel According to Walt Whitman, The" (Stevenson), 120

"Gospel According to Walt Whitman, The" (Wilde), 164

Gosse, Edmund, 148

Gottschalk, Louis Moreau, 38

Grant, Nelly, 102

Grant, Ulysses S., 63, 69, 86, 94, 101, 102, 125

Greek Slave, The, 17

Greene, Albert G., 9

Greenport, Long Island, xvii, 9, 17, 23, 30, 170

Grisi, Giulia, 24, 97

Griswold, Rufus, 10, 31

Gurowski, Count Adam, 72

Gutekunst, Frederick, 165

Hale, Edward Everett, 32

Hapgood, Lyman S., 50, 53, 58

Harlan, James, 70, 71

Harleigh Cemetery, 158, 166, 172, 179

Harned, Thomas B., xviii,

Harned, Thomas B.
(continued)
129, 155, 157, 161, 162, 172,
175, 177
Harper's Monthly, 101, 102,
133, 146, 148
*Harper's New Monthly Mag-
azine*, 164
Harper's Weekly Magazine,
42, 46, 149, 166
Harrison, Gabriel, 24
Harte, Bret, 88
Hartmann, Carl Sadakichi,
165
Harvard University, 133
Haskell, Mr. and Mrs. S. B.,
54
Hawthorne, Nathaniel, 11,
132, 135
Hay, John, 56
Hempstead, Long Island, 7
Heyde, Charles L., xvii, 23,
50, 170
Hicks, Elias, xvii, 5
Hine, Charles, 44, 92
Holmes, Oliver Wendell, 135,
150
Hoor, Ebenezer R., 86
Hospital Sketches, 55
Hotten, John Camden, 82, 83
Howells, William Dean, 27,
38, 71, 132, 164
Hubbard, Elbert, 144
Huneker, James Gibbons, 117
Hunkers, 14, 15
Huntington, Long Island,
xvii, 1, 2, 8, 168

Ingemann, Bernhard Severin,
22

Ingersoll, Robert, 107, 125,
126, 141, 158, 168, 169, 178
Irving, Henry, 146, 149
Ives, Percy, 127

Jackson, Andrew, 6
Jamaica Academy, 9
James, Henry, 71, 135, 152
Jefferson, Thomas, 97
Johnson, Andrew, 69
Johnson, John Newton, 155
Johnston, Alma Calder, 119
Johnston, Dr. John, xix, 155,
158, 168, 173
Johnston, John H., 107, 111,
114, 115, 116, 117, 118, 119,
120, 122, 123, 125, 128, 134,
136, 142, 149
Johnston, John R., 115

Kansas Magazine, 95
Kansas-Nebraska Act, 124
Keller, Elizabeth L., 175, 176
Kellogg, Clara Louise, 57, 89
Kennedy, William Sloane,
xix, 125, 127, 132, 148, 155,
167
Kilgore, Damon, 127
King, Preston, 51
Kings County Lunatic Asy-
lum, 64, 88
Kinnear, Dr., 157
Kossuth, Louis, 23

La Favorita, 113
Lafayette, Marquis de, 4
Laforgue, Jules, 154
Lanier, Sidney, 119, 137
Lathrop, George Parsons, 132
Lay, Tasker, 145, 146

Leaves of Grass: The Poems of Walt Whitman (Rhys), 157

Lee, John Fitzgerald, 137

Lee, Robert E., 53, 67

Leech, Abraham, 10

Lefrone, Charles, 89

Leggett, Elisa Seaman, 127

Lewis, Henry, 54

Life Illustrated, 24, 30, 31, 32, 34

Lincoln, Abraham, 41, 46, 53, 56, 61, 67, 68, 70, 107, 160, 167; "Death of Abraham Lincoln" (Whitman's lecture), 118, 119, 122, 125, 129, 132, 151, 152, 154, 167

Lincoln, Mary Todd, 68

Lind, Jenny, 24

Linda di Chamounix, 46

Linton, William J., 103

Lippincott's Monthly Magazine, 73, 104, 157, 167, 169, 171

Literary World, 125

Little Bay Side, Long Island, 9, 11

Little Journey to the Home of Whitman, A, 144

London, Ontario, xviii, 108, 118, 126, 144

London Advertiser (Ontario), 126, 150

London Daily News, 110, 111

Longaker, Dr. Daniel, 174, 178

Longfellow, Henry Wadsworth, 11, 35, 112, 131, 132, 135, 139, 146

Longfellow, Samuel, 35

Long Island Democrat, 8, 9, 10

Long Islander, 8, 13

Long Island Patriot, 5, 6

Long Island Rail Road, 17, 24

Long Island Star, 6, 7, 16

Long Swamp, Long Island, 7

"Love and Death," 95

Lovering, Henry B., 153

Lowell, James Russell, 42, 154, 159, 173

Lucrezia Borgia, 57

Lung, Mr. & Mrs., 128

Magazine of Art, 162

Mario, Giovanni, 24, 97

Marston, George, 140

Martí, Jose, 154

Martin, E. K., 123

Marvin, James B., 105, 112, 131

Mazzoleni, Francesco, 57

McAlister, Dr. Alexander, 174, 177, 178

McClure, J. F., 19

McClure's Magazine, 156, 167

McElheney, Jane (Ada Clare), 38

McKay, David, 141, 161, 163, 172

Meade, George, 53, 69

Medora, Giuseppina, 57

Merrill, Stuart, 154

Metropolitan Museum of Art, 171

Meyerbeer, Giacomo, 91

Millet, Jean-François, 133

Milnes, Richard Monckton, 106

Mitchell, Dr. S. Weir, 107, 118, 119

Modjeska, Helena, 119

Moffit, Eva, 134

Morris, Harrison S., 161

Morse, William Sidney, 121, 130, 156

Mount Lebanon (N.Y.) Shaker Community, 24

Mulvaney, John, 134

Munson's Magazine, 171

Munyon's Illustrated World, 167, 169

Murray, Samuel, 171, 178

Musgrove, William A., 162

Nación, La, 154

Nash, Michael, 105

National Industrial Exhibition, 93, 108, 110

National Teachers Reception, 123

National Theater, 75

Nature, 135

"Nature and the Powers of the Poet," 12

New Eclectic Magazine, 83

New Mirror, 15

New Orleans, 19, 20

New Orleans Daily Crescent, 19, 20

New Orleans Picayune, 20, 153

New Quarterly (London), 120

New York (Manhattan), 1, 5, 6, 7, 10, 11, 12, 13, 14, 15, 16, 19, 20, 21, 22, 23, 25, 27, 30, 31, 32, 34, 35, 36, 37, 41, 43, 45, 46, 47, 48, 51, 52, 56, 62, 63, 64, 68, 70, 74, 76, 77, 78, 84, 85, 90, 91, 92, 96, 97, 105, 111, 119, 120, 122, 123, 127, 134, 136, 138, 151, 154, 160, 171

New York Academy of Music, 46, 57, 97

New York Aurora, 8, 12

New York Criterion, 31

New York Daily Graphic, 98, 101, 102, 103, 160

New York Democrat, 14

New York Evening Post, 11, 21, 23, 102, 119

New York Evening Tattler, 13

New York Evening Telegram, 176

New York Herald, 48, 99, 131, 157, 159, 160, 161, 162, 165, 170

New York Leader, 46, 47

New York Ledger, 32

New York Morning Journal, 168

New York New World, 10, 13

New York Sun, 22, 105, 167

New York Sunday Courier, 42

New York Times, 45, 51, 54, 55, 64, 66, 67, 74, 76, 148

New York Tribune, 22, 27, 30, 31, 70, 78, 109, 110, 111, 113, 120, 123, 134, 140, 149, 160

New York Tribune Supplement, 22

New York Washingtonian and Organ, 14

New York World, 165

Nilsson, Christine, 91

Nineteenth Century, 149

Noel, Roden, 91

Norma, 97

North American Review, 32, 131, 141, 151, 152, 153, 169, 171

Norton, Charles Eliot, 30

Norwich, Long Island, 7
Nouvelle Revue, La, 161

O'Connor, Ellen Tarr Calder
    (Nellie), 43, 50, 51, 55, 71,
    78, 97, 101, 102, 143, 166,
    173, 176
O'Connor, William Douglas,
    xix, 40, 43, 48, 50, 55, 61,
    63, 64, 65, 70, 73, 74, 76,
    77, 78, 79, 82, 87, 88, 90,
    96, 99, 100, 101, 107, 111,
    112, 122, 129, 130, 139, 140,
    141, 143, 145, 150, 153, 157,
    158, 164, 166, 174
O'Donovan, William, 171, 178
O'Grady, Standish James, 106
Old Settlers of Kansas Com-
    mittee, 124
Olmsted, Frederick Law, 122
Once a Week, 176
O'Reilly, John Boyle, 133
Osgood, James R., 133, 138,
    139
Osler, Dr. William, 150, 164
Ottinger, G. M., 122
Outing, 149
Overland Monthly, 88

Paine, Thomas, xvii, 116, 173
Pall Mall Gazette (London),
    149, 162, 164
Parepa-Rosa, Euphrosyne, 76
Parker, Erastus O., 73
Parnassus, 104
Parton, James, 26, 36, 87
Parton, Sara (Fanny Fern),
    26, 32
Patti, Carlotta, 97
Paumanok, 23, 24

Peabody, George, 88
Perry, Commodore Matthew
    C., 45
Pfaff, Charles, 37, 134, 167
Pfaff's, 27, 37, 38, 48, 105,
    128, 134
Philadelphia, 109, 112, 113,
    114, 115, 116, 117, 118, 119,
    121, 123, 125, 127, 128,
    129, 132, 141, 142, 145,
    147, 148, 151, 152, 153,
    156, 158, 160, 167, 168,
    169, 173, 174, 178
Philadelphia Academy, 113
Philadelphia Athletics, 70
Philadelphia Press, 125, 126,
    147, 148, 152
Philadelphia Public Ledger,
    167
Philadelphia Times, 121
Pierce, Franklin, 32
Pilot, The, 133
Poe, Edgar Allan, 16, 105
Poems of Walt Whitman
    (Rossetti), 81, 82, 83
"Poètes modernes de
    l'Amérique, Walt Whit-
    man," 161
"Poetry of Democracy: Walt
    Whitman," 92
Poliuto, 89
Pond, James, 174
Powers, Hiram, 17
Price, Abigail (Abby), 27, 35,
    72, 73, 76, 84, 134
Price, Edmund, 73, 134
Progress, 121
Putnam's Magazine, 30, 82

Quarter Master's Hospital, 72

Radical, 88
Rand, Avery & Co., 135
Rawlins, John, 87
Raymond, Henry J., 74
Redfield, J. S., 90
Red Jacket, 147
Redpath, James, 54, 55, 105
Reed, Dr. & Mrs. T. K., 139
Rees Welsh & Co., 141
Reitzel, W. W., 123
Reminiscences of Walt Whitman, xix
Repplier, Agnes, 174
Republican Party, 49, 57
Revue Européenne, La, 47

Rhys, Ernest, 157
Riley, William H., 121
Ritter, Frederick Louis, 122
Robert le Diable, 91
Roe, Charles A., 9, 11
Rolleston, T. W. H., 137, 146
Rome, Andrew, 173, 174
Rome, James, 173
Rome Brothers, 28, 30
Romeo and Juliet, 135
Rossetti, Dante Gabriel, 77, 94
Rossetti, William Michael, 77, 78, 79, 80, 81, 82, 84, 87, 88, 92, 93, 95, 104, 106, 109, 110, 111, 112, 141, 152
Rossi, Ernesto, 135
Rossini, Gioacchino, 18
Round Table, 71
Rover, 14
Rowley, Charles, 154
Ruskin, John, 121
Russell, Dr. L. B., 54

Saint-Gaudens, Augustus, 154
Saintsbury, George, 103
Salesman, 23
Salesman and Traveller's Directory for Long Island, 23
Sanborn, Franklin B., 71, 111, 135
Sargent, Mrs. John T., 132
Sarony, Napoleon, 120, 138
Sarrazin, Gabriel, 161
Saturday Evening Post, 127
Saturday Press, 38, 41, 42, 44, 45, 71
Saturday Review (London), 110
Sawyer, Thomas P., 52
Schiller, Johann, 109
Schmidt, Rudolf, 91, 101
Scott, Sir Walter, 7, 22
Scovel, James Matlack, 104, 115, 144, 155
Scribner's Monthly, 100, 118, 127
Seas and Lands, 166
Selected Poems, 176
Seward, William H., 49
Shaw, Quincy, 133
Sheridan, Philip, 162
Sherman, William Tecumseh, 69
Shivers, Dr. George Henry, 151
"Shooting Niagara: And After?," 78
Sierra Grande Mines, 143
Skinner, Charles M., 148
"Sleeptalker, The," 22
Smith, Alys, 149
Smith, Edgar M., 134

Smith, Hannah Whitall, 142, 172

Smith, Logan Pearsall, 149

Smith, Mary Whitall, 142, 146, 149, 172

Smith, Robert Pearsall, 129, 142, 144, 145, 172

Smithtown, Long Island, 7

Society of Old Brooklynites, 128

Somnanbula, La, 57

Songs Before Sunrise, 92

Southern Literary Messenger, 46

Southold, Long Island, 10

Spooner, Alden, 6, 16

Spooner, Edwin B., 16

Springfield Republican, 102, 104, 111, 140

St. Louis Post-Dispatch, 124

St. Marie, Henry, 76

Stafford, Elmer, 116

Stafford, Eva Westcott, 147, 167

Stafford, George, xx, 107, 111, 112, 130, 145

Stafford, George Westcott, 167

Stafford, Harry, xx, 111, 112, 113, 114, 115, 116, 117, 120, 121, 123, 127, 129, 130, 131, 138, 142, 144, 147, 151, 153, 154, 162, 163, 164, 167, 170, 174, 175

Stafford, Susan, xx, 107, 111, 112, 130, 131, 145, 175

Stanbery, Henry, 73

Stanton, Edwin, 64

"Star-Spangled Banner, The," 17

Statesman, 14

Stedman, Edmund Clarence, 127, 176

Stevens, Oliver, 138

Stevenson, Robert Louis, 120, 152

Stoddard, Joseph M., 167

Stoddard, Richard Henry, 71

Stoker, Abraham (Bram), 109, 146

"Study of Walt Whitman, The Poet of Modern Democracy," 91

"Study of Whitman, A," 132

Sumner, Charles, 49, 51

Surratt, John H., 76

Sutton, Henry, 17

Swinburne, Algernon Charles, 81, 83, 92, 130, 138, 156

Swinton, John, 35, 38, 66, 111, 153

Swinton, William, 39

Symonds, John Addington, 84, 94, 95, 152, 156, 158, 168

Taney, Roger B., 51

Tarrytown Sunnyside Press, 125

Taylor, Bayard, 110, 112, 113, 119

Taylor, Father Edward, 43

Taylor, Zachary, 33

Tennyson, Alfred, Lord, 31, 81, 91, 95, 97, 102, 104, 106, 121, 149, 153, 157, 172, 173

Terry, Ellen, 148

Thayer, Dr. Samuel, 86

Thayer, William, 42

Thayer & Eldridge, 40, 45

Thompson, "Billy," 155, 161

Thoreau, Henry David, 26, 34, 35, 135

Three Tales, 166, 174

"To Walt Whitman" (Miller), 116

"To Walt Whitman in America" (Swinburne), 92

Traubel, Anne Montgomerie, 159, 171, 179

Traubel, Horace, ix, xii, xviii, xix, xx, 25, 31, 41, 79, 80, 137, 138, 153, 158, 159, 160, 162, 163, 164, 165, 169, 170, 171, 172, 173, 174, 175, 176, 177, 178

Trimming Square, Long Island, 9

Trinity College (Dublin), 137

Trovatore, Il, 57, 91

Trowbridge, John Townsend, 34, 40, 43, 58

Truth, 171

Tufts College, 81, 101, 102

Turgenev, Ivan, 97

Twain, Mark, 130, 150, 156

Tyndale, Hector, 36

Tyndale, Sarah, 26, 35, 36, 37

Union Magazine of Literature and Art, 20

United States Magazine and Democratic Review, 2, 8, 11, 12, 13, 15, 31

University of Dublin, 92

Van Buren, Martin, 1, 10, 21

Van Nostrand, Ansel (brother-in-law), xvii, 9

Van Velsor, Cornelius (grand-father), xvii, 7

Verdi, Giuseppi, 57, 75, 91

Visits to Walt Whitman in 1890–1891, xix

Wainwright, Marie, 145

Wallace, J. W., xix, xx, 155, 159, 173, 174

"Walt Whitman, A Brooklyn Boy," 30

"Walt Whitman, A Visit to the Good Gray Poet," 111

"Walt Whitman" (Freiligrath), 83

"Walt Whitman, His Life, His Poetry, Himself," 104

"Walt Whitman: Is He Persecuted?," 111

"Walt Whitman. Notes of a Conversation with the Good Gray Poet . . .," 165

"Walt Whitman" (Stedman), 127

Walt Whitman, the Man, 142

"Walt Whitman, The Poet of Joy," 106

"Walt Whitman as I Knew Him," 104

"Walt Whitman in Camden," 149

"Walt Whitman's Actual American Position," 108

"Walt Whitman's Life," 167

Walt Whitman Society, 165

Washington, D.C., 47, 51, 54, 55, 58, 61, 62, 65, 67, 68,

69, 70, 72, 73, 75, 84, 85, 90, 95, 97, 99, 100, 105, 121, 128, 157

Washington, George, 12, 72, 148

Washingtonian, 13

Washington Nationals, 70

Washington Saturday Evening Visitor, 88

Washington Star, 86, 124

Washington Sunday Chronicle, 87

Waters, George W., 117

Wells, Samuel R., 27, 32

West Hills, Long Island, 1, 2, 10, 24, 134

West Jersey Press, 106, 108, 109

Westminster Review (London), 92

When All the Woods Are Green, 119

Whitestone, Long Island, 10

Whitman, Andrew (nephew), 84

Whitman, Andrew Jackson (brother), xviii, 4, 14, 40, 41, 48, 50, 56, 58, 59, 81

Whitman, Edward (Ed, Eddie; brother), xviii, 7, 32, 37, 50, 59, 69, 76, 81, 86, 87, 96, 97, 98, 100, 126, 132, 146, 150, 159, 162, 169, 175

Whitman, George Washington (brother), xviii, 5, 7, 14, 37, 40, 46, 47, 48, 49, 51, 56, 58, 59, 61, 62, 63, 65, 66, 67, 68, 69, 70, 76, 81, 82, 86, 91, 92, 96, 97, 99, 100, 107, 114, 115, 117, 126, 128, 132, 146, 150, 175, 176, 178

Whitman, Hannah Brush (grandmother), xvii, 3

Whitman, Hannah Louisa (sister), xvii, 3, 23, 50, 59, 70, 86, 96, 159, 162, 170, 176

Whitman, Jesse (brother), xvii, 2, 3, 41, 50, 54, 55, 59, 64, 69, 81, 87, 88

Whitman, Jesse (grandfather), xvii, 1

Whitman, Jessie Louisa (niece), 53, 55, 113, 114, 117, 118, 119, 123, 144, 147, 162, 169, 170, 174, 176

Whitman, Louisa Orr Haslam (sister-in-law), xviii, 81, 82, 91, 96, 99, 100, 107, 110, 114, 115, 117, 120, 124, 126, 128, 132, 133, 146, 150, 162, 175, 176, 178

Whitman, Louisa Van Velsor (mother), xvii, 1, 2, 3, 20, 32, 35, 37, 38, 49, 50, 52, 53, 54, 55, 56, 59, 61, 63, 65, 70, 72, 74, 76, 77, 81, 84, 86, 87, 89, 95, 96, 97, 98, 99, 101, 117, 132

Whitman, Mannahatta (Hattie; niece), 50, 53, 113, 114, 117, 118, 119, 123, 129, 144, 147, 152

Whitman, Martha Emma Mitchell (Mattie; sister-in-law), 37, 50, 53, 77, 81, 82, 85, 95, 96, 98, 101

Whitman, Mary Elizabeth
Van Nostrand (sister), xvii,
3, 9, 14, 17, 30, 38, 159, 162,
175
Whitman, Nancy (sister-in-
law), xviii, 50, 84
Whitman, Naomi (Amy)
Williams (grandmother),
xviii, 4
Whitman, Thomas Jefferson
(Jeff; brother), xviii, 6, 14,
19, 20, 37, 41, 50, 55, 56,
58, 63, 69, 74, 75, 76, 77,
81, 82, 85, 86, 95, 98, 100,
102, 107, 113, 114, 124, 132,
138, 142, 143, 147, 152, 159,
161, 164, 169
Whitman, Walter, Sr., xvii, 1,
2, 3, 15, 26, 29, 173, 174
Whitman, Walter Orr
(nephew), xviii, 105, 107,
113
Whittaker, Daniel, 111
Whittier, John Greenleaf, 11,
150, 157
Wilde, Oscar, 129, 137, 138,
140, 164
Wilhelm, Kaiser of Germany,
160
Wilkins, Edward, 162, 163,
164, 166
Williams, Francis H., 145
Williams, Talcott, 148, 149
Wilmot Proviso, 18
Wilson, John L., 120
Wistar Institute of Anatomy
and Biology, 178
*With Walt Whitman in Cam-
den*, 161

Wolfe, Charles, 12
"Woman's Estimate of Walt
Whitman, A," xix, 88
Woodbury, Long Island, 10
Worthington, Erastus, 6
Worthington, Richard, 45,
127, 134
Wright, Frances, xvii
Wright, Silas, 14
Wroth, Caroline, 133

Young, John Russell, 174
Youth's Companion, 171

Title Index

"Abraham Lincoln, Born
Feb. 12, 1809," 160
After All, Not to Create Only,
108
"After All, Not to Create
Only" ("Song of the Expo-
sition"), 93, 108, 110
"After the Dazzle of Day," 160
"After the Supper and Talk,"
157
"Ah, Not This Granite, Dead
and Cold" ("Washington's
Monument, February,
1885"), 148
"America," 123, 160
"American National Litera-
ture," 171
American Primer, An, 25
"American War, The," 109
"Angel of Tears, The," 13
"Army and Hospital Cases,"
163

"Arrow-Tip" ("The Half-Breed: A Tale of the Western Frontier"), 15
"Art and Artists," 23
"Art-Music and Heart-Music," 16
As a Strong Bird on Pinions Free, 91, 95, 97, 108
"As a Strong Bird on Pinions Free" ("Thou Mother with Thy Equal Brood"), 96
"As I Ebb'd with the Ocean of Life" ("Bardic Symbols"), 42, 44
"As I Sit Writing Here," 161
"As One by One Withdraw the Lofty Actors" ("Death of General Grant"), 149
"As the Greek's Signal Flame," 157

"Backward Glance on My Own Road, A" ("A Backward Glance O'er Travel'd Roads"), 145
"Beat! Beat! Drums!," 40, 46, 97
"Bervance: or, Father and Son," 11
"Blood-Money," 22
"Booth and 'The Bowery,'" 149
"Boy Lover, The," 15
"Bravest Soldiers, The," 160
"Bravo, Paris Exposition!," 166
"Broadway, the Magnificent!," 34
"Broadway Pageant, A," 45

"Broadway Revisited," 123
"Brooklynania," 47
"Brother of All, with Outstretched Hand" ("Outlines for a Tomb"), 90
"Bumble-Bees and Bird Music," 133
"By Emerson's Grave," 140

"Calamus," 37, 44, 75, 95, 158, 168
"Calming Thought of All, The," 161
"Carol Closing Sixty-nine, A," 161
"Carol of Harvest, for 1867, A" ("Return of the Heroes, The"), 78
"Chant of National Feuillage, A," 42
"Children of Adam," 44, 75, 139, 141. *See also* "Enfans d'Adam"
"Child's Champion, The," 11
"Child's Reminiscence, A," 27, 38, 41, 44. *See also* "Out of the Cradle Endlessly Rocking" and "A Word Out of the Sea"
"Christmas Garland, A," 103
"City Notes in August," 134
"City Photographs," 47
"Columbian's Song, The," 10
"Commonplace, The," 171
Complete Poetry and Prose of Walt Whitman, 1855–1888, 158, 163 (publ'd.)
"Contralto Voice, A," 125

"Crossing Brooklyn Ferry," 33, 44

"Dalliance of the Eagles, The," 127, 139
"Darest Thou Now O Soul," 85
"Dead Emperor, The," 160
"Dead Tenor, The," 76, 147
"Death and Burial of McDonald Clarke, The," 12
"Death-Bouquet, A," 167
"Death in the School-Room (A Fact)," 11
"Death of Carlyle," 131
"Death of Longfellow," 139
"Death of the Nature-Lover" ("My Departure"), 14
"Death Sonnet for Custer, A" ("From Far Dakota's Cañons"), 113
"Democracy," 78, 80, 81
Democratic Vistas, 78, 81, 90, 91 (publ'd.), 92, 95, 101, 108, 141
"Dirge for Two Veterans," 122
"Dismantled Ship, The," 160, 162
"Drum-Taps," 90
Drum-Taps, 49, 51, 61, 63, 64, 67, 69 (publ'd.), 70, 71, 72, 74, 75
"Dumb Kate," 14
"Dusky Grisette, A," 19
"Dying Veteran, The," 156

"Each Has His Grief," 11, 13
"Edgar Poe's Significance," 140

"Effects of Lightning, The," 8
"Eidolons," 109
"Eighteen Sixty-One," 47
"Eighteenth Presidency, The," 26, 32
"Emerson's Books (the Shadows of Them)," 125
"End of All, The" ("The Winding Up"), 10
"Enfans d'Adam," 43, 44, 75. *See also* "Children of Adam"
"Ethiopia Commenting" ("Ethiopia Saluting the Colors"), 85

"Fabulous Episode, A," 146
"Fallen Angel, The" ("The Punishment of Pride"), 11, 13
"Fame's Vanity" ("Ambition"), 9, 11
"Fancies at Navesink," 149
"Fifty-First New York City Veterans," 63
"First Dandelion, The," 160
"First Spring Day on Chestnut Street," 121
"Five Thousand Poems," 155
"For Queen Victoria's Birthday," 167
"Fortunes of a Country Boy," 17
Franklin Evans, or, the Inebriate, 2, 13, 17
Franklin Evans or the Merchant's Clerk: A Tale of the Times, 13
"From Montauk Point," 160
"From Washington," 55

"Gathering the Corn," 120

"Going Somewhere," 129, 157

Good-bye My Fancy, 120, 159, 168, 169, 172 (publ'd.), 176

"Great Army of the Sick: Military Hospitals in Washington," 51

"Great Washington Hospital, The," 51

"Halcyon Days," 159

"House of Friends, The" ("Wounded in the House of Friends"), 22

"How I Get Around at 60, and Take Notes," 130, 132, 133, 134, 137, 141

"How I made a Book— or tried to," 152

"Human Voice, The" ("The Perfect Voice"), 69

"If I Should Need to Name, O Western World" ("Election Day, November, 1884"), 147

"Inca's Daughter, The," 9

"Indian Bureau Reminiscence, An," 75, 146

"Inscriptions" ("One's-Self I Sing"), 75

"In the Wake Following" ("After the Sea-Ship"), 103

"I Saw in Louisiana a Live-Oak Growing," 44

"I Sing the Body Electric," 44, 139

"Kiss to the Bride, A," 102

"Last Invocation, The," 85

"Last Loyalist, The," 13

"Last of the Sacred Army, The," 12

Leaves of Grass, 18, 22, 23, 25, 26, 27 (1st ed. publ'd.), 28, 30, 31, 32, 33 (2nd ed. publ'd.), 34, 35, 36, 37, 38, 40, 41, 42, 43–44 (3rd ed. publ'd.), 45, 58, 64, 65, 70, 73, 74, 75 (4th ed. publ'd.), 77, 78, 79, 80, 81, 82, 83, 84, 87, 88, 90 (5th ed. publ'd.), 91, 92, 93, 94, 95, 97, 103, 107, 108, 109, 111, 112, 119, 122, 129, 131, 134, 136 (6th ed. publ'd.), 137, 138, 139, 140, 141, 143, 146, 155, 157, 159, 164, 168, 169, 172, 173, 176 ("death bed ed.")

"Letter," 67

"Letter from Washington," 55

"Life," 161

"Life and Death," 161

"Little Bells Last Night" ("I Heard You Solemn-Sweet Pipes of the Organ"), 47

"Little Sleighers, A Sketch of a Winter Morning on the Battery," 15

"Live Oak with Moss," 37, 44

"Longings for Home" ("O Magnet-South"), 46

"Love of Eris: A Spirit Record," 14

"Love That Is Hereafter, The," 9

"Madman, The," 14

"Man-of-War Bird, The," 109

"Mannahatta," 160

"Memoranda During the War," 108

Memoranda During the War, 50, 55, 67, 82, 101, 105 (publ'd.), 141

"Memorandum at a Venture, A," 141

"Mississippi at Midnight, The," 20

"My Boys and Girls," 7, 14

"My Canary Bird," 148, 160

"My Departure" ("Death of the Nature-Lover"), 9, 14

"My Picture-Gallery," 127

"My 71st Year," 166

"Mystic Trumpeter, The," 95, 153

"Nay, Tell Me Not To-day the Publish'd Shame," 98

"New Orleans in 1848," 153

"New York Dissected," 31

"Noiseless Patient Spider, A," 85

"North Star to a South, A" ("A Christmas Greeting"), 167

"Not Meagre, Latent Boughs Alone," 157

"November Boughs," 157

November Boughs, 130, 142, 151, 152, 158, 162, 163 (publ'd.), 164, 176

"O Captain! My Captain," 70, 71, 154

"Ode.— By Walter Whitman," 17

"Of That Blithe Throat of Thine," 148

"Of the black question," 80

"Old Actors, Singers, Shows, & in New York," 171

"Old Age Echoes," 171

"Old Age's Lambent Peaks," 163

"Old Age's Ship and Crafty Death's," 167

"Old Bowery, The," 24

"Old Brooklyn Days," 168

"Old Chants," 171

"Old Ireland," 47

"Old Man's Rejoinder, An," 168

"Old Man's Thought of School, An," 103

"Old Poets— and Other Things," 169

"Old Salt Kassabone," xvii

"On, On the Same, Ye Jocund Twain!," 168

"Only a New Ferry Boat," 137

"Opera, The," 75

"Orange Buds by Mail from Florida," 160

"Orbic Literature," 91

"O Star of France," 92

"Our Brooklyn Boys in the War," 50

"Our Eminent Visitors (Past, Present, and Future)," 145

"Our Future Lot" ("Time to Come"), 8

"Out from Behind This Mask," 109

"Out of May's Shows Selected," 161

"Out of the Cradle Endlessly

Rocking," 38, 100. *See also*
"A Child's Reminiscence"
and "A Word Out of
the Sea"
"Over and Through the Bur-
ial Chant" ("Interpolation
Sounds"), 162
"Ox-Tamer, The," 103

"Pallid Wreath, The," 170
"Passage to India," 86, 88, 90
Passage to India, 81, 88, 90
(publ'd.), 91, 109
"Patroling Barnegut," 126,
133
"Paumanok," 160
"Pensive and Faltering," 85
"Personalism," 83, 91
"Pictures," 38
"Pioneers! O Pioneers!," 69
"Play-Ground, The," 17
"Poem for Asia . . . ," 33
"Poem of Apparitions in
Boston" ("Boston Ballad,
A,") 24
"Poem of Walt Whitman,"
33. *See also* "Song of
Myself" and "Walt
Whitman"
"Poetry of the Future, The"
("Poetry To-day in Amer-
ica—Shakspere—The
Future"), 131
"Poet's Recreation, A," 120
"Poet's Western Trip, A," 124
"Prairie Sunset, A," 160
"Prayer of Columbus," 81,
101, 102
"Proto-Leaf," 44
"Proud Music of the Sea-
Storm" ("Proud Music of
the Storm"), 85, 86, 90

"Queries to My Seventieth
Year," 161

Rambles Among Words, 39
"Real Summer Openings,"
123
"Red Jacket (from Aloft),"
147
"Resurgemus," 22, 28
"Reuben's Last Wish," 13
"Revenge and Requital; A
Tale of a Murderer Es-
caped" ("One Wicked
Impulse!"), 15
"Richard Parker's Widow," 15
"Riddle Song, A," 125
"Robert Burns," 142
"Robert Burns As Poet and
Person," 152

"Sea Captains, Young or Old"
("Songs for All Seas, All
Ships"), 98
Sequel to Drum-Taps, 61, 70
(publ'd.), 74, 75
"Shadow and the Light of a
Young Man's Soul," 20
"Shakspere-Bacon's Cipher,"
120, 157
"Ship Ahoy!," 171
"Shirval: A Tale of Jerusa-
lem," 15
"Sight in Camp in the Day-
Break Gray and Dim, A,"
49
"Singer in the Prison, The,"
88, 90

"Singing Thrush, The" ("Wandering at Morn"), 98

"Sketch, A," 13

"Slang in America," 151

"Slave Trade, The," 32

"Sleepers, The," 28

"Sobbing of the Bells, The," 62, 135

"So Long!," 136

"Some Diary Notes at Random," 151

"Some Fact-Romances," 16

"Some War Memoranda Jotted Down at the Time," 153

"Song for Certain Congressmen" ("Dough-Face Song"), 21, 22

"Song of Myself," 28, 136. *See also* "Poem of Walt Whitman" and "Walt Whitman"

"Song of the Exposition," 94, 108

"Song of the Redwood-Tree," 101

"Song of the Universal," 102

"Soon Shall the Winter's Foil Be Here," 160

"Spain, 1873–74," 98

"Spanish Lady, The," 9

Specimen Days & Collect, 49, 50, 51, 55, 67, 112, 129, 141 (publ'd.), 142, 163

"Spirit That Form'd This Scene," 135

"Spontaneous Me," 139

"Summer Days in Canada," 126

"Summer's Invocation, A" ("Thou Orb Aloft Full-Dazzling"), 133

"Sun-Down Papers," 8

"Sun-Down Poem," 33, 44. *See also* "Crossing Brooklyn Ferry"

"There Was a Child Went Forth," 136

"These May Afternoons," 123

"Thought of Columbus, A," 176

"Thought on Shakspere, A," 152

"Thoughts," 42

"Thou Vast Rondure, Swimming in Space," 86

"Three Young Men's Deaths," 122

"Time to Come" ("Our Future Lot"), 12

"'Tis But Ten Years Since," 101

"To a Common Prostitute," 139

"To a Locomotive in Winter," 109

"Today and Thee," 161

"Tomb Blossoms, The," 12

"To the Sun-Set Breeze," 169

"To Those Who've Failed," 159

"True Conquerors," 160

"Twenty Years," 162

"Twilight," 157

"Twilight Song, A," 168

Two Rivulets, 82, 104, 105, 106, 107, 108 (publ'd.), 122, 141

"United States to Old World
   Critics, The," 161

"Virginia—The West," 95
"Visit to the Opera, A," 24
"Voice from Death, A," 165
"Voice of the Rain, The," 149

"Walks in Broadway," 12
"Wallabout Martyrs, The,"
   160
"Walt Whitman," 136.
   See also "Poem of Walt
   Whitman" and "Song of
   Myself"
"Warble for Lilac-Time," 88,
   98
"Washington in the Hot
   Season," 54
"We All Shall Rest at Last," 9
"What Best I See in Thee,"
   124
"What Lurks Behind
   Shakspere's Historical
   Plays?," 147
"When Lilacs Last in the
   Door-Yard Bloom'd," 70,
   71, 122
"When the Full-grown Poet

Came," 109
"Whispers of Heavenly
   Death," 85, 90
"Wild Frank's Return," 11
"Winter Sunshine, A Trip
   from Camden to the
   Coast," 121
"With All Thy Gifts," 98
"With Antecedents" ("You
   and Me and To-Day"), 41
"With Husky-Haughty Lips,
   O Sea!," 144, 146
"Woman Waits for Me, A,"
   139
"Word about Tennyson, A,"
   152
"Word Out of the Sea, A," 44,
   153. *See also* "A Child's
   Reminiscence" and "Out
   of the Cradle Endlessly
   Rocking"
"Wound-Dresser, The," 69

"Year of Meteors," 45
"Yonnondio," 157
"You Lingering Sparse
   Leaves of Me," 157
"Young Grimes," 9